Assessing Listening

THE CAMBRIDGE LANGUAGE ASSESSMENT SERIES

Series editors: J. Charles Alderson and Lyle F. Bachman

In this series:

Assessing Reading by J. Charles Alderson
Assessing Languages for Specific Purposes by Dan Douglas
Assessing Vocabulary by John Read

Assessing Listening

Gary Buck

CAMBRIDGE
UNIVERSITY PRESS

PUBLISHED BY THE PRESS SYNDICATE OF THE UNIVERSITY OF CAMBRIDGE
The Pitt Building, Trumpington Street, Cambridge, United Kingdom

CAMBRIDGE UNIVERSITY PRESS
The Edinburgh Building, Cambridge CB2 2RU, UK
40 West 20th Street, New York, NY 10011–4211, USA
10 Stamford Road, Oakleigh, Melbourne 3166, Australia
Ruiz de Alarcón 13, 28014 Madrid, Spain
Dock House, The Waterfront, Cape Town 8001, South Africa
http://www.cambridge.org

First published 2001

Printed in the United Kingdom at the University Press, Cambridge

Typeface 9.5/13pt Utopia   *System* 3b2   [CE]

A catalogue record for this book is available from the British Library

ISBN 0 521 66162 5 hardback
ISBN 0 521 66661 9 paperback

I would like to dedicate this book to Aki, who made it possible, as a token of my love and gratitude.

Contents

Series Editors' Preface

The assessment of listening abilities is one of the least understood, least developed and yet one of the most important areas of language testing and assessment. It is important because of the potential wash-back effect onto classroom practices. After all, if we do not test the ability to understand spoken discourse in the second or foreign language, why would learners take seriously the need to develop and improve their listening comprehension? Even if teachers might be convinced of the importance of listening as a language-use activity, they will perhaps inevitably tend to concentrate on those specific aspects of listening that are eventually tested. Indeed, some have argued that it is crucial to test listening in settings where tests of speaking cannot be administered for practical and logistical reasons. The argument is that by teaching listening (in preparation for the test), teachers will necessarily have to engage in some sort of speaking activity in class, even if speaking itself is not assessed.

Thus, from a pedagogic point of view, the assessment of listening is central to our need to teach as well as to assess language proficiency.

It is all the more curious, therefore, that very little is written in the language assessment literature on the specific constructs, or abilities, that underlie listening, on how to go about designing listening assessment procedures, on how to validate and evaluate listening tests.

This book is therefore both timely and necessary. It represents a major addition to the language assessment literature, and is certain to be the standard reference work on the subject for years to come. We are confident in saying this, not simply because there is a clear need for the book, but also because it is written by an author who is one of the few true experts on the nature of listening. Dr Gary Buck's doctoral dissertation work on the testing of listening won the first TOEFL Award for Outstanding Doctoral Dissertation Research on Second/

Foreign Language Testing, in 1993. Dr Buck has since that time published a number of influential research articles on the topic. In addition to being an acknowledged expert in the field, he is also a very experienced language teacher, who has grappled for years with the problem of how to design suitable assessment procedures for classroom use as well as for larger scale proficiency tests. And, very importantly, he is able to write in a manner which is immediately accessible to practitioners as well as to researchers. Test-developers will find his account of the nature of listening clear, revealing, up-to-date, and of immense value in designing language tests. Classroom teachers interested in improving their tests of listening ability will find in the book very helpful advice on how to select, record and edit texts for their listening tests, and how to design suitable tasks to assess the construct. Applied linguistic researchers will find scholarly accounts of the construct of listening, that draw on the latest research as well as reflecting the progress made in the field over the past thirty years.

This book follows the tradition established in earlier volumes in the CLAS series, by drawing upon applied linguistic theory and the research literature in order to develop an understanding of the nature of listening. In addition, it calls on research results in the assessment of listening in order to reflect further on the nature of the ability being tested and the most appropriate ways of assessing it. In so doing, this offers suggestions for ways in which language testing research can contribute to a better applied linguistic understanding of the nature of listening, as well as to improved tests. And, as do other volumes in the series, this book presents detailed critical reviews of a number of published listening tests in order to evaluate the extent to which they reflect current theoretical views on listening, as well as the extent to which such tests represent the state of the art in assessing listening. As a result, many practical and constructive suggestions are made for ways in which we can improve the way in which we currently assess listening.

J. Charles Alderson
Lyle F. Bachman

Acknowledgements

The publishers and author are grateful to the authors, publishers and others who have given permission for the use of copyright material identified in the text. It has not been possible to identify, or trace, sources of all the materials used and in such cases the publishers would welcome information from copyright owners.

The Cambridge Encyclopedia of the English Language by D. Crystal, Cambridge University Press. Speech rates in British English by S. Tauroza and D. Allison, *Journal of Applied Linguistics*, Oxford University Press. On-line summaries as representations of lecture understanding by M. Rost in Flowerdew (ed.), *Academic listening: Research perspectives*, Cambridge University Press. *Modern Language Testing* by R. M. Valette, Harcourt Brace Jovanovich. *Measuring Listening Comprehension in English as a Second Language* by K. G. Aitken, British Columbia Association of Teachers of English as an Additional Language. *Understanding and Developing Language Tests* by C. Weir, Prentice Hall. Listening comprehension: approach, design, procedure by J. C. Richards, *TESOL Quarterly 17*(2), 1983, Teachers of English to Speakers of Other Languages. The sub-skills of listening: Rule-space analysis of a multiple choice test of second language listening comprehension by G. Buck, K. Tatsuoka, I. Kostin and M. Phelps, *Current Developments and Alternatives in Language Assessment*, University of Jyväskylä. Application of the rule-space procedure to language testing: examining attributes of a free response listening test by G. Buck and K. Tatsuoka, *Language Testing*, Arnold Publishers. Listening recall: A listening comprehension test for low proficiency learners by G. Henning, N. Gary and J. Gary, *System 11* (1983), Elsevier Science. *Certificate of Communicative Skills in English Level 3 and 4*, University of Cambridge Local Examination Syndicate, 1995. *Language Testing in*

Practice by L. F. Bachman and A. Palmer, Oxford University Press. *Writing English Language Tests (2nd ed)* by J. B. Heaton, Longman. *Cambridge First Certificate*, Listening Paper, December 1998, University of Cambridge Local Examination Syndicate. *Certificate of Communicative Skills in English*, December 1998, University of Cambridge Local Examination Syndicate. Does text matter in a multiple-choice test of comprehension? The case for the construct validity of TOEFL by R. Freedle and I. Kostin, *Language Testing*, Arnold Publishers. *Cambridge First Certificate*, University of Cambridge Local Examination Syndicate. *Finnish National Foreign Language Certificate*: English Intermediate Level, 1996, National Board of Education, Helsinki. *Certificate of Communicative Skills in English*, University of Cambridge Local Examination Syndicate. The TOEIC® Examination and TOEFL® Examination test questions are reprinted by permission of Educational Testing Service, the copyright owner. However, any other testing information is provided in its entirety by the author. No endorsement of this publication by Educational Testing Service or Chauncey Group International Ltd. should be inferred.

CHAPTER ONE

....

An overview of listening comprehension

Introduction

Listening comprehension is a process, a very complex process, and if we want to measure it, we must first understand how that process works. An understanding of what we are trying to measure is the starting point for test construction. The thing we are trying to measure is called a **construct**, and our test will be useful and valid only if it measures the right construct. Thus, the first task of the test developer is to understand the construct, and then, secondly, to make a test that somehow measures that construct. This is **construct validity**, and ensuring that the right construct is being measured is the central issue in all assessment.

The purpose of this book is to look at the listening process, and to consider how that should be measured. In this chapter, I will begin by examining the listening process, and how language is used to convey meaning. Much of this relates to reading as well as listening. Then, in Chapter 2, I will discuss what is unique to listening comprehension.

Different types of knowledge used in listening

If we consider how the language comprehension system works, it is obvious that a number of different types of knowledge are involved: both linguistic knowledge and non-linguistic knowledge. Linguistic knowledge is of different types, but among the most important are phonology, lexis, syntax, semantics and discourse structure. The non-linguistic knowledge used in comprehension is knowledge about the topic, about the context, and general knowledge about the world and how it works.

There has been much debate about how this knowledge is applied to the incoming sound, but the two most important views are: the **bottom-up** view, and the **top-down** view. These terms refer to the order in which the different types of knowledge are applied during comprehension.

The bottom-up vs. top-down views

It is my experience that when people start thinking about language processing, they often assume that the process takes place in a definite order, starting with the lowest level of detail and moving up to the highest level. So they often assume that the acoustic input is first decoded into **phonemes** (the smallest sound segments that can carry meaning), and then this is used to identify individual words. Then processing continues on to the next higher stage, the syntactic level, followed by an analysis of the semantic content to arrive at a literal understanding of the basic linguistic meaning. Finally, the listener interprets that literal meaning in terms of the communicative situation to understand what the speaker means. This is the bottom-up view, which sees language comprehension as a process of passing through a number of consecutive stages, or levels, and the output of each stage becomes the input for the next higher stage. It is, as it were, a one-way street.

However, there are some serious problems with this view of language comprehension, and both research and daily experience indicate that the processing of the different types of knowledge does not occur in a fixed sequence, but rather, that different types of processing may occur simultaneously, or in any convenient order. Thus, syntactic knowledge might be used to help identify a word, ideas about the topic of conversation might influence processing of the syntax, or knowledge of the context will help interpret the meaning.

It is quite possible to understand the meaning of a word before decoding its sound, because we have many different types of knowledge, including knowledge of the world around us. In most situations we know what normally happens, and so we have expectations about what we will hear. These may be very precise, or very vague, but while we are listening, we almost always have some hypotheses about what is likely to come next. In such cases it is not necessary to utilise all the information available to us – we can just take in enough to confirm or reject our hypotheses. To take a well known example, if we hear the following uncompleted sentence, *'she was so angry, she picked up the gun, aimed and* _____ *'* (adapted from Grosjean, 1980), we know what is going to happen, and we probably need very little acoustic information to understand the final word, be it *'fired'*, *'shot'* or whatever. As we listen, we will expect a word such as *fired*, and we will probably process only enough of the sound to confirm our expectations, or we may not even bother to listen to the last word at all. Our background knowledge about guns and what angry people do with them helps us to determine what the word is. This is a top-down process. Similarly, when we part from a friend, we hear the words of parting, not so much by processing the sound of what she says, but because she is waving to us and saying something as she leaves. We need very little acoustic information to determine whether she is saying 'good-bye', 'see you later', or whatever, and we may not even bother to find out.

Listening comprehension is a top-down process in the sense that the various types of knowledge involved in understanding language are not applied in any fixed order – they can be used in any order, or even simultaneously, and they are all capable of interacting and influencing each other. This is sometimes referred to as an interactive process, especially by reading theorists.

However, we should not underestimate the importance of the acoustic input, nor the importance of the linguistic information. The point is simply that listening comprehension is the result of an inter-action between a number of information sources, which include the acoustic input, different types of linguistic knowledge, details of the context, and general world knowledge, and so forth, and listeners use whatever information they have available, or whatever information seems relevant to help them interpret what the speaker is saying.

In the rest of this chapter we will look at each type of knowledge used in understanding spoken language. The chapter will be organised into five main sections:

i   the input to the listener;

ii   applying knowledge of the language;

iii   using world knowledge;

iv   the context of communication;

v   building mental representations of meaning.

The input to the listener

Listeners listen to spoken language, and this is very different from written language. There are three characteristics of speech that are very particularly important in the listening comprehension construct: firstly, speech is encoded in the form of sound; secondly, it is linear and takes place in real time, with no chance of review; and thirdly, it is linguistically different from written language. In this section we will consider each of these characteristics in detail.

The acoustic input

The external input into the listening comprehension process is an acoustic signal. This represents the meaningful sounds of the language, the phonemes. These phonemes combine together to make up individual words, phrases, etc. This acoustic signal is often very indistinct; in normal speech, speakers modify the sounds considerably and not all the phonemes are clearly and unambiguously encoded in the message.

Phonological modification

The process by which sounds are modified is regular and rule governed. It depends on a set of phonological rules which vary from one language to another. In normal-speed speech, some sounds are modified by the sounds next to them; some are simply dropped, others are combined in complex ways. For example, many words that are quite clearly intelligible within a text are difficult to recognise in isolation (Pickett and Pollack, 1963; Pollack and Pickett, 1963). In other cases words, or word clusters, which we assume to have different pronunciations often prove to be very difficult to distinguish in isolation. For example, the difference between the two sentences 'I wish she would' and 'I wish you would' is usually minimal, and most speakers could not even tell the difference between their own utterances if they heard them out of context. The fact is that many words are quite indistinct, and it is the surrounding context that enables us to identify them with little trouble.

Stress and intonation

However, while there is ample evidence that many of the individual sounds may be either indistinct or missing, there is also plenty of evidence to suggest that, at least in English, this is not the case with the prosodic features of the language, the stress and intonation. This remains important even in very fast speech. The English stress pattern gives each word an individual form, which is as much a part of the sound of the word as the actual phonemes. Furthermore, speakers stress what they think is important, and the most important words, those that express the core meaning, get additional stress (Brown, 1990). Similarly, the intonation pattern of the utterance is usually very important. In English, intonation patterns are closely related to the structure and meaning of the text. For example, intonation indicates clausal boundaries, marks questions, and also indicates when it is appropriate for the listener to respond (Cooper, 1976; Garro and Parker, 1982). One of the most important aspects of listening comprehension is paying attention to stress and intonation patterns.

Redundancy and shared knowledge

Language is by its nature extremely redundant (Cohen, 1975, 1977), and there are so many clues to what the speaker is saying that listeners can understand, even if speakers do not speak very clearly. Speakers know this and instinctively modify their speech depending on the situation, and their knowledge of the listener. Generally, people who share knowledge of a topic will tend to speak faster, run the words together more and be far less distinct when speaking to each other. But when they are speaking to someone who has less background knowledge, they will tend to speak more slowly and with much clearer enunciation (Hunnicutt, 1985). Thus, we find words with a high information content, that is non-redundant words, to be more clearly articulated than redundant words which have a low information content (Liebermann, 1963; Oakeshott-Taylor, 1977).

Given the fact that the acoustic signal is often indistinct, we might well ask how comprehension takes place. The answer is simple: we use our knowledge of the language to 'replace' any missing information. And this is where redundancy comes in – because language is redundant, we do not need all the information to be clearly expressed, we only need enough to activate our knowledge, we can then construct the meaning ourselves.

The real-time nature of spoken language

Speech takes place in real time, in the sense that the text is heard only once, and then it is gone. We cannot go back to a piece of speech and hear it again (although modern recording technology does actually allow this, most conversations take place without being recorded). Of course, we can often ask a speaker to repeat what they said, but strangely, speakers virtually never do. We almost never get the same words, but a re-statement in a different way: speakers realise that there is a problem, and usually try to help by re-phrasing or by offering examples. And even if we do get the same words, the stress and intonation are different for repeated information. In normal language use, we get just one chance at comprehension, and only one. There are two consequences of this. The first is that the listener must process the text at a speed determined by the speaker, which is generally quite fast. The second is that the listener cannot refer back to the text – all that remains is a memory, an often imperfect memory, of what was heard.

The necessity of automatic processing

Speakers generally speak very quickly: three words a second is quite normal. This leaves little time to think about the precise meaning of each word, or the way relative clauses are structured, or to speculate on what the pronouns might refer to. The words are flying past very quickly, and in order to understand speakers at this speed, the listening processes must be almost entirely automatic.

It is helpful to make a distinction between two types of cognitive process: **controlled processes**, which involve a sequence of cognitive activities under active control and to which we must pay attention; and **automatic processes**, which are a sequence of cognitive activities that occur automatically, without the necessity of active control and usually without conscious attention (Schneider and Shiffrin, 1977; Shiffrin and Schneider, 1977). This distinction is perhaps best illustrated in activities like learning to drive a car: at first the whole process is controlled and we have to pay conscious attention to everything we do, but after a while things become a little more automatic and we start doing things without having to think about them very much, until eventually the whole process becomes so automatic that we may not think about it at all. The difference between controlled and automatic processing is very important in second-language use. When second-language learners learn some new element of a language, at first they have to pay conscious attention and think about it; that takes time, and their use of it is slow. But as the new element becomes more familiar, they process it faster, with less thought, until eventually the processing of that element becomes completely automatic.

Given the speed and complexity of normal speech, the more automatic the listener's processing, the more efficient it will be, and the faster it can be done; and conversely, the less automatic the processing, the more time will be required. For language learners with less automatic processing, comprehension will suffer. As the speech rate gets faster, they will not have sufficient time to process everything, so they will start paying proportionally more attention to lexical and grammatical processing and less attention to the wider interpretation of the meaning (Lynch, 1998). Then, as the speech rate gets even faster, the listener will have insufficient time to process even the lexical and grammatical information, and they will begin to miss parts of the text. At a certain speed, their processing will tend to break down completely, and they will fail to understand much at all.

This rarely causes a problem for first-language listeners, but the normal state with many second-language listeners is that the language is only partly known, and so language processing will be only partly automatic. In such cases processing will periodically break down because the listener cannot process the text fast enough.

Interpretations vary

There are many reasons why the listening process may go wrong. This could be due to background noise, or listeners may have their attention distracted, or be thinking of something else. Second-language listeners could have other difficulties: unknown vocabulary, complex syntax, or the text could be just too fast, for example. In all these cases, when listeners try to recall the content of the text, their representation of what the text was about is likely to be incomplete – the listeners' interpretations will be inadequate, and will obviously vary.

Interpretations also vary even when the listening does not go wrong, and the whole issue of what listeners should understand from a text is very complex. Different listeners often understand different things from the same text (Brown, 1995a). This may be due to the effects of background knowledge. When we listen we use our background knowledge of the world to set up expectations, and then use those expectations to help us comprehend what we hear. If the topic of the text accords well with the listener's world knowledge, then it will be much easier to understand than a text with a topic that the listener knows nothing about (Spilich *et al.*, 1979; Pearson and Johnson, 1978). So, a talk on a subject about which the listener knows nothing will be more difficult to understand, and a talk which in some way violates or contradicts the listener's expectations will be even more difficult to understand, and could cause considerable confusion even though the language may not be linguistically challenging. It is difficult to assimilate and remember something that does not seem to make sense.

Different listeners often have different motives for listening, due to different interests and different needs. Listeners will pay more attention to those features of a text which they think are more interesting or more relevant. Thus what listeners get out of a text will depend on the purpose for listening as well as their background knowledge, and interpretations will therefore often differ from listener to listener. There is no such thing as the correct interpretation of many spoken texts, only a number of different **reasonable interpretations** (Brown and Yule, 1983).

While it is very true that interpretations reasonably vary, a note of caution is in order. Competent listeners will usually all grasp the same information from explicit statements, such as announcements, and they will usually share much common gist after hearing a piece of spoken discourse. If this were not the case, communication would be very difficult or even impossible.

Linguistic features of spoken texts

Most people assume that the language of speech is much the same as the language of writing. Well, this is not true. Speech and writing are both variants of the same linguistic system, but there are some considerable differences between them. Good descriptions of spoken language can be found in Carter and McCarthy (1997) and McCarthy (1998).

One important point, for example, is that people do not usually speak in sentences. Rather, spoken language, especially in informal situations, consists of short phrases or clauses, called **idea units**, strung together in a rather loose way, often connected more by the coherence of the ideas than by any formal grammatical relationship. The vocabulary and the grammar also tend to be far more colloquial and much less formal. There are many words and expressions that are only used in speech, never in writing.

Planned and unplanned discourse

The real-time nature of spoken language not only affects the listener, but also affects the speaker, who must speak in real time. This means that speakers must construct the text at a rapid rate, and attempt to organise and control the flow of information with little preparation time. Consequently most spoken texts are just a rough first draft. This is usually referred to as **unplanned discourse** (Ochs, 1979) – it is spontaneous and produced without taking much time for planning and organisation. **Planned discourse** may be thought of as polished, worked text. Often there is a considerable difference between planned and unplanned discourse. We think of something and then say it almost immediately; and what we produce, and what our listeners have to listen to, will consist of initial ideas, and first reactions, loosely or poorly organised, fragments of language, with hesitations, false starts, restatements, vocabulary repair, and even grammatically 'incorrect sentences' (Hatch, 1983).

The grammar of unplanned spoken discourse tends to be different from planned discourse. Normally in planned discourse the relation-

ship between the ideas or **propositions** (a proposition is a short statement that says something about something, i.e. one simple little fact)
is expressed by means of the syntax. However, in unplanned discourse
the context itself can be used to connect the propositions: they may
simply be placed next to each other, or strung together, so that the
listener has to make the right connections between the ideas in the
text. Similarly, referents are often missing, and the listener may have
to infer who, or what, the speaker is talking about.

Linguistic differences between speech and writing

Spoken idea units usually contain about as much information as we
can comfortably hold in working memory, usually about two seconds,
or about seven words (Chafe, 1985). They may consist of only one
proposition, but usually they will have a number of propositions. In
English, each idea unit usually has a single, coherent intonation
contour, ending in a clause-final intonation; it is often preceded and
followed by some kind of pause or hesitation. Idea units are often
clauses insofar as they contain a verb phrase along with noun phrases
and prepositional phrases. However, some idea units do not have a
verb, or the verb is understood but not explicitly stated. Other
languages have idea units that are structured differently.

Although idea units are a characteristic of spoken language, Chafe
also claims that they can be recognised in written texts. Probably the
nearest written equivalent to spoken idea units is not the sentence,
but the *t-unit*, which is one main clause plus all its dependent
clauses. If we regard these as the written equivalent of idea units, we
can then use these as a basis for examining the major linguistic
differences between spoken and written language (Chafe, 1985):

- In spoken language idea units tend to be shorter, with simpler
  syntax, whereas written idea units tend to be more dense, often
  using complex syntax, such as dependent and subordinate clauses,
  to convey more information.

- In spoken language idea units tend to be strung together by coordi-
  nating conjunctions (*and, or, but* etc.), whereas written idea units
  tend to be joined in more complex ways.

- Spoken language usually has hesitations: pauses, fillers and repetitions that give the speaker more thinking time, as well as repairs,

such as false starts, corrections in grammar or vocabulary, and afterthoughts.

- Spoken language tends to have more non-standard features such as dialect, slang, and colloquialisms, whereas written language tends to be far more formal, conservative and 'correct'.

- Spoken language tends to be far more personal, with more emotional involvement and much less precision. Speakers tend to indicate their feelings more, with expressions such as '*I think*' or '*I mean*', or by making direct reference to the listener. They also tend to be content with gross approximations, or use overstatements and exaggerations.

These differences were developed through study of English, and I am not aware of any research which addresses the extent to which they are universal. However, the differences between speech and writing seem likely to be important in most, if not all, languages, although the extent and significance of the differences may vary.

Such differences are of course really a question of degree, and Tannen has argued that texts can be ranged along an oral–literate continuum, with **oral texts** at one end, having more characteristics of spoken language that are typically associated with casual conversation, and **literate texts** at the other end, having more characteristics of written language that are especially associated with expository written prose (Tannen, 1982, 1985).

This idea of a continuum of features is very useful for our purpose. The features that determine where texts go on the continuum include linguistic features (the sound system, phonology, stress, intonation), paralinguistic features (tone of voice, gestures and facial expressions), vocabulary choice, grammar, degree of planning, the type and degree of shared context between the participants, and the function of the text. It is important to realise that spoken texts will differ in their degree of orality depending on the listening situation, and an important aspect of listening test construction is to identify those features of oral texts that need to be included on our tests.

The listening situation

The situation in which the listening takes place can have a considerable effect on various aspects of the listening process. Firstly, the situation can determine the topic. Talk in a bread shop is likely to be about bread, and in a chemistry lecture, about chemistry. Similarly, a chat with a friend will require listening to informal language, and a public speech will usually require listening to more formal language.

The degree of interaction between the listener and speaker

One of the most important aspects of the listening situation is the degree of interaction between the listener and the speaker. In some situations, the listener's role may be **non-collaborative** – requiring nothing more than interpreting the speaker's utterance. But in other situations, the listener's role may require **collaborative listening** – making appropriate requests for clarification, back-channelling, making responses to interactional language, or taking responsibility for organising turn-taking. This can be regarded as a continuum. At one end is the situation where there is no possibility of an interaction: listening to the radio, television or a lecture are examples of this. Other situations, such as classrooms or presentations, are mainly one-way, but there is some chance to ask clarification questions, or to intervene. Further along the continuum would be a situation where a group of people talk together, with one person doing most of the talking, and the others listening and saying very little, but able to intervene if they wished. At the other end of the continuum, there is a truly interactive conversation between two people, who collaborate equally to maintain the conversation, taking turns to speak with equal rights to participate.

The degree of interaction is related to the extent that the listener must collaborate with the speaker to maintain the conversation. In a typical two-way conversation, the listener and speaker change roles, back and forth, and they collaborate together to manage the conversation. In such conversations, decisions about who talks, and when, are not random, but are determined by a very complex set of shared, turn-taking rules (Rost, 1990). These rules depend on the relationship between the two interlocutors, the topics expected to be discussed, the context, and so on. Some conversations follow prescribed formulas, such as ordering a meal in a restaurant, and others have particular purposes which often determine interlocutor roles, such as a consultation with a doctor. But in other situations, turn-taking is negotiated between the participants.

Speakers generally use intonation and other markers to indicate when they want to pass on the turn, and listeners often indicate by verbal and non-verbal means when they would like to take a turn. And as topics shift in conversation, one contributor, and then the other, will take control of the conversation. Most groups have unspoken rules that determine how this should be done, and the listener must understand these and respond as appropriate.

The listener's responsibility to respond

In many situations, the listener also has responsibilities to respond in predetermined ways. For example, in the USA it is more or less obligatory to respond to *'thank you'* with *'you're welcome'*, and there are lots of other situations where some reasonably fixed response is expected: greetings, inquiries about health, compliments, and so on. If the listener fails to respond in the appropriate way, the interaction may not go well.

Another responsibility of the listener is to provide **back-channelling**. All the time we are listening we must give signs to the speaker that we are understanding what is being said, and that we are paying attention. This takes the form of formulaic expressions such as *'really'*, *'yeah'*, *'oh yes'*, *'I see'*, *'how interesting'*, *'well I never'*, and so forth. It will usually be accompanied by appropriate body language and other non-verbal signals. Back-channelling is very important, and if the listener ever stops providing this, the speaker will quickly sense that something is wrong, and will likely stop speaking.

The function of the interaction

We also need to consider the function of the interaction. We can make a distinction between two types of language use: **transactional language**, where the primary purpose is to communicate information, and **interactional language**, where the primary purpose is social interaction (Brown and Yule, 1983). Transactional language has a definite purpose, usually to get something done; it is important that the message be understood, and it matters that the listener gets it right. Examples are a teacher giving a homework task, a customer making a complaint, a doctor giving instructions to a patient, or two colleagues planning their work schedule.

Interactional language is quite different. Here the purpose is to maintain social relationships. What is important is not the content of what is said, but the fact that something is said. This includes greetings, comments about the weather, what is happening in the world and other phatic conversation. Generally the participants do all they can to make their conversation agreeable to each other: they express agreement, regardless of their real opinions, and pretend to understand, whether they do or not. In most listening situations, there is both transactional and interactional language use, although one will usually be more dominant in any particular situation.

Clearly, there are certain listening situations that make demands on the listener that are not normally thought of as listening skills: for example requests for clarification, taking responsibility for turn-taking, back-channelling, and making the appropriate responses to interactional language.

Applying knowledge of the language

In order to process language, we need to have knowledge of the language and the ability to apply that knowledge. It is useful to make a distinction between two types of knowledge: **declarative knowledge** and **procedural knowledge**. Declarative knowledge is the knowledge of facts or about things; procedural knowledge is knowledge about how to do things (Anderson, 1976). For example, knowing the fact that English relative clauses are introduced by *who*, *which* or *that* is declarative knowledge, but being able to string them together with other words to make relative clauses is procedural knowledge. In language use, declarative knowledge is of very limited value; in practical terms, something is not really known until it can be used, correctly and efficiently. This means that it is procedural knowledge which is important for listening performance, and as language testers this is what we should be mainly concerned with.

This section is divided into three parts: the first part deals with understanding individual words, the second part with understanding and processing sentences or idea units, and the third part with understanding longer discourse.

Understanding words

The process of understanding words can be conceptually divided into two parts: recognising the word and then understanding its meaning. Most scholars believe we have some sort of mental lexicon, where all the words are stored, both their forms and their meanings. The process of understanding words is then a process of accessing this mental lexicon. Two kinds of information are used: the perceptual/ acoustic information, and knowledge of the context.

One of the first problems is to determine exactly what the word is – the incoming signal does not indicate words by putting gaps between them, as happens in writing. Naturally, there are a variety of acoustic clues, such as pitch, loudness and timing, but we also use more than the words themselves; we use our general knowledge to help us decide what the words are. Otherwise we could not explain the fact that we hear only those words that the speaker intends us to hear. If someone tells us about a visit from a *guest*, we never confuse this with *guessed*, because our knowledge of grammar tells us that one is a noun and the other a verb. A spoken sentence often contains many words that were not intended to be heard. That last sentence, for example, contains *'Us poke can cent tense off in contains men knee words that were knot in ten did tube bee herd'* (Cole and Jakimik, 1980:139), but if we had heard the sentence, we would have recognised the right words from the topic of the discussion. Similarly, not only do we usually hear the right word, but we usually get the right meaning. For example, the word *'printer'* has two meanings, and if we hear *'the printer needs toner'*, we know this is referring to a machine because of our background knowledge about how these printers work, and if we hear, *'the printer is sick'*, we know that this is referring to a person because people get sick and machines do not.

The effect of context seems to work through what has been called **spreading activation**. Words are connected by their features and their associations into a complex semantic network. So that *'fire-engine'* will be associated with *'fire'*, *'red'*, *'truck'*, *'fireman'* and so on. Each of these will in turn have their own associations, and in this way a complex network is developed. When a concept or word is encountered, the other things associated with it are also activated. Things closely associated will be strongly activated, and things weakly associated will be weakly activated. Once a word is activated it becomes easier to process that word.

There has been a lot of research into word recognition, and some of this is relevant to test construction: (i) higher-frequency words are recognised faster than lower-frequency words; (ii) word recognition is faster if the words are in a helpful context; and (iii) the fainter the sound, the longer it takes to recognise the word (Garnham, 1985).

Processing idea units

We do not usually recognise words in isolation, but as part of idea units. Processing idea units somehow requires taking the meaning of individual words, and combining these together to construct the meaning of complete utterances. Establishing the relationship between the meaning of individual words and the meaning of whole utterances is called *parsing*. Generally, the listener constructs a meaning of the idea unit, and then forgets the actual words and the syntax, and so only a summary of the meaning, the gist, remains (Sachs, 1967). Then the gist of each idea unit is combined with the gist of other idea units, and is then added to the gist of the text heard up to that point. In this way a summary of the whole text is built up.

Parsing idea units means determining the relationship between the parts of the utterance: i.e. who does what, to whom, and with what. This is based on both semantic and syntactic clues. The semantic information comes from such things as knowing that for a particular verb the subject must be animate, the direct object can be either animate or inanimate, and the instrument is usually inanimate. Syntactic clues can come from the word order, which in English is usually subject–verb–object; or from subject–verb agreement, which means that the noun which governs the verb is the agent.

The ease with which idea units can be understood depends on both syntactic and semantic factors. Some structures are generally more difficult to process than others: in English, negative statements take more time to process than affirmatives, and passive statements take more time to process than active statements. In semantic terms, plausible events are easier to process than implausible events. If the events are very plausible and very predictable, then simply paying attention to the content words may be enough to process the meaning. Making inferences based on the common relationships between content words is a very common comprehension strategy. But if events are not so plausible, or if it is necessary to disambiguate the meaning, then the syntax is necessary to help determine the meaning. In the case of second-language listeners, syntactic skill tends to be low, and plausibility based on associations between content words is likely to play a greater role in language comprehension (Taylor and Taylor, 1990). Idea units are hardest to process when both the semantics and the syntax are challenging.

Processing connected discourse

Many people probably think of linguistic processing in terms of understanding sentences or short chunks of language. However, the rules and conventions of language use cover much larger linguistic units (for a review of research in discourse comprehension, see Graesser *et al.*, 1997). In typical conversations, speakers seldom organise complex thoughts into single utterances; instead, information may be spread out over many idea units and many conversational exchanges, as ideas are developed and expanded. Discourse level variables are important in the comprehension of spoken language.

Cohesion

One important variable is **cohesion**. Cohesion is a semantic relation between one element in a text and another element that has to be understood (Halliday and Hasan, 1976). One important type of cohesive device are **connectors** such as *'however'*, *'therefore'*, *'despite that'*, which indicate important semantic relations between the idea units they connect. In English, the definite article *'the'* is also very important – it indicates that the noun it modifies is a unique item already known to the listener and so, among other things, it serves to indicate what information is already shared between the speaker and the listener. Pronouns are another important type of cohesive device, and it is necessary for the listener to determine what a pronoun refers back to, in order to understand what it means. There are also pro-verbs – *do* in English or *suru* in Japanese, for example – that stand for other verbs, and are used to avoid repeating the main verb. The listener needs to understand which verb is being repeated.

Foregrounding

Related to the question of cohesion is the fact that not everything mentioned in a text is equally easy to refer back to; some things pass into the background while others remain in the foreground (Tyler and Marslen-Wilson, 1982; Anderson *et al.*, 1983). Those things which remain foregrounded are active as a focus of attention, and are very easy to refer to; these are things that have been recently mentioned, or are related in some way to the content of the current utterance. Pronouns refer back to items which are foregrounded rather than those in the background. Sanford and Garrod (1981) suggested that the things that have been mentioned in the text are in **explicit focus**, and the things implied by that are in **implicit focus**. Thus, for example, if a house were mentioned, then that would be in explicit focus, and aspects of the house would be in implicit focus. So it would be possible to follow mention of *'the house'* with a reference to *'the garden'*, and the listeners would be able to make sense of that and know which garden was being referred to.

Using world knowledge

It is already quite clear that any process of text comprehension presupposes a great deal of general non-linguistic knowledge about the world we live in, and how things work within it. This world knowledge can influence comprehension in several ways, but two are particularly important: (i) knowledge of the overall context restricts interpretations of the text; and (ii) knowledge of specific facts, or knowledge of how things usually happen, can be used to fill in details that are not explicitly stated in the text.

Inferencing

World knowledge is applied through the process of inferencing, and there is a wide variety of different types of inferences. For example, Hildyard and Olson (1978) classify inferences into three types: (i) **propositional inferences** are those that follow on logically and necessarily from any given statement; (ii) **enabling inferences** are related to the causal relationships between events or concepts; and

(iii) **pragmatic inferences** provide extra information which is not essential to the interpretation of the text, but which expands on it.

Inferences vary depending on how much background knowledge is needed to make the inferences, and these range from simple logical entailments, which follow on naturally from the meaning of words, to those that depend on very elaborate and extensive world knowledge. Inferences can also be classified according to how necessary they are to text interpretation: for example, **bridging inferences** must be made if a text is to be coherently interpreted, while **elaborative inferences** are not actually necessary to link together the parts of a text. Note also that inferences are not only made about situations described in the text, but can also be about the motives of the speaker, or the point the text is intended to illustrate.

Haviland and Clark (1974) and Clark and Haviland (1974) claim that the inferences necessary to understanding the meaning of a text, i.e. bridging inferences, are made while the text is being processed, although their research suggests that speed of comprehension is reduced when bridging inferences have to be made. Johnson *et al.* (1973) conducted a number of studies which suggested that elaborative inferences, i.e. those not necessary to understand the text but which add to it, are also made while a text is being processed, and are often incorporated into the comprehenders' mental representation of the text and what it is about. They found that after a lapse of some time, comprehenders were unable to distinguish between what was actually in the text and the inferences they had made while processing it.

However, world knowledge is used not only to expand interpretation, but also to restrict it. When the general topic is familiar, knowledge about that topic can be used to interpret the text. The importance of this topic-specific knowledge has been established in a series of famous studies by Bransford and Johnson (1972, 1973). They gave readers a number of passages which were rated as incomprehensible by the readers; when a simple hint about the topic was given however, a title or a picture, the passages were rated as very comprehensible by the readers.

Scripts and schema

In order to explain how world knowledge is stored in memory and utilised in the comprehension of text, a number of similar and related theories have been developed. Probably the most readily understood of these is the **script theory** of Schank and Abelson (1977). The idea is that an utterance sets up expectations, in the form of a script, about what normally happens in that context. The script is a mental structure which describes stylised, everyday situations; it is, in effect, 'a very boring little story' (Schank and Abelson, 1977:422).

Scripts are extremely numerous: we have restaurant scripts, birthday party scripts, football scripts, classroom scripts, library scripts and so on. In fact we probably have scripts for all the regularly occurring events in our lives. In listening to a story that calls up a script, the contents of the script automatically become part of the story, even if they are not spelled out. We know what happens in a restaurant, and there is no need to explain that the waiter brings the food, or that the customer pays the bill. Similarly, in a story about a Japanese public bath, the *sento*, we do not need to say that the bather undressed and went into a public room, washed thoroughly all over, and then got into a large communal bath of very hot water. This sequence of events is all part of the story because the *sento* script automatically includes it – that is what happens at the *sento*, everyone knows that, or at least everyone who has a *sento* script knows that. This example raises a very important point, namely that scripts tend to be culture bound. We probably all have a bathroom script, but these may vary considerably from one culture to the next.

Related to scripts are **schemata** (Rumelhart and Ortony, 1977; Rumelhart, 1980); in fact scripts are really a type of complex schema. Schemata are structures for representing knowledge in memory, and are assumed to exist for most things we would want to represent in memory, including general concepts, situations, events, sequences of events, actions, sequences of actions etc. In some sense they may be thought of as representing stereotypes of these concepts, and in others they are somewhat like a play, with the internal structure of the schema corresponding to the script of the play. Like scripts, schemata guide the interpretation of text, setting up expectations for people, places or events. According to Rumelhart and Ortony, schemata are the basic building blocks of the human information-processing system, and are the key units in the process of comprehension.

It is clear that background knowledge is very important in listening comprehension. If the listener shares the same knowledge as the speaker, much of what is being said can be understood by means of inferences based on shared background knowledge. However, if the listener has no knowledge relevant to the particular events being described in the text, then it will be more difficult to make inferences, and comprehension will be more dependent on interpreting the linguistic information. The question of whether, and to what extent, the listener shares background knowledge with the speaker is of particular concern in second-language situations, where the interlocutors will often come from very different backgrounds. Indeed Long (1990) found that schemata could hinder as well as help listeners of Spanish as a second language.

The context of communication

All language use takes place in a context, and context can be of different types. Psycholinguists have traditionally considered context in terms of **co-text**, or the other parts of the text accompanying that part being processed, whereas sociolinguists have tended to consider context in terms of the **context of situation**, or the social situation in which the communication takes place. Besides this, most language is accompanied by non-verbal information, especially visual information, which can either supplement or contradict the verbal message, and this provides a context which has a considerable influence on interpretation. It is also important to think in terms of the **cognitive environment** in which the language is processed. I believe that this is the context which includes all the others, and that it is the one that has the strongest influence on comprehension.

Sociolinguistic appropriacy

Work in sociolinguistics has led to the recognition that language use must not only be correct, but must also be appropriate to the situation in which it takes place (Hymes, 1972). There are sociolinguistic norms which are as much a part of the language as the grammatical system. For example, there are numerous ways of addressing people – some are appropriate to strangers, some to children, some to friends and some to employers. All these may be grammatically correct, but addressing a person in the wrong way can have very serious consequences. It is fine to tell children to 'shut up a minute', but addressing an employer in the same manner would generally be regarded as offensive. If we must ask our employer to be quiet, we need to do it in the appropriate way.

There are appropriate forms for greetings, requests, apologies, suggestions etc., and these vary in complex ways according to the context in which they are used, and according to the people using them. For example, when greeting people, a formal *'good morning'* would be appropriate in some cases, and in others a more casual *'hi'* might be better. The listener must understand the implications of the speaker's choice. The rules are very subtle, and each language community has its own ways of doing things. For example, in the USA it is polite to respond to a complement by saying *'thank you'*, but in Japan it is appropriate to deny what the person said. So if an American attempts to be complementary and tells a Japanese that they are very good at something, the Japanese is likely to make an embarrassed denial, and assert that they are not very good at all. Many Americans find it disconcerting to be contradicted in this way, especially as they were only trying to be nice. Even within the same speech community, different things are appropriate in different situations. For example, in a daily work situation in England, many would consider it inappropriate for a male office worker to tell a female colleague that he likes her dress and that she looks nice. At the annual office dinner party however, where everyone is dressed up, it might be quite appropriate, and even expected, that he should compliment her in this way.

Each speech community has its rules of appropriacy, and these vary according to the situation. Recognition of the various levels of formality, or appropriacy, can be an important variable in understanding the intent of the speaker, or the effect of an utterance.

Pragmatic interpretation

We interpret language in a context, and the interaction between what is said and the context in which it is said is an important aspect of comprehension. Even if we have understood the basic linguistic meaning of an utterance, we often need to know the context in order to understand what was meant. The study of how language is interpreted in context is called **pragmatics**, and constitutes a whole branch of linguistics in itself. We can illustrate the basic concern of pragmatics by the different uses of the verb *'to mean'* in the following sentences: if we ask, *'What does X mean?'* we would get one answer, but if we asked *'What do you mean by X?'* we would get a very different answer (Leech, 1983). It is this second meaning that concerns pragmatics.

Speech acts

Speech Act Theory shows how the listener must use the context to interpret the intent of a message (Austin, 1962; Searle, 1969). We can indicate our intention, for example, requesting, promising or ordering, in a number of ways: firstly, by announcing the intent (e.g. *'I request that you pass the salt'*), secondly, by using an appropriate syntactic form (e.g. *'Pass the salt'*), or thirdly by using an indirect speech act (e.g. *'Can you pass the salt?'*). The first two of these could be understood literally, but the third has the linguistic form of an inquiry regarding the listener's abilities, and yet listeners have to understand it as a request. It is an **indirect speech act**, in that a direct inquiry has the intent of an indirect request (Searle, 1975).

Similarly, *'Do that again and I'll hit you'* has the appearance of a command to do something again, but as every school child knows, in actual fact it is an injunction *not* to do it again. The context in which an utterance is used provides the background against which the intended meaning of the utterance has to be interpreted.

An indirect speech act is a case where the speaker communicates to the listener more than is actually said. The speaker does this by relying on the shared knowledge of the speaker and listener, both linguistic and non-linguistic, as well as relying on the general powers of inference on the part of the listener. Speech acts are not, in the ordinary sense, idioms, but their use is definitely idiomatic, and certain forms have become conventionally established as indicating indirect speech acts. In English, *'would you mind . . .'* is generally understood as a request or command, rather than an inquiry about whether the person actually minds. While most languages have indirect forms, the forms of one language will not always maintain their indirect speech act potential when applied to another. The problem for the listener is to decide whether an utterance is being used in its literal sense or not.

Grice's maxims

Grice argued that spoken interaction is a cooperative endeavour and the speaker and listener must share the burden of making the meaning clear (Grice, 1975). This means that the speaker does not need to make everything explicit, but can assume that the listener will try to infer what the speaker is intending to convey. Similarly, the listener can assume that the speaker is intending to convey something, and will try to infer what that is. This is the **cooperative principle**.

Grice developed a number of maxims that guide the operation of this cooperation in communication:

- the **maxim of quantity**, which suggests that speakers generally make their contributions as informative as is required, but no more than necessary;
- the **maxim of quality**, which suggests that speakers generally do not say what they believe to be false, or something for which they lack adequate evidence;
- the **maxim of relation**, which suggests that speakers generally say what is relevant; and
- the **maxim of manner**, which suggests that speakers generally avoid obscurity and ambiguity of expression, and are brief and orderly in what they say.

Of course, we all know that people tell lies or are deliberately obscure. That does not always mean that the speakers are being uncooperative, but rather they might be depending on cooperation from the listener to consider the violations of the maxim as a basis for interpreting what they are really saying. For example, if a statement seems irrelevant, the listener must imply something which will make this statement relevant, and hence will understand something which the speaker was unable or unwilling to state clearly. For example, if we asked a person to assess the ability of a senior manager of their company, and they replied that he was always very well dressed and wore nice ties, we could regard this reply as irrelevant to the important issue of his competence as a manager. However, if we assume that the speaker is being cooperative, but is loath to say anything openly critical of the manager, we could infer that the speaker had nothing complimentary to say about the manager's ability. So she said something complimentary, but irrelevant. From this we can imply that the speaker does not think highly of the manager. In this way, by skilful use of the cooperative principle, we can understand far more than the speaker actually said.

Principles of analogy and minimal change

Brown and Yule (1983) suggest that, when listeners encounter spoken language, the context provides them with a set of default values or stereotypical knowledge. For example, our knowledge of the particular street the speaker is talking about enables us to fill in many of the details of the text. This applies not only when we know the place, but also if we know the speaker, the situation, the topic or the language – which may all lead us to have expectations about what we will hear.

Brown and Yule further argue that listeners apply these expectations in accordance with two basic principles (1983:63):

a) The **principle of analogy**, which leads listeners to expect that things will be as they were before. For example, if a speaker refers to a street we know, we automatically assume that the street will be as we have always known it to be, unless we have a specific reason to think otherwise.

b) The **principle of minimal change**, which leads the listener to assume that things will be as like as possible to how they were before. For example, if we have been told that a house in the street has been changed, we will assume that this is the only change and other things will be as they were, unless we have reason to think otherwise.

The cognitive environment

As we have seen, the interpretation of utterances is often a matter of inference: listeners must make assumptions based on the literal meaning of the utterance in conjunction with their background knowledge. Sperber and Wilson (1986) have suggested that we do this based on what is relevant in the context. The context they are referring to is what they have called the **cognitive environment.**

It is not actually the co-text that forms the basis for interpretation of an utterance, but what the listener has understood from the co-text. Similarly, it is not actually the context of situation that is important, but what the listener thinks about that situation, and it is not the accompanying visual information, but how the listener interprets that. In other words, what is important is what is in the listener's mind, and the cognitive environment is everything the listener has in their mind that could influence the interpretation of the meaning.

In second-language listening situations, where listeners have only a partial knowledge of the language and also come from a variety of different backgrounds, there may be considerable differences between listeners in what they have in their cognitive environments, and this can lead to very diverse interpretations of the text.

Building mental representations of meaning

In previous sections of this chapter we have considered many different aspects of the listening construct. In the final section we will consider how all these aspects can be brought together into one overall activity: listening comprehension.

The flow chart approach

One way to think about listening comprehension is that it involves taking in an acoustic signal and then processing that in some way to produce an understanding of the text. We could construct a type of flow chart, with the acoustic signal going in at one end and comprehension coming out at the other. A number of scholars have characterised listening in this way, for example Nagle and Sanders (1986). They start off by first discussing three different types of memory commonly described in the research literature: (i) **echoic memory**, where the sounds are held very briefly, (ii) **working memory**, where the input is held for a few seconds while most of the processing takes place, and (iii) **long-term memory**, where things are stored for a much longer duration.

To simplify somewhat, they suggest that the acoustic input is held briefly in echoic memory, which captures the sound and passes this to working memory. At this stage affective factors, such as interest or motivation, may strengthen the input, or weaken it due to lack of attention. This input is processed in working memory by an executive processor, by means of either controlled processes or automatic processes, or any degree of combination between the two, and the result is then passed to long-term memory. There the input is compared to and synthesised with other knowledge – linguistic, contextual or relevant general knowledge – and a feedback loop relates the results back to the executive processor where it may be reprocessed and recycled as necessary. Thus, the basis for arriving at an interpretation of the meaning of a text is a complex synthesis of all the listeners' current knowledge states and a variety of inferences about the incoming information.

What is especially useful about this model of the listening process is that it is intended to be a model of second-language processing, and so the distinction between controlled and automatic processing is emphasised. While automatic processes are the norm in efficient language use, controlled processes are more common when performing new skills, and hence these will be particularly important in second-language processing where, by definition, listeners have not yet mastered the linguistic system and are likely to be performing new skills. As there is a limited amount of attention available for controlled processes, when this attention capacity is exceeded, tasks may be divided into smaller processing units if the speech rate is slow enough or processing will break down if the speech rate is too fast.

Despite the fact that this model is clearly an over-simplified metaphor for actual language processing, it does seem to bring together the most important elements into a coherent whole and provides a model of how the listening construct might work.

Mental models

One problem with the Nagle and Sanders model is that it does not show how the meaning of the text is built up in memory. To understand this we need to look at the body of work which looks at mental representations of texts (Johnson-Laird, 1983; 1985). There are three main ways in which texts can be represented mentally: as propositions, as **mental models** or as images. A proposition, it will be recalled, is a simple idea that consists of a concept (usually a noun) and something that describes or relates to that concept (usually a verb or adjective): it may help to think of propositions as one very simple fact. Storing a large number of propositions in memory would be a tremendous memory burden, although we clearly do that at times. Johnson-Laird has suggested that a better way is to make mental models based on the content. Thus, in processing texts, we do not store what we have heard in terms of the language or in terms of the propositions, but in terms of the events described in the discourse – the objects, the people and the situations. Thus we make mental models which are analogous to the structure of the corresponding state of affairs in the world. Images are simply visual representations of mental models. So, in fact, there are only two major ways of representing the contents of a text: propositional representations or mental models (Johnson-Laird, 1985), and mental models are by far the most common.

Mental models are created as the text is processed. They are obviously not complete, and are continually updated and revised as more information becomes available, or it is necessary to construct a better understanding of the text. Van Dijk and Kintsch (1983) use this idea as the basis of their influential model of comprehension. They claim that, while processing discourse, the comprehender constructs two things: a **textbase**, which is a semantic representation of the propositions in the text, and a **situation model**, which is a mental model of what the text is about.

This theory – that listeners construct mental models during discourse comprehension – can explain many of the known characteristics of text processing. Because mental representations are structurally similar to the world, rather than to linguistic representations of it, we do not remember either the language of the text, or the actual propositions – all we remember is the meaning. The theory also explains why information that is implicit in the text, but not explicitly stated, is often included in our memory of the text. Although many linguistic expressions are ambiguous, the theory explains how the mental models provide a context in which to determine the meaning of these ambiguous expressions. The theory also explains the fact that representations of a text are continuously created in the listener's mind as the text is being heard, and these representations are updated as the listening continues.

The listener is creating and updating a mental model while listening, and at any point during the listening process that mental model provides the context for the interpretation of the next part of the text.

Thus mental models constitute a very important part of the cognitive environment and help determine how later parts of the text will be interpreted.

Conclusion

In this chapter I have attempted to lay the foundation for an understanding of the listening construct. To summarise the process, the listener takes the incoming data, the acoustic signal, and interprets that, using a wide variety of information and knowledge, for a particular communicative purpose; it is an inferential process, an ongoing process of constructing and modifying an interpretation of what the text is about, based on whatever information seems relevant at the time.

It is very important for anyone intending to create listening tests to realise that listening comprehension is not simply a process of decoding language. Meaning is not something in the text that the listener has to extract, but is constructed by the listener in an active process of inferencing and hypothesis building. Within this view of listening, a number of themes seem to stand out as being particularly relevant to the task of assessing listening comprehension.

- Firstly, there is the importance of automatic processing. If listening is to be successful, it is clear that language processing must be fast and efficient, and there is little time to think about the meaning. Thus, knowledge of language must include the ability to process the language automatically in real time.

- Secondly, the normal process of listening comprehension allows the sum total of the listener's knowledge, past experience, current thoughts, feelings, intentions, personality and intelligence to interact freely with the acoustic input and with each other, to create the interpretation of the text.

- Thirdly, this leads to the question of context. Listening is a cognitive process and in reality the context is not external to the listener. Listening comprehension takes place within the mind of the listener, and the context of interpretation is the cognitive environment of the listener.

This leads to the fourth point, that listening is a very individual and personal process. Listeners make different inferences, and they have different interpretations of the texts they hear. Of course, when the task is simple and unambiguous, all competent listeners are likely to come to the same understanding, and there is usually a common core of similar interpretation between different listeners listening to the same text. However, when we examine comprehension in detail we often find considerable differences between listener interpretations of many texts; and the more complex and ambiguous the text, the more likely that interpretations will vary.

This chapter has been very theoretical, and has taken a wide focus. I have included many ideas that are relevant to all forms of comprehension, not just listening. The next chapter will focus more narrowly on listening itself, and what is unique to the listening situation. We will also look at the skills involved in successful listening.

CHAPTER TWO

....

What is unique to listening

Introduction

In Chapter 1 I reviewed work from a number of academic disciplines, mainly linguistics and psychology, to arrive at a broad overview of the listening comprehension process. I concluded that listening comprehension is an active process of constructing meaning, and that this is done by applying knowledge to the incoming sound. I further concluded that comprehension is affected by a wide range of variables, and that potentially any characteristic of the speaker, the situation or the listener can affect the comprehension of the message.

Many of the important characteristics of listening comprehension are actually characteristics of all forms of language comprehension, and while listening ability is unique in some respects, it also shares many characteristics with reading. This should be clear from the discussion in Chapter 1, but there is also research evidence for this conclusion. For example, Buck (1992a) and Bae and Bachman (1998) have established by statistical means that there is considerable overlap between listening and reading ability, while both also have unique aspects. Freedle and Kostin have examined the sub-skills involved in processing a variety of multiple-choice test items, and comparison of the listening sub-skills (Freedle and Kostin, 1999) with the reading sub-skills (Freedle and Kostin, 1994) supports a similar conclusion.

This has practical implications for test development. It will become

clear in later chapters that testing listening is technically more complicated, more time consuming and far less convenient than testing
reading: providing good quality recorded sound, for example, is just
not as easy as handing out pieces of writing. If the purpose is to
assess general language comprehension, it will usually be far easier to
do that through reading. In many cases, it is not worth going to all the
trouble of testing listening unless we are particularly interested in the
knowledge, skills and abilities that are unique to listening.

However, listening is an important skill, and due to the practical
complexities of providing spoken texts, it is neglected in many language-learning situations. One important reason to test listening,
even when it might overlap quite considerably with reading, is to
encourage teachers to teach it. In such cases, it is probably still better
to emphasise the knowledge, skills and abilities which are unique to
real-world listening, in order to encourage teachers to teach learners
to comprehend realistic spoken language in a realistic manner.

The chapter will be organised under three main headings:

i   the important characteristics of spoken texts;
ii   the differences between first- and second-language listening;
iii some common taxonomies of skills used in listening.

The important characteristics of spoken texts

In this section we will look more closely at those aspects of comprehension that are unique to listening. It is my belief that these are the
characteristics we need to pay particular attention to if we want to
create good listening tests. We will look at phonology, accents, prosodic features, speech rate, hesitations and discourse structure.

Phonological modification

The sounds of a language must be learned in order to understand
speech. This is obvious; it is not the sounds themselves, however, that
cause the most comprehension problems, but the way they vary in
normal speech. In rapid speech, adjacent sounds influence each
other. Such modifications take place according to a set of very
complex rules, and these rules vary from one language to another. A

good description of phonological modification in English, and its relevance for second-language education, is provided by Roach (2001).

The degree of phonological modification varies depending on the situation. For example, in formal situations speakers will tend to have less modification than in informal situations; similarly, in cases where the information is important, they will tend to pronounce the words with more care than they would with casual, throw-away information.

In English the most important phonological changes are:

Assimilation, when sounds influence the pronunciation of adjacent sounds. For example, *'won't you'* is generally pronounced something like *'wonchoo'*.

Elision, when sounds are dropped in rapid speech. For example, *'next day'* is usually pronounced something like *'nexday'*.

Intrusion, when a new sound is introduced between other sounds. For example, in standard British English the sound /r/ at the end of the word *'far'* is not normally pronounced, but if the word is immediately followed by a vowel, as in *'far away'*, then it is inserted between the two words.

Also in English, the little words with a grammatical function usually have two pronunciations, a **strong form**, which is used in isolation or when the word is receiving stress, and a **weak form**, which is used in connected speech when the word has no sentence stress.

The modifications to pronunciation that take place during fast speech, especially informal speech, are quite extensive. Hardly a word is left unaffected. Other languages also have phonological modification, but according to a different set of rules.

Phonological modification and language comprehension

The phonological system – the complex set of rules that determine the pronunciation of connected speech – must of course be learned. Any lack of such knowledge is likely to be reflected in reduced comprehension. Many students who have studied a foreign language are shocked when they go abroad and hear native speakers for the first time, because the pronunciation encountered in the classroom often differs considerably from that used by real speakers. In a research study, Henricksen (1984) found that most native speakers had little difficulty understanding words in their modified form, whereas the presence of phonological modification significantly reduces comprehension for second-language listeners. Even higher-level L2 listeners can fail to recognise language they actually know very well. Listeners need to know how the sound system works, in order to be able to process natural speech in real time.

Accent

Another occasion when listeners will encounter words pronounced in a non-standard manner is when listening to speakers with unfamiliar accents. It is very normal for different groups of language users to pronounce language in characteristic ways, and everyone has an accent. The most common accents are related to geography. In the case of English, Australians pronounce English differently from Americans, and this is different again from British English. Even within countries there can be considerable variation: the pronunciation in the north of England is very different from the south. Scotland and Wales have their own characteristic accents, as do Texas, Minnesota and New England in the United States. This is the case with most languages. Japanese is pronounced differently in the north than in Tokyo, and is different again in Osaka. Learners of Japanese as a second language will learn the standard Tokyo pronunciation, and will probably be unable to understand speech from rural areas in the provinces. Even Japanese native speakers from Tokyo or Osaka may not understand country folk from the far north or south. A similar thing happens with most languages that are dispersed across a geographical area, including French, Spanish, Arabic, Chinese and so on. In addition, accents not only vary according to geographical region, but also according to social groups. In England, for example, working-class English is different from middle-class English, which is different again from upper-class English.

Accent and language comprehension

Native speakers are generally used to hearing a wide variety of accents, but even then, when they hear a new accent for the first time, they may not understand it very well, and it can take a little while for them to get used to it. L2 listeners are usually much less familiar with the range of common accents, and they sometimes have considerable problems when they hear a new accent for the first time (Kennedy, 1978). Eisenstein and Berkowitz (1981) showed that standard English is more intelligible to ESL learners than either the local working-class accent of New York, or foreign-accented English, and Anderson-Hsieh and Koehler (1988) found that the stronger the accent, the lower the listeners' comprehension. It seems reasonable to suppose that it generally takes L2 learners much longer to adjust to a new accent than native speakers.

Accent is potentially a very important variable in listening comprehension. When listeners hear an unfamiliar accent – perhaps hearing an Australian for the first time after studying with American teachers – this can cause problems and may disrupt the whole comprehension process. An unfamiliar accent can make comprehension almost impossible for the listener.

Prosodic features

Understanding the sound system of a language involves far more than just knowing the pronunciation of individual sounds and how they change in rapid speech. The prosodic features, stress and intonation, also carry a great deal of communicative information. How this works varies from language to language (see Cruttenden, 1997).

Stress

Stress is very important. In English, stressed syllables are not only louder, they are usually more clearly enunciated, longer, and are often preceded or followed by a short pause. There are two types of stress which are important in English, word stress and sentence stress.

Word stress is the relative emphasis of the various syllables within a word, and it forms a very important part of the phonological shape of that word. In Japanese all syllables generally have the same stress, but in English they usually get different amounts of stress. Even if an English word is pronounced with the correct sound sequence, it will often be misunderstood if the relative stress of the syllables is incorrect. This is especially important with longer words.

Sentence stress is the relative emphasis of the words within an utterance. In English the most important words in an utterance are given more stress than the surrounding words. Words are stressed to indicate the point the speaker is making. For example, if a speaker says:

my SISTER returned yesterday

the stress is on the word *'sister'*, indicating that the topic of the utterance is the person, rather than what she did. However, if the stress changes to

my sister RETURNED yesterday

the topic is what she did, rather than who did it.

Another characteristic of stress, is that in some languages it determines the pace of the speech. This is the case in English, which is a **stress-timed** language. What this means is that the time between stressed syllables remains reasonably constant in any utterance. In the following, the words *'fax'* and *'now'* are stressed, and the time between them is the same in each utterance, and each utterance would take the same amount of time (Van Lier, 1995).

FAX NOW
FAX it NOW
FAX it right NOW

The result of this is that the words between the stressed syllables are pronounced very quickly, with no stress, and if there are more words they are pronounced even quicker to fit in the short time. To fit them in so quickly they are subject to considerable phonological modification, and sometimes may almost disappear.

This is a characteristic of English. In other languages the timing is determined in different ways. Japanese, for example, is a syllable-timed language: each syllable occupies the same amount of time regardless of how many phonemes there are in the syllable.

Intonation

Intonation is the variation in pitch that takes place within an utterance. Generally, in English, statements end with a falling intonation and questions with a rising intonation. The intonation can make a considerable difference to the meaning.

Intonation has a number of very important functions. According to Crystal (1995) the most important ones are:

- **Emotional**: the intonation is used to express the speaker's attitudinal meaning, such as enthusiasm, doubt, or distaste.

- **Grammatical**: the intonation is used to mark the grammatical structure of the utterance, rather like the punctuation in written language.

- **Informational**: the intonation indicates the salient parts of an utterance, rather like sentence stress, so a higher pitch marks the important information.

- **Textual**: the intonation is used to help larger chunks of discourse to contrast or cohere, rather like paragraphs in written language.

- **Psychological**: the intonation is used to chunk information into units which are easier to deal with. For example, lists of words, or telephone and credit card numbers are grouped into units to make them easier to memorise.

- **Indexical**: the intonation is used by certain groups of people as a sort of identifier. For example preachers and newscasters often use a recognisable intonation pattern.

Intonation patterns do tend to vary from one language group to another, and they also change over time. A new intonation pattern is spreading across the English speaking world at present. This is a rising intonation at the end of statements. Women use it more than men, young people more than older people, and working-class more than professional-class people. Crystal (1995) suggests that it seems to have started in Australia or New Zealand, but I have heard it frequently among young people, especially women, in the United States. Perhaps in a few years it will become standard.

Prosody and comprehension

Stress and intonation are very important in word recognition. Dirven and Oakeshott-Taylor (1984) claim that they are more important to word recognition than the actual sounds, and Gimson (1980) suggests that 'a word pronounced with the correct sound sequence may well be misunderstood if the relative prominence of the syllables is in-correct.' Among their collection of **slips of the ear**, when people thought they heard something that was different to what was actually said, Bond and Garnes (1980) found that listeners usually understood the prosodic features of words, even when they did not catch the actual sounds.

Word stress, sentence stress and intonation are all important in comprehension. Lynch (1998) suggests that prosodic features have a direct impact on how listeners chunk and interpret discourse seg-ments. Furthermore, these prosodic features can carry considerable meaning that supplements, or in some cases contradicts, the literal meaning of the words. Much of the communicative effect of utter-ances is expressed by the stress and intonation, and listeners need to be able to understand that to construct a reasonable interpretation.

Speech rate

All second-language listeners have probably had the experience of listening to something and not quite understanding it because it seemed too fast, of feeling that they could have understood if only it had been a little slower. Listener perceptions that speech is too fast are often due to a lack of processing automaticity, and as listeners get better, and as they learn to process the language more automatically, speech seems to become slower. So just because speech appears fast, it does not mean it is. However, the actual speech rate does affect comprehension, and there is a whole body of research that looks at the relationship between speech rate and comprehension. Results generally support the common-sense belief that the faster the speech, the more difficult it is to comprehend.

Typical speech rates

It is useful to start by getting an idea of typical speech rates. Tauroza and Allison (1990) looked at average speech rates for British speakers: radio monologues, conversations and interviews aimed at native speakers, as well as lectures intended predominantly for a non-native speaking audience. Table 2.1 summarises their findings.

The most common measure of speech rate is words per minute (wpm), which is obviously problematic when we consider that some

Table 2.1. *Average Speech Rates for British English (Tauroza and Allison, 1990)*

Text Type	words/ minute	syllables/ minute	syllables/ second	syllables/ word
Radio Monologues	160	250	4.17	1.6
Conversations	210	260	4.33	1.3
Interviews	190	250	4.17	1.3
Lectures to NNS	140	190	3.17	1.4

words are much longer than others, and further that there are systematic differences in word length between text types. Table 2.1 shows how word length varies, with the conversations and the interviews having a shorter word length, 1.3 syllables per word, whereas the monologues have 1.6 syllables per word. It is quite likely that serious academic lectures would have had even longer average word length. Syllables are a much better unit of measurement whenever precision is necessary (Sticht, 1971; Tauroza and Allison, 1990). However, counting syllables is complex and time-consuming, whereas counting words is relatively easy (especially with a word processor), so words per minute continues to be widely used.

Looking at the speech rates, we can see that the average is about 170 wpm, or about 4 syllables per second (sps). Interactive speech – the conversations and the interviews – is a little faster, and monologues are a little slower. The lectures to the non-native speakers are much slower, at about 140 wpm or 3.17 sps, which suggests that the lecturers are probably slowing down their speech to aid comprehension. It is important to remember that these are averages, and that there will be considerable variation between different speakers: the speaker in Example 2.2, later in the chapter, normally speaks at about 230 wpm, which is very fast.

Relationship between speech rate and comprehension

What is important for us is the relationship between speech rate and comprehension. Looking first at the situation with native speakers, in an early study Foulke (1968) modified the speed of recordings from a talking book and found that comprehension was relatively unaffected by increases up to 250 wpm, but above this point it began to drop off rapidly. Foulke and Sticht (1969) and Sticht (1971) reviewed a number of other studies and concluded that there is indeed a gradual decline in comprehension, until a threshold level is reached at about 275 wpm, after which comprehension drops off far more steeply. Carver (1973) found similar results and interpreted them as follows:

> The data suggest that when an individual is presented with speech at increasingly high rates, there will be little decrease in his understanding of the thoughts until the minimum amount of time required to process each word, each group of words, or each thought is exceeded. Then, the decrease in thoughts understood will drop abruptly because little or nothing is understood or comprehended below the threshold.   (Carver, 1973:124)

Anderson-Hsieh and Koehler (1988) looked at speech rate and foreign accent. Predictably they found that native English speakers had lower comprehension at faster speech rates, but more interestingly, they found that the decrease in comprehension was most dramatic when the speaker had a more pronounced accent. This suggests that speech rate is more critical to comprehension when listening to speakers with less standard accents.

There is less research on the effects of speech rate on second-language comprehension. Stanley noted that the thing that gave listeners most difficulty when listening to everyday speech was 'quite simply, those areas which were spoken most rapidly' (1978:287). He adds that when speech was faster, language learners 'constantly failed to perceive individual phonemes and hence words with which they were already familiar' (1978:289). Griffiths (1992) looked at the effects of three different speech rates (127, 188, 250 wpm) on the comprehension of second-language speakers and concluded that comprehension was significantly better at the slowest speech rate and worse at the higher rates.

To summarise, the research has shown speech rate to be clearly an important variable in listening comprehension. Comprehension declines as the speaker talks faster, and the weight of the evidence suggests that the decline in comprehension is rather slow until a threshold level is reached, at which time an increased speech rate leads to a much more rapid decline in comprehension. As for the particular speech rate at which this rapid decline takes place, the weight of the evidence suggests that this varies from one listener to another and is affected by a variety of factors. There is strong evidence to suggest that the language ability of the listener is important

– non-native speakers seem to have a lower threshold – and that the accent of the speaker is also important. Based on this, we can probably assume that other text variables, such as vocabulary, syntax or topic, would also interact with speech rate.

Hesitation and language comprehension

One important characteristic of spoken texts are hesitations. There are four main types of hesitations: (i) unfilled pauses, which are just periods of silence; (ii) filled pauses, where the speaker uses fillers such as *'uh'*, *'um'*, *'ah'*, *'mm'* or *'well'*, *'anyway'*, *'let me see'*; (iii) repetitions, where the speaker repeats the same word or part of a word; and (iv) false starts, where the speaker stops and then replaces the previous word or phrase with another choice.

There is evidence to suggest that hesitation phenomena can present a major comprehension difficulty to non-native speakers who are listening to spontaneous speech. Voss (1979) asked 22 non-native speakers of English to listen to a passage of spontaneous speech, about 210 words long. The passage included a variety of hesitation phenomena: repeats, false starts, filled pauses and unfilled pauses. Results indicated that nearly one-third of all perception errors were connected with hesitation phenomena. These errors were due to listeners either misinterpreting hesitation phenomena as words, or parts of words, or to misinterpreting parts of words as hesitations.

However, there is also evidence to suggest that certain types of hesitation phenomena can aid comprehension. When one-second pauses were introduced into a text at the juncture between clauses, comprehension improved, while pauses inserted randomly into the text resulted in lower levels of comprehension (Friedman and Johnson, 1971; Johnson and Friedman, 1971). Blau (1990) inserted pauses into a variety of passages and found that comprehension of the text with the pauses was significantly better. However, Blau's results could have been because the listening passages with the pauses were slower and hence easier to understand. In a follow-up study, Blau (1991) used a new version of the recording in which pauses were filled with hesitation markers. Results indicated that comprehension scores for both hesitation passages, that is with un-filled pauses and filled pauses, were significantly higher than for the normal passages, but did not differ significantly from each other.

To summarise, the research on hesitation phenomena is quite clear in indicating that these occur as a regular and normal part of spoken English. Hence the ability to comprehend spoken English must include the facility to deal with these hesitation phenomena. As for how they affect comprehension, there are indications that in some cases they can aid comprehension, and in others they may cause problems. But the research suggests that pauses inserted at meaningful syntactic boundaries can aid comprehension, whereas random pauses do not. Hesitations that slow down the speech rate do aid comprehension for L2 listeners, and this applies to both filled and unfilled pauses, as long as the listener recognises the fillers as fillers. However, if the listener does not recognise these as fillers, then comprehension can be adversely affected.

Discourse structure

In Chapter One I reviewed work on important aspects of discourse comprehension, most of it conducted on first-language reading. There is also a body of work that looks at the effect of discourse on second-language listening comprehension, the work on academic lectures. This is important for our purpose because a common reason for testing listening comprehension is to determine whether students are ready for academic study.

I will also illustrate aspects of spoken discourse structure by presenting transcripts of actual speech samples. However, there are some problems connected with this. When speech is transcribed, many of its important characteristics are lost. Most importantly it loses stress, intonation and timing, and as we have seen these convey a great deal of important information. However, writing speech down does have the important advantage of making it clear just how different it is from writing. Some of the following examples may be difficult to read, but they are normal speech, and they made perfectly good sense when they were spoken.

Lecture comprehension

Many researchers believe that discourse variables are very important in lecture comprehension. For example, Olsen and Huckin (1990) point out that ESL students can understand all the words of a lecture and still fail to understand the main points, and Dunkel and Davis (1994) claim that lecture comprehension depends less on the meaning of the individual sentences, and more on their inter-relatedness and the structure of the whole text. Devices that explicitly signal the micro- and macro-structure of the text are assumed to be very important, and it is claimed that effective speakers make use of appropriate structuring and organising cues to help listeners understand the meaning of the lecture (Chaudron and Richards, 1986). Research suggests that both L1 listeners (Kintsch and Yarborough, 1982; Meyer and Freedle, 1984) and L2 listeners (Hron *et al.*, 1985; Chaudron and Richards, 1986) can benefit from explicit discourse markers within the text.

Lectures can be very challenging for second-language listeners, and some research has tried to discover how to make them easier: redundancy (using repetition and paraphrase) and the use of clear rhetorical markers are assumed to aid comprehension. Chiang and Dunkel (1992) found that added redundancy benefited higher ability students more than lower ability students, and Dunkel and Davis (1994) found that rhetorical signal cues did not aid comprehension.

Tauroza and Allison (1994) found that students have difficulty following more complex discourse structures. However, it is possible that lectures with the more complex structure also imposed a greater cognitive load on the listeners, and Brown (1995b) has argued that cognitive load is one of the most important determinants of difficulty in listening.

Speech sample one

The following is a transcript of a typical lecture, taken from Rost (1994). It is the beginning of an introductory lecture on social psychology.

Example 2.1

1 hello everybody. today i would like to continue our discussions of
2 social psychology. by talking about some of the major influences on
3 our attitudes and our behaviours. i think the place to start is by in-
4 troducing the idea or the concept of a norm. N-O-R-M. and I am
5 sure you are all familiar with this concept. a norm is an accepted or

6   expected standard of behaviour. or standard of thinking in a given
7   group of people. and we find that all groups of people have norms.
8   for an array of things. for basic things like the food they eat, the
9   clothes they wear, to much more complex types of behaviour and
10 decisions.

Although lectures are more formal than many other speech events, and although this is a very short extract, the discourse patterns are clearly different from written language. The speaker strings together direct statements, in a rather loose way, by just adding more information, and following on from one idea to the next. This is the most basic characteristic of discourse structure in spoken language.

Speech sample two

Academic lectures form a separate domain of language use, and are somewhat different from more informal speech. Example 2.2 is more typical of daily interaction. Here, a young American man is describing the time he arrived to take part in a tennis tournament and discovered that there was only one other person besides himself entered for the tournament.

Example 2.2

1   and i got there, and it turned out i was only the second person
2   signed up for the entire tournament. and so there_ the people who
3   ran it were like 'do you even want to bother playing the tournament?'
4   and i was like_ 'let's it a great opportunity because if i win then i've
5   won a tournament only with one match. so i can beat one guy, and
6   even if i don't, like who cares.' so_ and_ cuz you get points for when
7   you finish. so a runner-up gets the points anyway. so i was kind of
8   hoping that the other guy i was gonna playing against was gonna
9   dropout, and just give me the trophy. but he didn't. so anyway we
10 went out and played, and we didn't even start_ we started like way
11 after_ because i got there for a seven o'clock match. we didn't start
12 playing until like ten at night.

There are no significant pauses in the original, but obviously the stress, intonation and timing make the structure of the passage quite clear. This passage illustrates some noteworthy characteristics. Firstly there are a number of false starts. In line 2, there is a repair after *so there*', and later, on line 6 after *'so and'*, he changes his mind and offers an explanation of why he doesn't mind if he gets beaten. In line 10 too there is a repair after *'even start'*, and in line 11 one after *'like way after'*. He also appears to make a grammatical error in line 8, *'the other guy I was gonna playing against'*, although in rapid speech the two words *'playing'* and *'against'* run together and it is hard to be sure what was said.

Probably the most interesting aspect of this text, however, is the use of the word *'like'* to introduce a direct or indirect quotation, or even just a thought. He first uses this word when he explains how the organisers were asking the two players whether they actually wanted to play or not. In this case he uses it to introduce a direct quotation, *'the people who ran it were like do you even want to bother'*. He uses the same *'like'* to introduce his reaction, *'and i was like let's it a great opportunity'*. It seems likely that he is not necessarily quoting himself directly, but probably explaining his thoughts on the reasons that motivated him to continue with the match. He then uses *'like'* again in line 6, when he says, *'like who cares'*. In this case, however, this is clearly not a quotation, but an expression of his own attitude to the situation.

The point here is not to go into details of the usage of this word *'like'*, but to note that this is not a standard use of the word. Some would consider it slang, or think it incorrect usage, but the point is that this is very common among young Americans. This is not street slang, nor is this a conversation between two young teenagers. The speaker is an undergraduate at Princeton University, an Ivy League university with very high admission standards and, although the situation was relaxed and relatively informal, he is speaking to an older male who was a relative stranger.

Speech sample three

The third example is of a young American woman, a 19-year-old student at a state university. She is talking to a relative stranger, an older male, and telling him about how she got into serious debt with her credit cards.

Example 2.3

1   um now here comes August, and i'm thinking okay i'm getting bills.
2   they're saying eight hundred dollars, and six hundred dollars and

3   I'm like 'wow oh my goodness.' so yaknow i haven't stopped yet,
4   though, because i have them_ i have_ i keep one_ i stopped_ i put
5   two away_ i acquired another one mid- summer, used about three
6   hundred dollars on that one. and . . . uh i had one more that i was
7   still using because it was my A-T and T card, it was also a phone
8   card, so it was very helpful. um but anyway, um i finally started
9   using_ i i_ continue to use to that A-T and T card. and i saw little
10   sales that just yaknow i couldn't resist. they were perfect sales and_
11   they were good sales, but i didn't have money. it was_ using_ i was
12   using the credit cards, so i finally yaknow i called one day, i tried to
13   use the A-T and T card and it said no.

Again it is important to stress that this is normal informal speech and quite intelligible. Again there are no significant pauses in the original, but the rhythm, stress and intonation make the structure very clear. There are numerous fillers (e.g. *'um'*, *'uh'*), repetitions (e.g. line 9: *'i i'*), repairs (line 4: *'i have i keep one'* or line 11: *'it was using i was using'*), as well as exclamations (*'wow!'*) and non-standard forms (*'like'*, *'yaknow'*). What is most interesting however, is the discourse structure. This is really a stream of ideas, connected not so much by grammatical devices, but more by their juxtaposition in the text and the coherence of the ideas. In fact on reading this it appears very ungrammatical.

This is what much spoken language is really like. Reading a theoretical description as in Chapter 1 may be helpful, but it does not have the same impact as actually seeing normal speech written down in this way. These are not extreme examples of the spoken genre – readers can be assured that a group of close friends, chatting informally over a cup of coffee, would likely produce language with many more oral characteristics than the examples here.

Non-verbal signals

Before concluding this section on the characteristics of spoken texts, it is important to note that in many spoken interactions, the relevant linguistic information is conveyed not only by the sound. Kellerman (1990) has argued that looking at the speaker's mouth – the lips, jaw and tip of the tongue – provides information about what the speaker is saying, and listeners use that to help them understand. And not all the relevant information is conveyed by the language. As Abercrombie suggests, 'we speak with our vocal organs, but we converse with our bodies' (1967:55). Visual information is important in communication, and of particular interest given the increased availability of video and multimedia.

Work on teaching second-language listening suggests that visual support can aid language learners, especially less proficient learners, and is particularly helpful with more difficult texts (Rubin, 1995). However, whether visual information generally increases comprehension is still open to doubt, although test-takers certainly seem to prefer it (Progosh, 1996). Lynch (1998) suggests that it may increase motivation and attention levels, and comprehension of gist, but that it probably has little effect on understanding detail, and there is no firm evidence that it increases long-term retention.

Bostrom (1997) notes that the non-verbal signals sometimes contradict the verbal information, and in such cases listeners 'accept the non-verbal as a more valid expression of the feelings of the interactant' (Bostrom, 1997:24). There is research to indicate that listeners vary in their ability to understand these non-verbal cues (Burgoon, 1994), but Bostrom claims that visual cues are decoded with much greater accuracy than many verbal messages.

Non-verbal communications can take a number of forms, and they may be deliberate, for the purpose of communication, or unintentional. Firstly, there are actions or movements that are obligatory in certain types of social situations. For example, greetings such as bowing and handshaking are executed in a certain way, and in some social groups there is often a correct way to hold oneself while speaking to an employer or high-ranking superior officer. Refusing to behave in that respectful manner will have a very strong communicative effect, however polite one's words.

Secondly, certain general body movements express the mood of the speaker: depression or happiness are often very apparent in the posture and movements of the speaker, and our assessment of the speaker's mood can have a considerable influence on how we interpret what they say.

Thirdly, there is kinesics, which we might define as message-related body movements (Antes, 1996; Kellerman, 1992). Gestures or facial expressions can substitute for a verbal message, as in the case of a shoulder shrug to indicate that the speaker doesn't know or doesn't care. Sometimes body movements might reinforce a message, as in the case of emphatic gestures stressing important points, or at other times they might be intended to completely modify the interpretation of the spoken message, as in the case of gestures or facial expressions to indicate disbelief or sarcasm.

Although the effect of visual information may vary considerably from one listening situation to another, it certainly has the potential to influence or change the listener's interpretation of the speaker's words in a significant way.

The differences between first- and second-language listening

The view of listening comprehension described in Chapter One was developed mainly through first-language comprehension. In the last section we looked at what is unique about listening compared to other types of comprehension. In this section we will look at the difference between first- and second-language listening.

Although there is not much work that looks explicitly at the difference between first- and second-language processing (see Lynch, 1998), the existing work suggests that the processes are similar. For example, Fishman (1980) found that both first- and second-language test-takers made similar types of errors. Voss (1984) looked at slips of the ear, and also found that both natives and non-natives made similar types of errors.

I believe that the evidence to date gives no reason to suppose that second-language listening is in any fundamental way different from first-language listening. The same processes seem to apply. Dunkel (1991a), for example, makes a similar assumption in her review of native- and second-/foreign-language listening. Faerch and Kasper (1986) claim that first- and second-language listening differ only in that the second-language listener has a restricted knowledge of the language, and that they might be influenced by transfer from their first language.

There is, however, a difference in emphasis. When problems arise in native-language listening, they are often due to such factors as the listener being distracted, disinterested or responding to the content by thinking about something else. While these will obviously be of importance to all listeners, with second-language listening more problems arise due to insufficient knowledge of the linguistic system, or a lack of knowledge of the socio-cultural content of the message.

They may lack crucial content or textual schemata to help them understand the text (Long, 1989; Chiang and Dunkel, 1992), and because they generally come from a different background, second-language learners often lack important background knowledge that would help them compensate for their lack of linguistic skills (see Aitchison, 1994; Bremer *et al.*, 1996).

First-language knowledge

All normal human beings successfully acquire their first language. In our first language, we are all capable of understanding complex and subtle ideas. Indeed, first-language listeners become very adept at detecting affective cues about the speaker's state of mind or attitude towards the message (Bostrom, 1997). This is not always the case with second-language listeners.

First-language knowledge is largely implicit, by which I mean that it is outside conscious awareness. It is procedural knowledge rather than declarative knowledge. We do not consciously learn most of our first-language skills, we just acquire them automatically as we grow up and interact with the world around us. In our first language, we all know many complex rules and can use them correctly without being aware of them, and usually we could not explain these rules if we tried. The cognitive processes that are involved in first-language comprehension are almost entirely automatic – it is as if the language were transparent: we just do not notice it is there. When we hear something in our first language, we just automatically understand.

Second-language knowledge

In the case of a second language, we usually learn things differently, especially when we learn it as an adult. Knowledge of the language varies considerably: from those who can understand only a few isolated words in their second language, to those who appear to be indistinguishable from native speakers. Rarely do second-language learners develop the same high level of ability as in their first language. In most cases, second-language listeners have huge gaps in their knowledge of the language. Although some second-language knowledge is implicit, much of the knowledge is explicit, by which I mean that it is to some extent consciously known and consciously applied.

For example, in a study which examined dictation errors, Angela Oakeshott-Taylor (1977) found evidence that proficient subjects were able to process the sound quickly and derive meaning from what they were hearing, whereas weaker subjects had to spend so much time on basic linguistic analysis that they had no time for interpretation of the meaning. She concludes, 'the process that takes place with the native speaker in a matter of milliseconds may occur over a longer period of time with the less proficient L2 speaker' (1977:148).

If we think of language as a window through which we look at what the speaker is saying, in the case of first-language listening, the glass is very clean and we see through it without even noticing it is there; but in the case of second-language listening, the glass is dirty: we can see clearly through some parts, other parts are smudged, and yet other parts are so dirty we cannot see through them at all. We are very aware of the glass because it gets in the way.

When second-language learners are listening, there will often be gaps in their understanding. In some cases, these gaps will be just a small part of what they hear, an occasional word or nuance; but in other cases the gaps will form a significant proportion of the message, and in more extreme cases, the listener may only understand a few isolated words or expressions. Of course, gaps occur in first-language listening too, but the gaps in second-language listening usually have a far more significant impact on comprehension.

Compensatory skills

As we have seen, listeners use their understanding of the communicative situation – the speakers or the topic under discussion – to help them understand what is being said. Therefore, when there is a gap in their linguistic knowledge, second-language listeners will naturally tend to compensate for that by using any other available information – including visual information, general background knowledge or their common sense. A second-language listener who knows the situation well and who knows what to expect, will often be able to understand a great deal even when there are considerable gaps in their knowledge of the language. These compensatory skills are a significant aspect of second-language listening.

However, this may not always be so easy for second-language listeners who come from different backgrounds: what is significant in one cultural situation may not be significant in another. Similarly, non-verbal information may have different meanings from one culture to another. For example, in certain situations in Japan, it is common to laugh as an expression of extreme embarrassment; Americans would never laugh in such situations and so they could easily misinterpret this as indicating a lack of concern. The second-language listener may be at a considerable disadvantage, because the background knowledge necessary to understand and interpret the language may not be available.

I believe that the difference between first- and second-language listening is not that the processes are fundamentally different in any way, but only that the knowledge necessary to understand is often grossly inadequate for the second-language listener. This may often be a double disadvantage, in that they lack both the knowledge of the language and also the background knowledge to compensate for that.

Listening sub-skills

Listening comprehension is a complex, multidimensional process, and a number of theorists have attempted to describe it in terms of taxonomies of sub-skills that underlie the process. However, it should be stressed at the outset that the empirical support for these taxonomies is usually lacking. While there is no doubt that many of the components are crucial in listening, there is no evidence to suggest that any of these taxonomies constitute a complete unified description of the listening process. Collectively they are useful because they tell us what scholars in the field have come to think is important in listening comprehension.

The two-stage view

One very common taxonomy is the division of listening into a two-stage process: a first stage, in which the basic linguistic information is extracted, and then a second stage in which that information is utilised for the communicative purpose. This division of listening comprehension is a theme that occurs again and again in the literature, and for this reason I believe it has considerable value.

Probably the clearest example is Carroll (1972), who describes listening comprehension as a two-stage process: first the apprehension of the linguistic information contained in the message, and second the application of that linguistic information to the wider communicative context. Rivers (1966) suggests that listening to a foreign language may be analysed into two levels of activity: 'the recognition level, involves the identification of words and phrases in their structural inter-relationships' and 'the level of selection, where the listener is drawing out from the communication those elements which seem to him [sic] to contain the gist of the message' (1966:199).

In a very influential text on speech processing, Clark and Clark (1977) make the distinction between the 'construction process', which is the way listeners construct an interpretation of a sentence from the speaker's words, and the 'utilisation process', which is concerned with how listeners utilise this interpretation. In the construction process the listener understands the underlying propositions which the speaker meant to express, and then in the utilisation process the listener uses these to understand what the speaker intended to communicate by that. Oakeshott-Taylor (1977) proposes a similar distinction between what he calls 'micro-comprehension' which is the perception of a short section of a text, and 'macro-comprehension' which is the understanding of a text in its totality (Oakeshott-Taylor, 1977:94).

Clark and Clark (1977) make the point that the distinction between the two processes may not be very clear. They stress that this does not infer a serial or sequential model of listening, and that in actual practice it may not be possible for a listener to infer the meaning of the propositions without simultaneously being aware of the speaker's purpose in using them. There will obviously be feedback between them, and the two aspects of listening comprehension will be capable of interacting and influencing each other.

Despite some differences, these scholars seem to have arrived at similar conceptualisations of listening comprehension, and the fact that they use different terminology suggests that they have arrived at this understanding more or less independently. This adds considerable credibility to the two-stage view of listening.

A cognitive skills approach

Quite a different approach underlies a taxonomy from Valette (1977:20), which is interesting because she intended this to form the basis for developing listening tests. Although she makes no reference to Bloom, the categories do seem heavily influenced by Bloom's (1956) taxonomy of educational objectives in the cognitive domain. Her taxonomy has five levels; it does not attempt to describe the processing of listening *per se*, but describes a series of increasingly complex cognitive skills that can be used to show increasing facility with listening comprehension.

- **Mechanical skills**: the listener performs by rote memory, rather than by understanding. For example, perceiving differences between two or more sounds and making distinctions between them.
- **Knowledge of the language**: the listener demonstrates this by showing knowledge of facts, rules etc. This can be done by answering simple questions about the language.
- **Transfer**: the listener uses this knowledge in new situations, for example taking information from one source and using it for a new purpose.
- **Communication**: the listener uses the language as a natural vehicle for communication, for example when a message containing new information is understood.
- **Criticism**: the student analyses or evaluates a piece of language in terms of its effectiveness, appropriacy, style, tone etc.

Communicative approaches

Given the interest in communicative language teaching, it is not surprising that some scholars have attempted to describe listening skills in communicative terms. An early attempt to do this was Aitken (1978). His taxonomy goes beyond basic linguistic processing and takes into account a variety of skills which are concerned with relating the basic linguistic processing to the wider communicative situation. He does not claim that these constitute a complete description of the skills used in listening, but he does claim that the skills needed to process and comprehend speech include at least the following:

- Understanding the vocabulary and being able to guess the meanings of unfamiliar or unclear words from their context.
- Understanding the syntactic patterns, the morphological forms characteristic of spoken language, and following the discourse patterns of spoken language.
- Understanding the flow of stressed and unstressed sounds, as well as intonation cues and other cues of oral punctuation.
- Identifying the speaker's purpose.
- Drawing correct conclusions and valid inferences about the social situation, the speaker's intent or the general context.
- Recognising the speaker's attitude to the listener and the subject of their discussion.
- Identifying the techniques and rhetorical devices the speaker used to convey the message.

A later, and more comprehensive taxonomy of communicative listening sub-skills is provided by Weir (1993). He does not call this a taxonomy as such, but a checklist of operations that listening tests should require. Like Aitken, he makes it clear he does not regard this as a complete list of listening sub-skills.

Direct meaning comprehension

- listening for gist
- listening for main idea(s) or important information; and distinguishing that from supporting detail, or examples
- listening for specifics, including recall of important details
- determining a speaker's attitude or intention towards a listener or a topic

Inferred meaning comprehension

- making inferences and deductions
- relating utterances to their social and situational contexts
- recognising the communicative function of utterances
- deducing meaning of unfamiliar lexical items from context

Contributory meaning comprehension

- understanding phonological features
- understanding grammatical notions such as comparison, cause, result, degree etc.
- understanding discourse markers
- understanding the main syntactic structure of clauses or idea units
- understanding cohesion, especially reference
- understanding lexical cohesion, especially lexical set membership and collocations
- understanding lexis

Listening and taking notes

- ability to extract salient points to summarise the text
- ability to select relevant key points

It is interesting that neither Aitken nor Weir attempt to provide exhaustive lists of communicative skills, but rather seem content to point out the important skills that they think should be included on listening tests.

More detailed taxonomies

However, other theorists have taken a different view and tried to present a far more complete taxonomy of sub-skills. One of these is Richards (1983). He asserts that 'listening purposes vary according to whether learners are involved in listening as a component of social action (e.g. conversational listening), listening for information, academic listening (e.g. lectures), listening for pleasure (e.g. radio, movies, television), or for some other reason' (1983:228). He suggests that different lists of 'micro-skills' (1983:228) would be required for each of these, and his suggestions for conversational listening are given in Table 2.2, and for academic listening in Table 2.3.

Table 2.2. *Conversational Listening (Richards, 1983)*

1. ability to retain chunks of language of different lengths for short periods
2. ability to discriminate between the distinctive sounds of the target language
3. ability to recognise the stress patterns of words
4. ability to recognise the rhythmic structure of English
5. ability to recognise the functions of stress and intonation to signal the information structure of utterances
6. ability to identify words in stressed and unstressed situations
7. ability to recognise reduced forms of words
8. ability to distinguish word boundaries
9. ability to recognise the typical word order patterns in the target language
10. ability to recognise vocabulary used in core conversational topics
11. ability to detect key words (i.e. those which identify topics and propositions)
12. ability to guess the meaning of words from the contexts in which they occur
13. ability to recognise grammatical word classes
14. ability to recognise major syntactic patterns and devices
15. ability to recognise cohesive devices in spoken discourse
16. ability to recognise elliptical forms of grammatical units and sentences
17. ability to detect sentence constituents
18. ability to distinguish between major and minor constituents
19. ability to detect meanings expressed in differing grammatical forms/ sentence types (i.e. that a particular meaning may be expressed in different ways)
20. ability to recognise the communicative functions of utterances, according to situations, participants, goals
21. ability to reconstruct or infer situations, goals, participants, procedures
22. ability to use real-world knowledge and experience to work out purpose, goals, settings, procedures
23. ability to predict outcomes from events described
24. ability to infer links and connections between events
25. ability to deduce causes and effects from events
26. ability to distinguish between literal and applied meanings
27. ability to identify and reconstruct topics and coherent structure from ongoing discourse involving two or more speakers
28. ability to recognise coherence in discourse, and to detect such relations as main idea, supporting idea, given information, new information, generalisation, exemplification
29. ability to process speech at different rates
30. ability to process speech containing pauses, errors, corrections
31. ability to make use of facial, paralinguistic and other clues to work out meaning
32. ability to adjust listening strategies to different kinds of listener purposes or goals
33. ability to signal comprehension or lack of comprehension, verbally and non-verbally

---

Table 2.3. *Academic Listening (Richards, 1983)*

1. ability to identify purpose and scope of lecture
2. ability to identify topic of lecture and follow topic development
3. ability to identify relationships among units within discourse (e.g. major ideas, generalisations, hypotheses, supporting ideas, examples)
4. ability to identify role of discourse markers in signalling structure of a lecture (e.g. conjunctions, adverbs, gambits, routines)
5. ability to infer relationships (e.g. cause, effect, conclusion)
6. ability to recognise key lexical items related to subject/topic
7. ability to deduce meanings of words from context
8. ability to recognise markers of cohesion
9. ability to recognise function of intonation to signal information structure (e.g. pitch, volume, pace, key)
10. ability to detect attitude of speaker toward subject matter
11. ability to follow different modes of lecturing: spoken, audio, audio-visual
12. ability to follow lecture despite differences in accent and speed
13. familiarity with different styles of lecturing: formal, conversational, read, unplanned
14. familiarity with different registers: written versus colloquial
15. ability to recognise relevant matter: jokes, digressions, meanderings
16. ability to recognise function of non-verbal cues as markers of emphasis and attitude
17. knowledge of classroom conventions (e.g. turn-taking, clarification requests)
18. ability to recognise instructional/learner tasks (e.g. warnings, suggestions, recommendations, advice, instructions)

One very influential taxonomy of language skills is Munby (1978), who provides a very detailed taxonomy of what he calls 'enabling-skills'. This includes both productive and receptive, spoken and written skills, and provides the most exhaustive list of sub-skills, a list too long to be quoted here.

Research-based taxonomies

The taxonomies described above are based primarily on theoretical speculation, but there are a small number of taxonomies based on research. Using a newly developed research methodology, Buck *et al.* (1997) looked at 30 listening items from Part Three of the TOEIC: short dialogues followed by one multiple-choice comprehension question. They found 14 abilities which they claimed were most important:

- the ability to process faster input
- the ability to process lower-frequency vocabulary
- the ability to process text with higher vocabulary density
- the ability to process more complex structures
- the ability to process longer segments
- the ability to process text with a higher information density
- the ability to scan short segments to determine listening purpose
- the ability to synthesise scattered information
- the ability to use redundant information
- the ability to use word-matching strategies
- the ability to resist superficial word associations
- the ability to recall (arbitrary) names
- the ability to make text-based inferences
- the ability to use background knowledge to make inferences

In a similar study, Buck and Tatsuoka (1998) looked at a test with 35 short-answer comprehension questions, taken by a group of Japanese test-takers. They found 15 abilities that accounted for most of the test-taker performance:

- the ability to identify the task by determining what type of information to search for in order to complete the task
- the ability to scan relatively fast spoken text, automatically and in real time
- the ability to process a relatively large information load
- the ability to process a relatively medium information load
- the ability to process relatively dense information
- the ability to use previous items to help information location
- the ability to identify relevant information without any explicit marker to indicate it
- the ability to understand and utilise relatively heavy stress
- the ability to process relatively fast text automatically

- the ability to make text-based inferences
- the ability to incorporate background knowledge into text processing
- the ability to process L2 concepts with no literal equivalent in the L1
- the ability to recognise and use redundant information
- the ability to process information scattered throughout a text
- the ability to construct a response relatively quickly and efficiently

All the taxonomies in this section should be treated with caution. Those based on theory are only lists of what scholars think are likely to be important, whereas those based on research use complex statistical techniques that are still not fully understood. They give no indication of the relative importance of individual skills, nor do they provide guidance on how they should be sampled for test construction. Furthermore, the unspoken assumption is that these sub-skills described here are in fact skills – namely that they are things that somehow exist within the listener. There is reason to question whether this is the case. As we have seen, language use can be defined at almost any grain size – from broad sub-skills, such as the ability to listen for gist, to small detailed sub-skills, such as the ability to recognise the stress patterns of specific words. The research seems to suggest that we are able to identify them statistically at almost any level of detail. Perhaps these sub-skills are just ways of describing language-use activities. In other words, they may not be something we have within us, but may just be something we do with language. Nevertheless, what these taxonomies of sub-skills do is help us think about what processes we should be including in our listening tests.

Overall, what do these taxonomies tell us about the listening construct? The first point is that listening is a multi-faceted process, with a large number of sub-components that can be viewed from a number of different perspectives. The short taxonomies make the point that we need to test both the ability to extract the basic linguistic information, and the ability to interpret that in terms of some broader context. We need linguistic processing, which should include phonology, stress and intonation, word meanings, syntax and discourse features. We also need interpretation in terms of the co-text, the context of situation and world knowledge, which would include summarising, making inferences, understanding sociolinguistic implications, following the rhetorical structure and understanding the speaker's communicative intent.

Conclusion

In Chapter 1 we looked generally at how comprehension works, whereas in this chapter we have concentrated on the characteristics unique to the listening situation.

We have seen how the sounds of the language often undergo considerable modification in rapid speech; and that there is considerable redundancy in the input, and much of the information is provided in a number of different forms. Stress and intonation are important and carry vital information. Stress is used to mark important words or ideas, and intonation is used to mark the grammatical structure of the text as well as indicating the attitude of the speaker to the content of the message.

Speech is usually a quick first draft, and often contains a variety of hesitations, repetitions and corrections. Spoken texts usually consist of a series of short utterances, strung together in a simple linear manner. Ideas may be developed over a number of utterances. The relations between ideas are often expressed less through grammatical structure but more through the juxtaposition and coherence of the ideas. Often it is not clear exactly what pronouns or cohesive markers refer to.

Spoken texts exist in real time and need to be processed very rapidly as they are heard. We have seen how the listeners' understanding of a passage depends very much on the purpose for listening and the background knowledge of the listener. Then, having been spoken, the text is gone, and generally all the listener has left is a memory of what they understood.

I have examined a number of ways of defining the listening construct in terms of its sub-components. In the next chapter, Chapter 3, I will look at how language testers have developed notions of the listening construct, and how they have attempted to use these to develop test items. Then, in Chapter 4, I will describe how to provide construct definitions useful for test development.

CHAPTER THREE

....

Approaches to assessing listening

Introduction

The purpose of Chapters 1 and 2 was to describe the listening construct. The rest of this book will be concerned with how to measure ability on that construct. For those who would prefer a simpler introduction to this topic, or who would like to read a brief summary, there are overviews of the assessment of listening comprehension. I would recommend Brindley (1998), Buck (1988, 1997) and Thompson (1995).

The basic task in making assessments is to take theoretical notions about a construct and to **operationalise** those, that is to turn them into actual practice, in a set of **test items**. (A test item is the part of the test that requires a scorable response from the test-taker.) Historically, there have been three main approaches to language testing: the discrete-point, integrative and communicative approaches. Associated with each of these approaches are a set of theoretical notions about language and what it means to comprehend spoken language, and certain testing techniques. These approaches do not constitute a precise, coherent set of ideas, but a tendency to emphasise particular aspects of language ability, and when we examine the testing techniques associated with each approach, we will see considerable overlap between them.

The theoretical notions underlying testing practice are not always explicit. However, each test item is based on particular theoretical notions about the nature of the construct being measured. In some cases, test-developers may be fully aware of what these theories are, and in other cases they may not. They often do things in a way that just feels right, or in the way that people have always done them. Implicit in their practice are ideas about listening and how it should be tested, even though test-developers may not know what they are. We can often look at a test, or test items, and say with some certainty what theoretical notions underly that practice – although it is not always possible. The chapter is divided into three sections:

i   the discrete-point approach and associated techniques;

ii   the integrative approach and associated techniques;

iii   the communicative approach and associated techniques.

The discrete-point approach

During the period when the audio-lingual method was the preferred way of teaching language, structuralism was the dominant linguistic paradigm and behaviourism the dominant psychological paradigm, discrete-point testing was the most common approach to language testing. The most famous advocate of this approach was Lado, who defines language in behaviourist terms. He maintains that language is a 'system of habits which operates largely without our awareness' (Lado, 1961:13). The basic idea of the discrete-point approach is that it is possible to identify and isolate the separate bits, or elements, of language – the units of linguistic knowledge – and test each one of these separately. There are too many elements to test them all, and so test-developers sample the most important ones, and then assume that knowledge of these is representative of knowledge of the whole language.

Lado considered listening comprehension to be a process of recognising the sounds of the language. The basic testing technique is 'presenting orally to the students an utterance in the goal language and checking to see if the students understand the complete utterance or crucial parts of it' (1961:208). As for what the items should measure, he recommends segmental phonemes, stress, intonation, grammatical structure and vocabulary. He suggests using true/false, multiple-choice questions and pictures. He also cautions against the use of too much context, 'the context should be enough to resolve any ambiguity as to the crucial problem, and no more' (1961:218). Thus, for Lado, testing listening comprehension means testing the ability to recognise elements of the language in their oral form.

Discrete-point tests generally use selected responses. True/false items are quite common, but the three- or four-option multiple-choice format has become so closely associated with discrete-point testing that some people do not distinguish between the two. There are a number of multiple-choice tests, most notably the TOEFL, that were first created under the influence of discrete-point ideas, which now focus more on overall comprehension and even inference, while still keeping the same multiple-choice format. Although the test items look almost the same, the construct is quite different. Nevertheless, many people still refer to them, mistakenly, as discrete-point tests.

The most common tasks for testing listening in the discrete-point tradition are phonemic discrimination tasks, paraphrase recognition and response evaluation.

Phonemic discrimination tasks

Perhaps the listening task that is the most extreme example of the discrete-point approach is the phonemic discrimination task. Test-takers listen to one word spoken in isolation, and have to identify which word they have heard. Often the words are what are called **minimal pairs**: two words that differ only in one phoneme, such as *'ship'* and *'sheep'*, *'bat'* and *'but'*, or *'buff'* and *'puff'*. Such items really do come quite close to testing one bit of language knowledge.

In Example 3.1, test-takers listen to a recording and select the word they heard.

Example 3.1

Test-takers hear:
  i hear they have developed a better vine near here.

They read:
  *I hear they have developed a better **vine/wine** near here.*

This is a discrete-point item in the sense that the test-taker is given no clue at all to the correct interpretation, except for the phonetic information being tested. This is a somewhat unnatural task because in most listening situations, listeners do not use just the phonetic information to determine what was said, they also use the context.

However, in this particular case, even if there were some context, such as a conversation about new developments in the local wine trade, it may not help.

Minimal pairs are very unfashionable at the present time, but it may be appropriate to use them if the test-takers share a first language that has particular problems distinguishing certain sounds. For example, for Japanese learners who often have difficulty distinguishing between /l/ and /r/, or for Hungarian learners who have difficulty distinguishing /v/ and /w/.

Paraphrase recognition

The basic idea of discrete-point testing is that test items focus on one small part of the utterance, but in most discrete-point listening items it is necessary to understand more than just the point being tested.

In Example 3.2 test-takers listen to a statement and then choose the option that is closest in meaning:

Example 3.2

Test-takers hear:
John ran into a classmate on his way to the library.

They read:
   (a) *John exercised with his classmate.*
   (b) *John ran to the library.*
   (c) *John injured his classmate with his car.*
   (d) *John unexpectedly met a classmate.*

The item focuses on the meaning of the idiom *'ran into'*, and the rest of the language is only there to provide context for that idiom. However, while each of the options offers a different meaning of the word *'ran'* or *'ran into'*, it is still necessary to understand the other language that accompanies it. Such paraphrase recognition items are typical of discrete-point listening tests.

Response evaluation

In many cases though, items focus on more than one point. In the following item test-takers hear a question followed by four possible responses and choose the most appropriate response.

Example 3.3

Test-takers hear:
   how much time did you spend in Boston?

They read:
   (a) *Yes, I did.*
   (b) *Almost $250.*
   (c) *Yes, I had to.*
   (d) *About four days.*

The correct response is (d) *'About four days'* and the item is focusing on whether listeners have understood the expression *'how much time'*. Whereas option (b) *'Almost $250'* seems to be testing whether people are misunderstanding the common idiom *'how much'*, and option (a) *'Yes, I did'* is probably testing whether people are misunderstanding the purpose of the expression *'did you'* in the stem. This item is no longer testing one discrete point, but a number of different points.

In Example 3.4, we see an item that appears superficially similar; test-takers hear a statement followed by three alternative responses and have to choose the best response.

Example 3.4

Test-takers hear:
   Male 1:   *are sales higher this year?*
   Male 2:   (a) *they're about the same as before.*
              (b) *no, they hired someone last year.*
              (c) *they're on sale next month.*

However, this item is quite different. It is not attempting to focus on any one linguistic point, nor even a number of particular linguistic points, but simply requires understanding the literal meaning of a number of short, decontextualised utterances. If the language is understood, there is no difficulty choosing the correct option; the three options are quite different from each other, and the two incorrect options are unrelated to the question. Another interesting point: the options are not written down, but are given orally and so this item will require holding the options in memory, while the correct one is selected.

Discrete-point items are usually scored by giving one mark, or point, for each correct item, and using the total number of correct items as the total test score. (In British practice, test items are said to be marked, and in US practice they are scored by giving points. These terms mean essentially the same thing, and I will use them interchangeably.)

The theoretical view of listening implicit in discrete-point tests

Although it is rarely found in listening tests, two particularly noteworthy theoretical notions seem to be implicit in the strongest form of the discrete-point approach. The first notion is that it is important to be able to isolate one element of the language from a continuous stream of speech. The second notion is that spoken language is basically the same as written language, only presented orally, and so listening is just a process of recognising the elements of the language in this alternative form. These notions are clearly mistaken given the review of listening comprehension in Chapters 1 and 2.

However, while putting the focus on one individual element, most discrete-point tests also require other elements to be processed and interpreted in order to understand the element of interest. Such items take little account of the fact that language is redundant, or that language processing involves sampling the incoming stream of speech and using that to make predications and inferences. Comprehension is seen as understanding language on a local, literal level, and meaning is treated as something that is contained within the text, and the listeners' task is to get it out.

We will see in the next section how the ideas underlying discrete-point testing were criticised, and how this led to the integrative and communicative testing movements.

Integrative testing

In the early 1970s scholars, notably Oller, started arguing for what have become known as *integrative* tests. Oller explained, 'whereas discrete items attempt to test knowledge of language one bit at a time, integrative tests attempt to assess a learner's capacity to use many bits all at the same time' (Oller, 1979:37). He based his ideas on what he called a **pragmatic expectancy grammar** (Oller, 1979). By this he means that there are regular and rule-governed relationships between the various elements of the language, and that to know a language it is necessary to know how these elements relate to each other. Oller was claiming that in terms of language use, the whole is greater than the sum of its parts. He offers a definition of these pragmatic or integrative tests as 'any procedure or task that causes the learner to process sequences of elements in a language that conform to the normal contextual constraints of that language' (Oller, 1979:38).

Oller is talking about *using* language, rather than just knowing about it, but there is no mention of communication in Oller's definition, only of processing sequences of linguistic elements. The main difference from the discrete-point approach is that integrative testing puts the emphasis on assessing the processing of language as opposed to assessing knowledge about the elements of the language.

Reduced redundancy

As noted in Chapter 1, redundancy is one important way the elements of language relate to each other, and it is useful to see exactly how redundancy works. Consider the following sentence, *'I walked to work yesterday'*. There is a past-tense marker, *'-ed'*, on the verb *'walk'*, and this tells us that the action took place sometime in the past. Yet the word *'yesterday'*, also indicates that the action took place in the past. The past-tense marker is redundant. If the topic of the whole conversation were how the speaker had been travelling to work recently, we would now have three ways of knowing that the walking took place in the past. If the *'-ed'* on the end of *'walked'* were omitted for some reason, the listener would understand quite well, and could even replace the missing part, based on an understanding of the other parts of the text.

Speech is redundant on many different levels: it is redundant on the acoustic, phonological, morphological and syntactic levels, and this is also increased by the context, through the co-text, the topic and the situational context. Furthermore, there is a large amount of predictable material in normal usage, such as idiomatic expressions, stock phrases, collocations and regular patterns of expression (Cohen, 1977).

Because of this regularity and redundancy, those who know the language well will be able to make predictions about the language based on this pragmatic expectancy grammar, and this ability to make predictions can be used as a measure of proficiency in the language. Such tests of **reduced redundancy**, in which elements are removed thus reducing the redundancy of the text, became widely used, and have come to be very closely associated with the integrative testing movement.

Noise tests

One early recommendation for creating reduced-redundancy listening tests was the noise test (Gradman and Spolsky, 1975). Test-takers listen to a passage which has been mutilated by the addition of background noise. This partly masks the text. The added noise is usually what is called **white noise** – that is, noise which covers most of the frequency range of the spectrum, a sort of continuous hiss. Test-takers listen, and respond by repeating what they have heard – either speaking aloud, or writing it down during appropriate pauses.

Noise tests have never been popular, and it is not difficult to see why. Apart from the practical problems of collecting responses, making the tapes requires good equipment and a level of technical expertise. Also, the white noise is irritating, and test-takers tend to dislike these tests. It might be worthwhile attempting to replace the white noise with more realistic background noise, the hum of conversation from a room full of people, perhaps. However, probably the most telling objection to noise tests is that, if we are going to ask students to respond by writing what they have heard, we are giving them a type of dictation; which is more or less the same as a noise test without the noise.

Listening cloze

Cloze tests are reading tests based on the idea of reduced redundancy. The basic cloze procedure is very simple. A text is selected, and words are replaced by blanks in a systematic way, usually every 5th, 7th or 10th word. The test-taker has to fill in the blanks by writing down the word they think fits best. Given the popularity of cloze tests, it is not surprising that there have been a number of attempts to adapt this basic technique to listening.

The practical problems of making the cloze test entirely aural – a pure listening cloze – are considerable. The text must somehow be presented, the blanks indicated and the responses recorded, all in audio. Templeton (1977) did this: he recorded lectures and inserted beeps on top of every 15th word in order to mask the word and create the blanks. He then made a second recording of the text, with a short pause inserted into the tape at the next suitable syntactic boundary after each bleep. When the test was administered, the recording was played twice: the first time without the response pauses, when test-takers just listened to the text the whole way through, and the second time with pauses, during which test-takers wrote down the words masked by the bleeps. Example 3.5 is an extract from one test used in his study:

Example 3.5

by way of introduction let's have some information on just how far british industry .... commerce have been computerized // how many machines are in use here compared with other .... of the world // well the statistics of national computer populations are notoriously difficult to .... // differences in the ways different countries make up their figures lead to further problems .... making comparisons // (Templeton, 1977:293)

// indicates pauses of four seconds

Templeton claimed that reliability was high, as were correlations with other listening tests. He suggests that such a test takes little administration time, and that item writing is easy, the only problems being the technical problems of making the recording. He concludes, 'the above experiments seem to suggest it [i.e. the listening cloze test] has high validity on both theoretical and practical grounds' (1977:298).

This is certainly encouraging. There is considerable evidence that the standard reading-cloze procedure can be used to make good tests, and there is every reason to think that the listening cloze would work as well. Test-takers would clearly have to understand a short piece of spoken language, at least on the linguistic level, even if they did not have to apply this to a communicative situation. It seems likely that the ability to replace the blanks would be directly related to the degree of successful language processing.

The main problem is the difficulty of making the recordings: those who have tried to edit recordings using traditional analogue tape will know just how complex and difficult it is, and how poor the results often are. However, digital audio-editing software is now cheap and easy to use, and as explained in Chapter 6, it is very easy to cut and paste sound files to make such recordings, so more people may start to experiment with this technique.

Other gap-filling techniques

Templeton's technique preserves the basic rationale of the cloze – to delete words in a systematic or semi-random manner – and I have therefore continued to call it a cloze test. However, many of the other attempts to adapt the cloze technique to listening have modified the original technique to such an extent that I agree with Alderson (2000) that it is not appropriate to call them cloze tests. I will refer to them as gap-filling tests.

One simple way of making a gap-filling test is to give test-takers a transcript of a spoken text, with words deleted, then play a recording of the text and ask test-takers to fill in the blanks based on what they have heard. The most obvious problem with this is that test-takers could treat the passage as a normal cloze test, and fill in the blanks without listening to the passage, in which case it is no longer a listening test at all, although it may still be a perfectly good test of reading or general language ability. Alternatively, other test-takers may not try to understand the passage at all, but may just listen for the missing words and respond based on word recognition.

Henning *et al.* (1983) have tried to get around this problem by putting the blanks on content words, which have a high information load, and which are the least predictable words in the passage, and hence the most difficult to guess. They call this a **listening recall** test. The text of their test is given below.

Example 3.6

> The Porters live in Dartmouth a <u>small</u> English town at the <u>mouth</u> of the River Dart. Mr Porter is a lecturer in <u>engineering</u> at the local <u>college</u>. Mrs Porter is a <u>nurse</u> and works in a <u>nearby</u> hospital. The Porters have their <u>friends</u>, the Saids, visiting them from Egypt. They've been there a <u>week</u> now. What they really enjoy doing is taking a <u>large</u> boat out and <u>spending</u> an hour or two <u>fishing</u>. Yesterday, Mr Porter caught <u>two</u> fish, and Mrs Porter caught <u>three</u> nice <u>ones</u>. Mr Said <u>caught</u> a fish too, but it got away.

The underlined words are deleted; test-takers must write them in the blanks.

Henning *et al.* (1983) claim that the listening recall had better reliability, better discrimination and better validity than the other sections on a battery of tests, and they recommend it for low-level listeners. Weir (1993) also recommends its use, although he does admit that it is difficult to say what it measures. It seems clear that some test-takers might fill in the blanks based on their overall comprehension of the passage, but other test-takers would surely listen specifically for the individual words, in which case the test will be a test of word recognition. Furthermore, looking at the content of the blanks in Example 3.6, some of the blanks could probably be filled without hearing the passage: *'college'*, *'nurse'*, *'friends'*, *'spending'*, and *'caught'* for example.

It is difficult to claim that the listening-recall test provides evidence of comprehension. Anderson (1972) has argued that texts can often be processed on a perceptual or phonological level without bringing to mind the actual meaning of the words, and that this does not constitute comprehension. He maintains that unless tests provide clear evidence of semantic processing of the content we cannot claim they are measuring comprehension. He points out that items on gap-filling tests, such as the listening-recall test, can often be completed without actually processing the meaning of the text, and therefore they do not provide definite evidence of comprehension.

Gap-filling on summaries

If we want to prevent test-takers filling in blanks without actually understanding the meaning, we can ask them to fill in blanks on a summary of the passage. This forces them to process the meaning in order to fill in the blanks. The testing procedure is quite simple: test-takers are given a summary of the passage they are going to hear, in which some of the important content words have been replaced by blanks. After looking at the summary for a while, test-takers then listen to the original passage. They should be discouraged from writing while listening; their task is to use their understanding of the passage to fill in the blanks.

As an example, we could use the short speech sample Example 2.2 from Chapter 2 (p. 44), where the young man talks about entering a tennis tournament and finding there were only two entrants. We then write a short summary, and replace some words by blanks. A draft is given in Example 3.7 (overleaf).

Example 3.7

*On arrival at the _____, he discovered there were only _____
people signed up. The _____ wondered whether they should even
bother to play or not, but the speaker thought it was a good opportunity
to get easy _____ for just one game, or even that his opponent
would _____. But he didn't, and they _____ the match at 10
o'clock in the evening.*

The technique has much to recommend it. Buck (1992a) explored the
technique and found it reliable; it had good construct validity in that
it was more closely related to other tests of listening than to tests of
reading that used a similar format. Lewkowicz (1991) found that the
technique could be used with a variety of texts and topics, that a large
number of items could be developed on one passage, and that the
marking was relatively objective. She also notes that such tasks are
not so easy to make, and do require pre-testing. There are two
dangers – first the test-takers could fill in the gaps without understanding the text, and second, it might not be clear what information
should go in each gap. Thus, it is always a good idea to ask a few
people to try to fill in the blanks without listening to the passage,
early in the development stage, before pre-testing.

This technique can be used as an integrative test of short sections
of text, but the gaps can also be selected so that listeners are required
to understand discourse features, summarise parts of the text or make
inferences about the overall meaning.

Scoring gap-filling tests

Gap-filling tests are usually scored by counting the number of gaps
that are correctly filled, and using the sum as the total test score. In
cases where the test-taker has to replace deleted words – for example,
in listening-recall tests – there are two methods of scoring: firstly, to
score the item as correct only when the actual deleted word is replaced, or secondly, to count any acceptable alternative. Research on
traditional reading cloze suggests that both methods provide similar
results (Oller, 1979), but the exact-word method results in far fewer
correct answers. However, test-takers generally feel they ought to be
given credit for any acceptable word, and may complain that it is
unfair to ask them to guess the exact word.

Determining which responses are acceptable can be problematic, and this is always necessary when tasks require finding an appropriate word rather than replacing a deleted word, such as with gap-filling on summaries. Some responses will be obviously correct, or obviously incorrect, and these are not difficult to score, but the problem is what to do with the borderline cases. This will depend largely on the purpose of the test, but in most cases we are interested in listening comprehension, not production, and it is better to make acceptability dependent on whether the response indicates that the listener understood the text, rather than on whether the response fits appropriately into the text.

Processes involved in gap-filling tests

We obviously need to consider what processes are involved in gap-filling tests, if we want to determine what construct they measure. This depends on both the type of gap-filling task, and the nature of the information that has to be inserted into the gap. For example, in a listening cloze, filling some gaps may test listening in the narrower sense of understanding clearly stated information, whereas other gaps may only require word recognition skills. In other cases, especially when function words have been deleted, filling a gap may test general linguistic knowledge, rather like a reading cloze. Listening-recall tests that delete words with a high information content seem more likely to test word-recognition skills than general listening ability. In the case of gap-filling on summaries, they could test general linguistic knowledge, discourse knowledge or even inferencing, depending on the nature of the information to be inserted. They may also require some metacognitive processing (see Chapter 4) in order to determine what information the test-developer intends for the blank. It is almost impossible to make general statements about what these tests measure, and individual gaps must be examined closely in order to determine what construct is being assessed.

Dictation

Without doubt the most widely used integrative test of listening is the dictation. Before the integrative testing movement, dictation was considered to be little more than a test of spelling and punctuation

(Lado, 1961; Valette, 1967), but advocates of integrative testing argued that it was a good test of expectancy grammar (Oller, 1971; 1979; John Oakeshott-Taylor, 1977). Angela Oakeshott-Taylor (1977) examined the errors test-takers made when taking dictation tests and found they related to interpretation of the acoustic signal, phonemic identification, lexical recognition, morphology, syntactic analysis and semantic interpretation. On the basis of this she argued that dictation tests assess performance at all stages of the 'speech perception' process.

More recent writers have also recommended dictation. Hughes (1989) and Weir (1990, 1993) recommend dictation as providing a good supplement to other listening tests, and Cohen (1994) even suggests it can serve as a communicative test if the speech rate is fast enough. There is also evidence that dictation works for languages such as Japanese that have a close correspondence between the spelling and the pronunciation (Kaga, 1991).

The basic idea of dictation is simple: test-takers listen to a passage and write down what they have heard. Usually this involves listening to the passage twice: the first time, test-takers just listen and try to understand; the second time, the passage is broken into a number of short segments, with a pause between each, and during these pauses test-takers write down what they have heard. Below is a teacher-made dictation, intended for low-level language learners.

Example 3.8

Test-takers hear:

> Mary lives with her mother and father in a small town just outside London. every day from Monday to Friday she works in a large office in the centre of London. she always gets up at half-past six. first she has a shower, then she has a good breakfast. she always has eggs on toast for breakfast. while she is eating her breakfast she usually reads the morning paper. after she's finished breakfast she puts on her make-up, gets changed and leaves the house at about eight o'clock. it only takes her five minutes to walk to her local station, where she catches the twelve-minutes-past-eight train. she has to change trains once before she gets to London Bridge Station. from there to her office is about a ten-minute walk. she starts work at half-past nine and always gets to the office about five minutes early.

Test-takers hear the text again, segmented in the following manner, and write down what they have heard in the pauses.

Segment	# Words
Mary lives with her mother and father	[7]
in a small town just outside London	[7]
every day from Monday to Friday	[5]
she works in a large office	[6]
in the centre of London.	[5]
she always gets up at half-past six	[8]
first she has a shower	[5]
then she has a good breakfast	[6]
she always has eggs on toast for breakfast	[8]
while she is eating her breakfast	[6]
she usually reads the morning paper	[6]
after she's finished breakfast she puts on her make-up	[9]
gets changed and leaves the house at about eight o'clock	[10]
it only takes her five minutes to walk to her local station	[12]
where she catches the twelve-minutes-past-eight train	[9]
she has to change trains once	[6]
before she gets to London Bridge Station	[7]
from there to her office is about a ten-minute walk	[11]
she starts work at half-past nine	[7]
and always gets to the office about five minutes early	[10]

There are a number of ways of scoring dictations, but it is important to remember that they are not designed to be tests of spelling. Spelling mistakes should therefore be ignored in cases when it is obvious that the mistake is indeed a simple spelling mistake (not always an easy decision). It is common to score each word written correctly; the total available score for each segment is the total number of words, and the total test score is the sum of those. Words out of order or omitted are marked as incorrect. Unfortunately this does not take account of intrusions – words written down that were not in the original passage. A better way to score dictations, therefore, is to delete marks. Starting with the number of words for each segment, one mark is subtracted for each mistake. Intrusions count as one mistake each, as do omissions. This could result in a minus score for some sections, in which case it is customary to score this as zero. When scoring the responses of higher ability test-takers, the replacement of individual words by synonyms is a common occurrence and should be marked as correct.

Hughes suggests that scoring dictations for low-ability test-takers can be very difficult when they make many mistakes, because it is not always clear exactly which part of the text their responses refer to. He recommends partial dictation, in which some of the text is already written down on the answer sheet (Hughes, 1989). This gives test-takers anchor points so that it is easier for them to keep oriented within the passage. Each section is scored in the same way as in a normal dictation. Example 3.9 is an unpublished example, used in a college entrance exam in Japan.

Example 3.9

Test-takers hear:

> *i am an englishman and i live in Japan. one thing which i think is very strange is the use of microphones on japanese television. on english television you never see a microphone, they are always hidden. but people talking on japanese television very often have a microphone in their hands which they hold in front of their face, rather like they are eating a large ice-cream. at first I thought this was because japanese television was not as advanced as english television, but then I realised this was not true. a strange thing happened. i was watching a man on television, and he was standing speaking, holding a large yellow micro-phone in front of his face. at the same time he was trying to open a large envelope. it was impossible to hold the microphone and open the en-velope at the same time so he put the microphone on a nearby table, and continued talking without it. i expected the sound of his voice to become much lower, but strangely it didn't. i realised then that the microphone was not necessary at all, it was only for show. i wonder why so many people on japanese television hold large microphones in front of their faces which they don't need?*

Test-takers listen to the text again and write the underlined part; the other part is already provided in written English.

Segment	# Words
I am an Englishman and I live in Japan. One thing	
which I think is very strange	[6]
is the use of microphones on Japanese television.	
on english television you never see a microphone,	[8]
they are always hidden.	
but people talking on japanese television	[6]
very often have a microphone in their hands	
which they hold in front of their face,	[8]
rather like they are eating a large ice-cream. At first I thought this was because Japanese television was not as advanced as English television,	
but then i realised this was not true	[8]

A strange thing happened.
i was watching a man on television,   [7]
and he was standing speaking, holding a large yellow microphone in
front of his face.
at the same time he was trying to open a large envelope.   [12]
It was impossible to hold the microphone and open the envelope at
the same time
so he put the microphone on a nearby table,   [9]
and continued talking without it.
i expected the sound of his voice to become much lower,   [11]
but strangely, it didn't. I realised then
that the microphone was not necessary at all,   [8]
it was only for show. I wonder why so many people on Japanese
television hold large microphones in front of their faces which they
don't need?

Processes involved in dictation

Oller claims that dictations are pragmatic tests because they 'require
time constrained processing of the meanings coded in discourse'
(Oller, 1979:263). He further claims they are 'language processing
tasks that faithfully reflect what people do when they use language for
communicative purposes in real life contexts' (Oller, 1979:267). I am
not convinced that they *do* faithfully reflect what people do, and it is
interesting to consider exactly what processes are involved.

In my view, dictation works in a number of different ways, depending on how long the segments are and how much they challenge
the test-taker. First, when the segments are very short, and they do
not challenge the test-taker, writing down a few words of spoken text
is little more than a simple transcription exercise. The listening skills
involved are probably just word recognition.

As the chunks of language get longer, test-takers need to rely more
on their short-term memory: they must recognise what they have
heard, and keep that in memory long enough to write it down. There
is a limit to the capacity of working memory, which seems to be
restricted to about seven units, or chunks, of information (Miller,
1956), so as the segments get even longer, working memory capacity
will be strained. More advanced students will be able to use their
language ability to group these words into meaningful units, such as
phrases or idea units, and then retain about seven of those chunks in

memory. The better the language ability, the better the chunking ability (Ellis, 2001), and the longer the segment of text that can be remembered and written down.

This has nothing to do with reduced redundancy. It is, however, a well recognised characteristic of language processing that listeners tend to remember the content of a message, rather than the words used (Sachs, 1967), and as the segments get longer, listeners may start forgetting the exact words, even if their comprehension is good. In order to write down what they have heard, they need to use their linguistic knowledge to reconstruct the words they have forgotten, and replacing missing words brings us back to the idea of reduced redundancy. Those with a good knowledge of the language can fill in the missing words and reconstruct the text better.

Thus, the length of the segments is important in constructing dictations. Each of the sections needs to be long enough to place a certain amount of load on the working memory. The ideal size of each chunk will vary depending on the ability level of the test-takers, but a good strategy is to make the chunks of differing lengths, with shorter chunks near the beginning, getting progressively longer throughout the test. This ensures that at least some of the chunks will be of an ideal length for each test-taker, and it makes the test more useful – either for a group of test-takers with slightly different abilities, or when we are not sure of the exact ability level. This is what happens in Example 3.8 above; the test was very reliable and discriminated well among a group of low-ability Japanese language learners.

Clearly the cognitive processes required by dictation are important in general language processing, but the more important question is how well it operationalises the listening construct. In my view, if the segments are very short and do not challenge the test-taker, then dictation is probably testing little more than the ability to recognise simple elements; but if the segments are a little longer, it will be testing understanding on a local, literal, linguistic level, in which case it clearly is an integrative test, as we have defined the term.

Given the lack of context and no obvious communicative situation, dictation does not seem to require the ability to understand inferred meanings, or to relate the literal meaning to a wider communicative context. Dictation operationalises listening in the narrower of the two-level view of listening. Dictation also clearly tests more besides listening: it requires good short-term memory as well as writing ability, and it seems fair to say that it is far more than a test of listening skills.

Sentence-repetition tasks

A variation on the dictation test, useful for testing non-literate language users, such as children, is the sentence-repetition task. It is basically the same as a dictation, except that students repeat the text orally during the pause between each section.

Often test-takers are given a series of unconnected sentences rather than a unified passage. In this case, they usually hear each sentence once and repeat it back immediately after they have heard it. This task has been given various labels: sentence elicitation, sentence repetition or response elicitation. The responses are usually tape-recorded and then scored later. In Sri Lanka, sentence-repetition tasks were used in the National Certificate in English as part of an oral test. The sentences were spoken by the test administrator, who then scored the repetitions as they were made by the test-taker. In the report on the first administration, researchers remarked that the procedure worked well and the scoring was reliable (Alderson *et al.*, 1987).

Although sentence-repetition tasks work through listening, they require more than just listening skills. If the sentence is short and can be repeated immediately, it might test no more than the ability to recognise and repeat sounds, and this may not require processing of the meaning at all. This clearly fails Anderson's (1972) criteria for proof of comprehension. If the sentence gets a little longer, or the delay between listening and repeating increases, the task will begin to test working memory. As the sentences get even longer, it seems likely that chunking ability and the ability to deal with reduced redundancy will begin to become more important and, as with dictation, these are closely related to general linguistic competence. As listening tasks they require no more than understanding short sections of decontextualised language on a literal level.

I would argue that sentence-repetition tasks are not just tests of listening, but tests of general oral skills. They are integrative tests in that they test the ability to use language rather than just knowing about it, but only as long as the segments actually challenge working memory capacity. And they do require speech production.

Statement evaluation

We can test the ability to understand simple statements without asking the test-taker to repeat them. We can ask test-takers to show that they have understood either by evaluating the truth of the statement, or by comparing two statements and saying whether they mean the same thing or not.

Emery (1980) notes that native speakers 'will be able to say without hesitation that a statement like "The sun rises in the west" is false, while "A square has more sides than a triangle" is true' (1980:97). If the question is understood the answer is immediately obvious to all. He suggests that a number of such statements would provide a good measure of listening ability.

Example 3.10

Test-takers hear:

> *we choose our shoes according to where we intend to go. strong boots are better for hiking than beach sandals.*

There are two drawbacks with this technique: they test background knowledge, and they sound very contrived. An alternative is to provide two statements, and to ask test-takers to evaluate whether they have the same meaning or not. It is probably easier to think up sets of suitable matching sentences than self-evidently correct or incorrect statements.

Example 3.11

Test-takers hear:
 a *the snow delayed the flight.*
 b *the plane arrived on time despite the snowstorm.*

This technique has been used on the Japan Association of College English Teachers (JACET) Listening Comprehension Test. The technique requires the processing of short, decontextualised sentences, and as such it is more a test of basic sentence-processing skills rather than communicative-listening skills. It does, however, provide firm evidence that the test-taker has processed the semantic meaning of the texts. I believe this technique has the promise of making very simple tests, with very little trouble, and may be quite suitable for classroom use.

Translation

Translation is not usually thought of as an integrative test, but Oller suggests that 'it still remains a viable pragmatic procedure' (1979:50).

Although translation is not usually thought of as a listening test, I carried out a number of studies in which I looked at translation tests, including listening tests (Buck, 1992b), and results were very encouraging. Scott *et al.* (1996) also examined a summary translation test of Spanish into English and reported that it had very satisfactory construct validity.

I constructed a translation test of listening as follows. First, a Canadian was asked to record a short description of Canada, in English. This recording was then cut into 20 short sections at natural pauses, and sufficient time was included to allow the test-takers to write down what they had heard; rather like a dictation, except that they write in their first language, Japanese. The test-takers were asked to listen to the recording and, then during the pauses, write down a translation of what the man had said, for the benefit of a friend who was considering a trip to Canada. The text is given below:

Example 3.12

1 *the most striking feature is its size*
2 *it's so large unbelievably large*
3 *especially if you come from a small country*
4 *so if you want to come to Canada for a vacation*
5 *you have to consider very carefully just a small part of Canada to visit*
6 *even for a week you must choose a small area otherwise it's impossible to see anything*
7 *Canada has different regions*
8 *starting from the west there's British Columbia British Columbia is a little like Canada's California*
9 *the city of Vancouver is a nice city*
10 *it's located beside a beautiful sea coast*
11 *right behind the city are beautiful mountains*
12 *it's perhaps Canada's nicest city perhaps*
13 *as you go across the Rocky Mountains westwards you come to a large flat area the prairies*
14 *for most Canadians who don't live there it's considered boring*
15 *the summer times are dreadfully hot and the winters are freezing cold*
16 *there are no hills almost no trees just huge farms*
17 *boring . . . I don't recommend it*
18 *as you come east you come to a huge province called Ontario*
19 *the western half of this province a very large area is largely only trees*
20 *trees lakes rivers rocks and almost no people*

The translation was scored by awarding one mark for each important idea expressed. What constituted 'an important idea' was decided on the basis of my own intuition. All the translations were marked by the same rater, and reliability was found to be quite acceptable. The test correlated well with other tests of listening, much higher than it did with a reading test that also used translation (Buck, 1992b). In other words, this was a listening test more than a translation test.

In many ways this is like a dictation in which test-takers write down what they have heard in their native language. The obvious disadvantage is that it requires the test user to know the test-takers' native language, and it will be most useful when all the test-takers share the same native language.

There are two advantages to this technique. First, having a speaker talk freely about his home country produced a reasonably spontaneous text. Second, the requirement to translate ensures that test-takers have to process the semantic content of the text, which clearly meets Anderson's (1972) criteria of a test of comprehension.

The theoretical view of listening implicit in integrative tests

Generally, the theoretical notion of listening comprehension associated with integrative testing, as we have defined it, is clearly the first of the two-level view of listening: that is, listening in the sense of processing texts in real time, to understand the literal, semantic meaning. It is more of a sentence-processing approach. There is very little attempt to relate the linguistic information to a wider context, or to ask the test-taker to process inferential meanings. However, it is often very difficult to identify exactly what construct is being measured by these integrative tests, either by a whole test or by individual items.

The basic theories about language processing which underlie integrative tests, ideas about a pragmatic expectancy grammar, have never been seriously challenged. The problem with integrative testing is not that the skills they test are not important – clearly they are fundamental – but that the tests tend to measure too narrow a range of language skills. As we have seen, language extends over much longer pieces of text than sentences, and always takes place in some sort of communicative situation. Integrative tests tend to see language processing as an isolated event, where the listener grasps the basic linguistic information in the message, but then is not required to relate that to the context.

Communicative testing

At the same time as Oller was arguing for integrative tests, Carroll (1972) was arguing that comprehension of a message is adequate, or satisfactory, to the extent that the listener both apprehends whatever linguistic information is in the message, and then is also able to relate that information to the wider communicative context.

This had little effect at the time, but eventually the movement for **communicative testing** developed primarily in response to the trend towards increased 'communicative' second-language teaching. The basic idea underlying communicative teaching is that language is used for the purpose of communication, in a particular situation and for a particular purpose, and the important thing is not what a person knows about the language, nor how grammatically correct they are, but whether they can actually use it to communicate in the **target-language use situation**, the real-world situation in which the language will be used. Language proficiency is thus seen as communicative competence (Hymes, 1972). This idea influenced testing, namely that testers should be less concerned with how much a person knows about the language, and more about whether they can use it to communicate effectively.

The move towards communicative testing was not the work of one scholar, but was more a general shift in attitudes. It was characterised by strong criticism of discrete-point testing, but unlike the integrative movement, it was never quite made clear exactly what should replace the old tests. There was a strong feeling that communicative tests should test **use** of the language for its communicative function, rather than **usage**, a distinction made by Widdowson (1978). As Carroll put it, 'the *use* of language is the *objective*, and the mastery of the formal patterns, or *usage*, of that language is a *means* to achieve that objective' (Carroll, 1980:7, italics in original). Oller had attacked the idea of testing the elements of language, and argued for tests that actually required processing the language. The advocates of communicative testing felt he had not gone far enough – they argued for testing the use of language for a communicative purpose.

In a well known paper, Morrow (1979) illustrates both the

aspirations of the movement, and at the same time the inability to clarify the criteria for determining exactly what a communicative test should be. Morrow criticises the discrete-point view of language, and suggests that 'conventional tests' (which he never defines) fail to measure certain important aspects of language use: namely, that language use is interaction-based – it is unpredictable, contextualised, purposeful, it has authentic characteristics, it is a performance, and it is actual behaviour. He makes much of Chomsky's (1965) distinction between **competence**, the users' knowledge of the language, and **performance**, the actual use of the language in concrete situations, and argues that communicative tests must be tests of performance rather than competence, in other words, that language tests should test the 'use of language in ordinary situations' (1979:148).

There is a problem with this position which Morrow himself recognises, namely, if you test performance on one particular language-use task, in one particular target-language use situation, how do you know that performance generalises to other similar tasks in other situations? You need to have some evidence that the competence underlying performance on one task is in some way similar to that required by the others. Morrow claims that Munby's (1978) taxonomy of enabling skills are the common characteristics of different performances, and these are what makes generalisation possible. However, it is difficult to determine what the enabling skills are for a particular task (Alderson, 1981a); furthermore it seems that determining the underlying enabling skills is conceptually little different from determining the underlying competencies, in that enabling skills can be regarded as one particular way of describing competencies.

There are two practical measurement issues that tend to become more problematic when making communicative listening tests. Firstly, in most domains of language use, there are many communicative situations and many contexts, as well as a large variety of topics. Tests sample from these, and performance on those test tasks is assumed to generalise to performance across the whole domain. Unfortunately, successful performance on one complex communicative task does not always indicate the ability to perform well on others, so the sample often does not generalise as well as the test-developer would like. Furthermore, due to the necessity of creating the context, communicative test tasks often take more time than less context-embedded tasks, so the sample of texts, tasks, topics and so forth tends to be smaller. Thus more communicative tests will often have lower generalisability. The second issue is already familiar to us, namely the fact that there is often more than one reasonable interpretation of many texts. This becomes especially problematic when we attempt to assess broader communicative skills by asking test-takers to make pragmatic inferences regarding a speaker's implicit meaning, or to assess the sociolinguistic appropriacy of a particular response.

To summarise, the basic problem with communicative testing is that language use varies considerably from one individual to another, and one situation to the next. The linguistic system, on the other hand, is relatively systematic, and therefore much more amenable to testing (Alderson, 1981b). Despite the theoretical difficulty of determining what a communicative test is, and the practical difficulties of doing it, communicative testing has had a very powerful and pervasive influence on language testing for more than two decades.

Characteristics of communicative test items

Probably the best way to understand communicative testing is to look at communicative test items. This is an obviously circular process: if we do not know what communicative tests are, we cannot reasonably select communicative test items. However, a few themes do stand out, although they may not provide a clear definition.

Authentic texts

Probably the most common theme running through communicative testing is the idea that the texts should be reasonably authentic – by which most people probably understand that they should either be taken from the target-language use situation, or should have the characteristics of target-language use texts. Widdowson (1978), however, argues that although texts may be **genuine**, in the sense that they are taken from the target-language use situation, they are not **authentic** unless the test-taker is required to deal with them in a way that corresponds to their use in the target-language use situation: thus, genuineness is a characteristic of the text, whereas authenticity is a characteristic of the relationship between the text and the listener. However, even though the term authenticity is often used somewhat loosely, it is still a powerful notion underlying much communicative testing. This issue is addressed in greater detail in Chapter 4.

Below is a test used in a research study (Buck, 1990). Test-takers are told to imagine they are in London on vacation, and they telephone the Tourist Information office to ask about tours of London. They listen to the man in the office, and based on that they fill in the missing information in the grid. Note that four of the slots are already filled in as a guide, which leaves 12 items to be completed by the test-taker.

Example 3.13

Test-takers look at the grid.

	Departure Time	Duration	Price	Speaker's Recommendation
Bus: Full Day Tour	9.00	Q1	£6.50	Q2
Bus: Half Day Tour	9.00	Q3	£3.50	Q4
Private Car Hire	Q5	Q6	Q7	Q8
Thames River Tour	Q9	Q10	Q11	Q12

Test-takers listen, just once, and then fill in the slots after listening.

mm well the London Transport full-day tour leaves Victoria Coach Station at nine o'clock, and takes about_ it takes eight hours. and gets back at five o'clock. ya? there's an hour's stop for lunch, and it costs six pounds fifty. it's quite a good tour, but in my opinion it's much too tiring. i think it's much better for you to take the half-day tour. ya? this also leaves from Victoria Coach Station at nine o'clock, and visits all the famous places in the centre of London. it finishes at one o'clock, and costs three pound fifty. and it's_ i i_ well i think it's probably the best of all the tours. ya? you see all the well-known places and it's not too tiring. ya? as for the_ mm the hiring a private car, there are three companies here in uh London which arrange private tours. ya? they're all nice cars, and the cars pick you up from your hotel, and they take you around to where ever you want to go. the drivers are all proper trained tour guides, you can arrange to start your tour when you want, and the price is five pounds an hour. but you must have a minimum of two hours, so the minimum charge is ten pounds. ya? personally after what you've said i think it's much too expensive for you. mm. as for the boat tour, mm it leaves Westminster Pier at ten o'clock every morning, and travels down the river to Greenwich, and there . . . you see down the river side, and you see the observatory at Greenwich, and then you return. it takes about four hours. ya? um . . . it's a little more expensive than the bus tour, at five pounds twenty-five, and you only get to see the river, so i_ well i think this is not so interesting for you. okay. uhm anyway which ever one you choose, i hope you have a pleasant day. bye.

This is what is called a semi-scripted text (I will discuss these in Chapter 6). The text is not completely authentic, in fact it is a simulation and perhaps not a good one at that, but it does contain many characteristics of genuine real-world texts, such as phonological modification, hesitations and speaker repairs. The speaker also has a common habit of using *ya* or *okay* as a tag question.

There are two problems with providing more authentic texts. The first concerns the fact that speakers need to speak spontaneously to produce realistic spoken language, but test-developers need to control what the speaker says in order to make test items. This is a dilemma we will discuss at length in Chapter 6, but as a result, many test-developers who want to develop communicative tests often look for genuine texts that are also scripted, and this usually means broadcast material such as radio programmes. No one can deny these are genuine listening texts, and they may even be used in an authentic manner, but they represent only one text-type, and one with relatively few oral features. The result is that the developers of such tests will be able to claim that they use authentic texts, but the selection of texts across the whole test will not be an authentic representation of the range of texts the listener will have to deal with in the target-language use situation.

The second problem with more authentic texts is that they are often too difficult for lower-level language learners. To illustrate this, first look at Example 3.14 below. Test-takers listen to the words of a song (which the examiners claim is an authentic task for modern-day young people). This task is for intermediate test-takers taken from the

Certificate of Communicative Skills in English Level 3 and 4 (University of Cambridge Local Examinations Syndicate, 1995:82):

Example 3.14

Test-takers listen to the song twice.

> *Don't know when I've been so blue*
> *Don't know what's come over you*
> *You've found someone new*
> *And don't it make my brown eyes blue.*

> *I'll be fine when you've gone*
> *I'll just cry all night long*
> *Say it isn't true*
> *And don't it make my brown eyes blue.*

> *Tell me no secrets, tell me some lies*
> *Give me no reasons, give me alibis*
> *Tell me you love me and don't make me cry*
> *Say anything but don't say goodbye.*

> *I didn't mean to treat you bad*
> *Didn't know just what I had*
> *But honey now I do*
> *And don't it make my brown eyes, don't it make my brown eyes*
> *And don't it make my brown eyes blue.*

They then write responses to the following questions:

> How is the singer feeling?
> Why does she feel like this?
> What colour are her eyes?

This task clearly requires an understanding of the message, and seems to be testing important skills. However, the same song was also given to lower-ability students, but with a different task. The task for lower-ability test-takers is given in Example 3.15 taken from the same test, but the beginners' level (University of Cambridge Local Examinations Syndicate, 1995:81). Test-takers listen to the song and fill in the blanks.

Example 3.15

> *Don't know _____ I've been so blue*
> *Don't know _____'s come over you*
> *You've found someone new*
> *And don't it make my brown eyes blue.*

> *I'll be _____ when you've gone*

I'll just _____ all night long
Say it isn't true
And don't it make my brown eyes blue.

Tell me no secrets, tell me some lies
Give me no reasons, give me alibis
Tell me you _____ me and don't make me cry
Say anything but _____ say goodbye.

I didn't mean to treat _____ bad
Didn't know just _____ I had
But honey now I do
And don't it make my brown eyes, don't it make my brown eyes
And don't it make my brown eyes blue.

This task requires listening and recognising words in a stream of speech (or a song in this case). Such a task may not even require language processing, let alone communicative language use. In fact it may not even require listening at all. Many of the blanks could be filled in without listening; the first two seem particularly obvious. This task operationalises listening as recognising isolated elements within a stream of language, which in Widdowson's (1978) terms is surely not an authentic use of such a text. This text seems to have been included in a test of 'communicative skills' largely because the text is genuine.

As regards the types of authentic texts that should be used in communicative tests, Brindley suggests they would include: conversations, announcements, service encounters, answering machine messages, directions, lectures, narratives, anecdotes, personal reports, news broadcasts, interviews, advertisements, announcements, debates and talkback exchanges (Brindley, 1998:175).

Providing a communicative purpose

Another common theme in communicative testing is that language use takes place for a definite communicative purpose, and so test-tasks should also provide a purpose for listening. Example 3.16 below is taken from the Certificate of Communicative Skills in English (University of Cambridge Local Examinations Syndicate, 1995).

Example 3.16

Test-takers read:

Your friend is in Scotland on a walking holiday. You want to know what the weather is like there. You listen to the weather forecast on the radio.

1. What's the weather like in Eastern Scotland?
Tick (✓) the correct boxes.
Dry ☐   Rainy ☐   Sunny ☐   Cloudy ☐   Foggy ☐   Thundery ☐

2. Where in Scotland is the weather best for walking?
Tick (✓) the correct boxes.
Western Scotland ☐   Eastern Scotland ☐   Northern Scotland ☐

Test-takers hear:

and here's the weather forecast from Peter Cockcroft.

good morning. a cloudy day for Western Scotland with outbreaks of rain and some of them heavy over the hills. the chance of some hail, perhaps even the odd rumble of thunder. for Northern Ireland a rather cloudy and wet start here but the rain will turn showery during the day. across in Eastern Scotland rather cloudy here too but at least it will be dry and there will be a bit of brightness now and then. for the rest of England and Wales [fades]

We could just ask test-takers to listen to a recording of a weather forecast, and then ask comprehension questions, or give them a grid to fill in. In this example, however, a communicative situation is described, and test-takers are given an explicit purpose for listening. Obviously, the whole task is still rather contrived: they do not actually have a friend walking in Scotland, and if they did, they probably would not check the weather, and if they did check the weather, they certainly would not tick boxes with the information. Nevertheless, the task gives test-takers a clearer idea of what they should be listening for, and allows them to choose the most appropriate listening strategies and determine what information they should target in the text. It seems likely to better replicate the skills used in real-world listening.

A similar function can be performed when using comprehension questions, by allowing test-takers to know the questions in advance, so they know what to listen for.

Authentic tasks

Another theme that occurs in communicative listening tests is the use of more authentic tasks. While test tasks can never be entirely authentic replications of target-language use tasks, the idea is that they should be as much like them as possible. This is illustrated by another item from the CCSE (University of Cambridge Local Examinations Syndicate, 1995:89).

Example 3.17

Instructions:

> You read an article about a journalist called Jocelyn Stephens. Then you hear a radio programme about him.
>
> From the introduction to the interview you realise that there are a number of mistakes in the article so you decide to write to the newspaper.
>
> Circle anything in the article that differs from what you hear. Write corrections in the space to the right of the article. You will hear the interview twice.

Test-takers read:

> Jocelyn Stephens is now 70 years old. He has achieved a great deal in his long lifetime. As a public servant, entrepreneur and newspaper man, he brought new life to Vogue magazine. He then ventured into broadcasting and was a major force behind the launching of Radio Caroline. He is ex-chairman of the Independent Television Commission and Rector of the Royal College of Music. He works in Edinburgh and spends his weekends in Gstaad. Later this year he takes over as Chairman of Scottish Heritage.

Then test-takers hear:

> *and now Desert Island Discs with Sue Lawley. my castaway this week is an entrepreneur newspaperman and public servant. he's now sixty. during his lifetime he's revitalised Queen magazine, launched Radio Caroline, saved the Evening Standard and served as managing director of Express Newspapers. at the moment he is deputy chairman of the Independent Television Commission and rector of the Royal College of Art. that he's done so much is due to two things, his great wealth and his enormous energy. he works in London but spends the weekends in Gstaad. flamboyant and glamorous, he epitomized the jet set. hard working and anxious to do a worthwhile job, he's looking forward to taking over as chairman of English Heritage later this year. he is Jocelyn Stephens. there's only one question to ask, Jocelyn after an introduction like that, which is aren't you exhausted? how have you managed to pack so much in?*

Instead of just asking the test-taker to find the mistakes, the test-developer has created a task which requires more purposeful language use. People do write to newspapers and complain about the inaccuracy of articles – although it is not a very common practice. The point is that the test-developer has attempted to make the task a more realistic simulation of real-world language use.

However, one problem with providing authentic tasks is that in many real-world listening situations, the listener does not perform any task at all, but simply listens and stores the information for later use. Requiring a task of any nature will often place a very inauthentic demand on the listener.

The theoretical view of listening implicit in communicative tests

We can now consider exactly what a communicative test is. There are two answers to this question: one a practical, rough-and-ready answer, based on popular usage, and the other a rigorous theoretical response.

On a practical, or even popular level, a communicative test is one that better simulates the characteristics of target-language use in the real world, and as such it is just an attempt to test a richer, more realistic listening construct.

However, strictly speaking, there is no such thing as a communicative test. Every test requires some components of communicative language ability, and no test covers them all. Similarly, with the notion of authenticity, every test task shares some characteristics with target-language use tasks, and no test task is completely authentic, however genuine the text, simply because it is a test and not a real-world communication. All items require some aspects of authentic communicative language ability, but none of them is truly communicative. The problem is that we have no criteria to determine when items are communicative or authentic enough.

In reality we should not be looking at the test, but at the interaction between the test tasks and the test-taker. If a test is well designed, it will allow us to make inferences about the test-taker's communicative language ability, and that is what we are interested in. As Douglas put it, 'a test is thus not, in my opinion, inherently communicative; rather, to belabor the point, we make inferences about communicative language ability on the basis of a particular performance' (personal communication, October 1999). A good test is one that allows us to make useful inferences about the test-taker's communicative language ability.

Despite the difficulties of deciding what we mean by communicative testing, I should stress that the communicative testing movement has been, and still is, a very positive influence in language testing. Indeed, as Davies suggests, 'there is much to be said for fuzzy concepts that we cheerfully (and properly) operationalise even though they do not lend themselves to confinement within a definition' (personal communication, October 1999). I think communicative testing is one such fuzzy concept, as is authenticity. It has led to a much broader notion of what it means to know a language, and has reminded test-developers that language use takes place in a context, and for a communicative purpose, and tests need to take account of that. In terms of listening comprehension, it has taken us from the idea of testing listening in the narrow sense of constructing a linguistic representation of the text to the idea of testing listening as the application of that understanding to a wider communicative situation.

Conclusion

This chapter has been organised around three main approaches to language testing and the ideas associated with them. In many ways it is possible to see these ideas as representing the development of an expanding view of the listening construct: from the narrow view of listening as recognising elements, through listening as language processing, to the more current idea of listening as interpreting meaning in terms of a communicative context. I have also discussed a number of different testing techniques that have been historically associated with these approaches, and examined a number of actual test items.

The question arises, which of these is the best way to assess listening comprehension, and that is the topic of the rest of the book. Test-developers need to consider the needs of the situation and determine which construct and which operationalisation of that construct will be the most suitable for their purpose. The following chapters will begin the process of considering how to make listening tests. Chapter 4 will discuss how the listening comprehension construct can be defined and operationalised in ways useful to test construction; Chapter 5 will discuss the design of test tasks, Chapter 6 will examine listening texts, and Chapter 7 will show how to bring this all together to construct complete assessments.

CHAPTER FOUR

....

Defining the construct

Introduction

In Chapter 3 I discussed some of the most important historical ideas in language testing, and described the techniques that have commonly been used to test listening comprehension. I also discussed the constructs implicit in those common practices. In this chapter, I will discuss what should be the first stage of test development: defining the construct.

When we make a test, we do it for a particular purpose and for a specific set of test-takers, and these form the starting point for test development. The first step is defining the construct. This is a two-stage process: firstly, we define it on a theoretical or conceptual level, and then secondly, we operationalise that through the texts we select, and the tasks we ask our listeners to perform. The conceptualisation of our listening construct will be based on both our theoretical understanding of listening comprehension, and from our knowledge of the target-language use situation. The operationalisation of the construct will be based on our knowledge and experience as test-developers. Operationalisation of the construct could be inadequate for two reasons: we could omit something that should be there, or add something that should not. Messick (1989, 1994) has provided two useful terms for these: **construct-underrepresentation**, which occurs when the operationalisation of the theoretical construct is incomplete and parts of it are not represented in the test, and **construct-irrelevant variance**, which occurs when the test assesses abilities which are not included in the theoretical description of the construct.

It is important to get the construct right, both theoretically and operationally, because the construct is what our test is measuring, and this determines what our scores mean. This in turn determines whether the decisions we make based on those test scores will be valid and fair.

Practical constraints on construct definition

There are a number of constraints on construct definition that need to be taken into account. The first, and most important, is the purpose of the test, but there are also a number of other constraints that will be discussed below.

Purposes of assessing listening comprehension

Tests are always made for a purpose, and the purpose has considerable influence on the construct we want to measure. There are a number of common purposes for testing listening.

General language proficiency

One of the most obvious reasons to test listening is that traditionally language ability has been considered to comprise four skills, and listening comprehension, along with speaking, reading and writing, is one of those. Feyten (1991) claims that more than 45 percent of our total time communicating is spent listening, which suggests the tremendous importance of listening skills in overall language ability. Whenever people are interested in general language proficiency, they usually want to know about listening ability. Hence, listening is found in most general proficiency tests, as well as most tests of academic language ability, and tests of language for business purposes.

Representing oral skills

Listening is not only included in language tests for its own sake; I believe it is also used as a substitute for other oral skills. Although speaking ability is the skill that is most commonly associated with language proficiency in the popular mind, speaking tests are expensive and time consuming. They require obtaining a representative sample of spoken language, and then having that evaluated by one, or preferably two, trained raters. In many testing situations there are too many candidates, too few resources and too little time to do this well. Different test-developers address this issue in different ways. For example, there tends to be a feeling among British test-developers (perhaps more influenced by the demands of classroom teachers) that a speaking test must be included in a proficiency test, even if there are not enough resources for a very reliable one – the idea being that, from an educational perspective, almost any test is better than no test. On the other hand, US test-developers (perhaps more influenced by the traditions of psychological measurement) tend to be more inclined to avoid having a speaking test unless they can guarantee very high levels of reliability – the idea being that, from a measurement perspective, all tests must be very reliable. This is a philosophical difference, and both positions have advantages and disadvantages. In the latter case, however, the result is that there is only one test of spoken language, and the listening test becomes the *de facto* test of oral skills. For example, the Test of English as a Foreign Language (TOEFL), the Test of English for International Communication (TOEIC), and the Comprehensive English Language Test for Learners of English (CELT) are all used as general proficiency tests, and all contain a listening section but no speaking section.

Assessing achievement

There are also classroom teachers who feel that if they are teaching listening, they ought to assess it. This is basic achievement testing, and tests are commonly used to provide grades, give credit for course completion or to determine whether students are ready to proceed to the next level of instruction.

Another reason why teachers might want to test listening is to encourage students to practise listening. Many theorists of second-language pedagogy have advocated teaching methods which concentrate on providing large quantities of listening during the early stages of language learning (Asher, 1969; Gary and Gary, 1981; Krashen, 1982; Krashen and Terrel, 1983; Postovsky, 1974; and Winitz, 1981).

Feyten (1991) claims some research evidence for the importance of listening ability in language acquisition. While there are many who may not agree with the stronger claims of listening-first teaching methods, it is probably fair to say that there is no theorist of second-language pedagogy who denies the tremendous utility of large amounts of listening comprehension practice in the early stages of second-language learning. Given this, many teachers use tests to motivate students.

Making achievement tests is an important responsibility for many teachers. Yet testing is often neglected during teacher training, and overworked teachers sometimes resent the time it takes to make them. One of the principal aims of this book is to show teachers how to make better achievement tests.

Diagnostic testing

The other main purpose for testing is diagnosis. There is a strong imperative in education to find out where student knowledge is deficient so that teaching can more effectively target their needs. There are currently few diagnostic tests of listening, largely because we still do not fully understand what the important sub-skills of listening are; nor are we sure what information educators need to teach listening better. Statisticians and researchers are developing new research techniques that will enable testers to diagnose learners on important sub-skills of language performance including listening (for example Freedle and Kostin, 1996; Buck *et al.*, 1997; Buck and Tatsuoka, 1998).

We can in fact imagine a whole range of purposes for assessing listening. First, there are assessments made by the teacher to motivate study or to evaluate achievement. Then there are what we might call school or district-based tests, for the purpose of admissions, placement, or even achievement and graduation. Then there are even larger-scale tests, general proficiency tests, often made by large organisations and available at regular intervals in a variety of locations. There are also specific-purpose tests, most commonly academic listening or listening tests for business use. Finally, listening tests are often made for specific research purposes.

Practical constraints

Before defining our construct, we need to consider a number of constraints that will have a considerable impact on our construct definition.

Collaborative or non-collaborative listening

A listener is a participant in a communicative interaction, and the degree of interaction between the participants can vary considerably. As noted in Chapter 1, the degree of collaboration forms a continuum, and the communicative skills necessary will vary depending on the collaboration the listener must provide.

Virtually all work in testing listening comprehension, both research and actual test construction, has been concerned with non-collaborative listening, that is listening as a process of understanding what speakers mean in non-interactive situations. The ability to perform the listener's role in an interactive, collaborative situation has generally been tested as a speaking skill, usually in interactive, interview-type assessments. The reason for this is simple: it is relatively convenient and cheap to test non-collaborative listening in large-scale situations, where many test-takers can take the test at the same time. However, assessing how well listeners can perform in collaborative, interactive situations requires an actual communication between two or more participants, and then one or more people to rate the test-takers' performance.

Setting up such interactive assessments is both expensive and time consuming, as well as requiring expertise generally associated with testing speaking rather than listening. I think it makes more practical sense to stick with the traditional practice of testing non-collaborative listening, and that is what I intend to do in this book. However, interactive listening skills are important, and it is sensible to ensure that they are included on interactive assessments such as oral interviews (Brindley, 1998).

Differing interpretations of texts

There is a major practical problem in designing tests: there is often no one correct interpretation of a text. In the case of simple explicit statements, for example when two people hear an announcement that a train will depart at 8 a.m., there is little room for individual interpretation. Even in longer texts, competent listeners usually share the same gist; after all if they did not, daily communication would be totally chaotic. However, much of what is conveyed and understood in communication is not explicitly stated, but depends on cooperation and inference. Effective daily communication does not usually need precise understanding, and listeners often manage quite well with a rough approximation of the speakers' intended meaning. Listening tests tend to look much more closely at exactly what people have understood from a text, and the normal variation in interpretation can cause serious problems in item design. This is especially difficult when testing listening in the sense of understanding implied meanings. When defining a listening construct, it is important to define it in such a way that it can be operationalised in workable test items.

Intervening variables

Another problem is that the product of listening comprehension is a construction or representation of meaning in the mind, and there need not be any external evidence that the listener has understood. In the case of writing or speaking we can examine what the test-taker has produced, but with listening comprehension we cannot. We have to give the test-taker a task to complete – filling in blanks, answering questions, following directions, for example – and then we make inferences about the degree of comprehension from performance on that task.

The thing to note is that completion of the task will always require other abilities besides listening comprehension – and these will often be construct-irrelevant skills. For example, if the questions on a listening test are presented to the student in written form, then the ability to answer the questions will depend partly on second-language reading ability. Quite a lot of reading can be involved in some listening tests, especially multiple-choice tests. We can avoid this by giving the questions orally. Test-takers could listen to a recorded passage, and then listen to recorded questions. This works quite well when the test-takers have to construct their own responses, but it is a little more complicated with multiple-choice items, which offer a number of different options.

Presenting the questions orally will solve the problem of second-language reading ability affecting listening scores, but introduces memory effects. Some students may have better working memories than others (Just and Carpenter, 1992), and students with poor memories could suffer. This is less of a problem if the options are short, and not very complex. Furthermore, such items also call for a high level of concentration by the test-taker. One short moment of inattention can result in test-takers not hearing the question, or one of the options, and failing to answer even though they understood the passage quite well.

Open-ended questions that require the test-taker to construct a response would require less reading, or less memorisation, but then writing becomes necessary. This can be avoided in cases where all the test-takers share the same first language, as in many foreign-language teaching situations. In such cases it is possible to ask questions and allow test-takers to respond in their native language. Although students vary in their first-language abilities, the difficulty of the language used can be kept to such a basic level that it is unlikely to tax the ability of even the least proficient student. However, test-takers may find it irritating to move backwards and forwards between two languages.

The decision regarding which of the many tasks or question forms to use will depend largely on the purpose of the test, and the priorities of the test-maker. Some test-makers, for example, may be quite happy to have answers written in the L2, and others may be quite happy to have reading ability influencing listening scores. After all, listening and reading are both important language skills, and a test that measured both could well be a good test of general language comprehension.

When we think of construct-irrelevant abilities we need to be aware of whether or not they cause **variance** – which is the variability between test-takers, or put another way, the extent to which the test-takers are spread out from the average. Even though there will always be construct-irrelevant abilities required to complete listening-test tasks, if test-takers have similar levels of ability on these, then all the test-takers will be equally affected, and these construct-irrelevant abilities will not lead to differences in test scores. In other words, they will not lead to variance in test performance. Remember that it is construct-irrelevant variance that we would like to avoid. So when considering the other abilities to include in a listening test, it is better to choose those that will lead to the least variance between test-takers – all other things being equal.

Furthermore, it is usually a good idea to have a variety of task types. It has long been accepted that test-item performance consists of both construct-relevant variance, and construct-irrelevant task variance (Campbell and Fiske, 1959); and there is reason to believe that test-taker performance can vary depending on the type of task (Brindley, 1998). Thus, as a general principle, it makes sense for test-developers to use a wide variety of item types in order to reduce the effects of any one type of task.

Available resources

In discussing and evaluating tests, the purpose of the assessment is important. Purpose not only determines the type of test that needs to be made, but the required quality of the test. High-stakes decisions (such as entrance examinations) require good tests – in terms of reliability and validity – whereas low-stakes decisions (for example, part of a class grade) do not put such demands on test quality.

To a considerable extent, the quality of the test will depend on how much time, effort and resources go into making it. In many cases resources for test-development are limited, and in such cases, we have to have reasonable expectations about the quality of the outcome.

The resources needed to make a test are of three main types: people with the right skills, material resources and sufficient time (Bachman and Palmer, 1996). Consideration of resources is important for two reasons. First, as Bachman and Palmer noted, the practicality of a test-development project is a function of the relationship between the resources that are required and the resources that are available. It is not practical to make a test if we do not have the resources to do it well enough. However, in the harsh world, it often happens that test-developers have to do the best they can, even though they may lack the resources to do as well as they would like.

The second reason resources are important is that the available resources provide one basis for determining the success of a test-development project. As noted, many test-developers, especially teachers, have limited resources, and it is unreasonable to expect people with limited resources to develop top-quality tests. While we should not condone unacceptable tests, we need to be realistic and fair. Some tests may seem quite ordinary, but represent a considerable achievement considering the limited resources available for their development.

Developing the construct

There are two basic ways of defining a construct (Chapelle, 1998). The first is to define the competence – the knowledges, skills and abilities – we think test-takers should have, and the second is to define the tasks we think test-takers should be able to perform. Both methods represent different philosophical positions, and both have advantages and disadvantages. The third option is to try to combine both of these methods.

Defining a competence-based listening construct

It is possible to use a description of listening ability as the basis for defining the listening construct. This is most appropriate when we think that consistencies in listening performance are due to the characteristics of the test-taker, and that test performance is a sign of an underlying competence that manifests itself across a variety of settings and tasks. In most testing situations, it is the ability of the test-taker that we are most interested in, and this is probably the more traditional way of defining test constructs.

The central problem is to come up with a suitable description of listening competence. There have been a number of descriptive models of communicative competence, for example Canale and Swain (1980), Canale (1983), Bachman (1990), and Bachman and Palmer (1996). These attempt to describe all the knowledge and skills that learners need in order to use the language effectively. I have developed a similar descriptive model to describe listening ability.

The model, or framework, for describing listening ability is given in Table 4.1. It is adapted from Bachman and Palmer (1996), which is currently the most widely accepted general description of language ability among language testers. Determining the components of such a framework is largely a definitional problem, and I have tried to keep as much consistency with their work as possible. The basic division into language competence and strategic competence, as well as the sub-categories of linguistic competence, are taken from their model, although I have changed the names slightly to fit in better with discussion within this book. They are based on the main sub-fields within linguistics, and represent traditional ways of looking at language ability. It is important to stress that the term **knowledge**, as used in the framework, refers to procedural knowledge – the ability to apply the knowledge in efficient and automatic language processing.

The description of strategic competence is based on the work of Purpura (1997, 1999), and has also been influenced by McNamara (1996). On the basis of empirical research, Purpura suggests that strategic competence consists of (minimally) both **cognitive strategies**, which are the conscious or unconscious mental processes related to comprehending, storing and using linguistic knowledge, and **metacognitive strategies**, which consist of self-management activities that oversee and manage the cognitive activities.

It is important to point out that this framework is intended to help test-developers think about the various aspects of the listening construct, and provide a basis for discussion. It is not intended to be exhaustive; it is work in progress, and no doubt other scholars will be able to improve on it.

This framework is intended to aid test development by describing the components of listening comprehension, but it does have limitations. It does not offer the test-developer any guidelines regarding which of the components are most important, nor which components should be included in a particular test and in what relative proportions. Nor does it provide criteria to determine what is an adequate operationalisation of the components. All it does is provide a framework. The job of the test-developer is to fill in the details. The purpose of the test should be the major determiner of which components should be included in the test, in what relative proportions, and in what way.

The listening framework has two parts, language competence and strategic competence. The distinction between these is not very clear, because it is difficult to separate knowledge of the language from the general intellectual ability to apply that knowledge (McNamara, 1996). This is a complex issue, but I believe it is something on which first-language and second-language performance differ. In the case of first-language use, at least in adults, both language competence and strategic competence are relatively well developed, and are linked

Table 4.1. *A framework for describing listening ability*

Language competence: the knowledge about the language that the listener brings to the listening situation. This will include both fully automated procedural knowledge and controlled or conscious declarative knowledge. Language competence consists of:
 	
    Grammatical knowledge: understanding short utterances on a literal semantic level. This includes phonology, stress, intonation, spoken vocabulary, spoken syntax.
 	
    Discourse knowledge: understanding longer utterances or interactive discourse between two or more speakers. This includes knowledge of discourse features, such as cohesion, foregrounding, rhetorical schemata and story grammars, and knowledge of the structure of unplanned discourse.
 	
    Pragmatic knowledge: understanding the function or the illocutionary force of an utterance or longer text, and interpreting the intended meaning in terms of that. This includes understanding whether utterances are intended to convey ideas, manipulate, learn or are for creative expression, as well as understanding indirect speech acts and pragmatic implications.
 	
    Sociolinguistic knowledge: understanding the language of particular socio-cultural settings, and interpreting utterances in terms of the context of situation. This includes knowledge of appropriate linguistic forms and conventions characteristic of particular sociolinguistic groups, and the implications of their use, or non-use, such as slang, idiomatic expressions, dialects, cultural references, figures of speech, levels of formality and registers.
 	
Strategic competence: includes the cognitive and metacognitive strategies, or executive processes, that fulfil the cognitive management function in listening. This is the ability to use language competence, and includes all the compensatory strategies used by second-language listeners. It consists of:
 	
    Cognitive strategies: those mental activities related to comprehending and storing input in working memory or long-term memory for later retrieval;
 	
        Comprehension processes: associated with the processing of linguistic and non-linguistic input;
 	
        Storing and memory processes: associated with the storing of linguistic and non-linguistic input in working memory or long-term memory;
 	
        Using and retrieval processes: associated with accessing memory, to be readied for output;
 	
    Metacognitive strategies: those conscious or unconscious mental activities that perform an executive function in the management of cognitive strategies;
 	
        Assessing the situation: taking stock of conditions surrounding a language task by assessing one's own knowledge, one's available internal and external resources and the constraints of the situation before engaging in the task;
 	
        Monitoring: determining the effectiveness of one's own or another's performance while engaged in a task;
 	
        Self-evaluating: determining the effectiveness of one's own or another's performance after engaging in the activity;
 	
        Self-testing: testing oneself to determine the effectiveness of one's own language use or the lack thereof.

together in a long-term, stable relationship. They are likely to be closely correlated. Thus, when testing first-language ability, it is not as important to separate language competence from the cognitive skills required as to use that competence effectively.

In second-language testing, the situation is quite different. In adult second-language learning, cognitive abilities will be relatively developed and stable, whereas language knowledge is, by definition, only partially developed. Language competence will usually vary considerably from one second-language user to the next, and their knowledge of the second language may be changing rapidly, as learning progresses. Differences in performance capability between individual listeners, or between the same listener on different occasions, will generally be due to differences in linguistic competence, rather than differences in strategic competence. In applying the framework to test second-language listening ability, it makes more sense to put the emphasis on testing language competence rather than testing strategic competence.

We can use the framework to envisage a number of different definitions of the listening construct, for different testing purposes. The following are a number of illustrative examples, and form a sort of expanding definition of the listening construct. Test-developers would choose those aspects of language competence which met the requirements of their test.

- *Knowledge of the sound system:* would just include those relevant aspects of grammatical knowledge, namely phonology, stress and intonation.

- *Understanding local linguistic meanings:* would include the whole of grammatical knowledge – not only phonology, stress and intonation, but also vocabulary and syntax, as well as the ability to use that knowledge automatically in real time.

- *Understanding full linguistic meanings:* would include grammatical knowledge plus discourse knowledge, and would require understanding longer texts.

- *Understanding inferred meanings:* would include grammatical knowledge, discourse knowledge and pragmatic knowledge – that is understanding inferred meanings and unstated implications.

- *Communicative listening ability:* would include grammatical knowledge, discourse knowledge, pragmatic knowledge and sociolinguistic knowledge; this would be communicative language ability.

Unfortunately, determining the competencies that underlie performance on a set of test tasks is a complex and indirect process, and we have no way of knowing for certain which competencies are required by any particular task. Thus, the main problem of the competence-based approach to construct definition is ensuring that the test items actually assess the competencies of interest.

Defining a task-based listening construct

The alternative is to define the listening construct in terms of the tasks the listener can perform. This is most appropriate when we think that consistencies in listening performance are due to the characteristics of the context in which the listening takes place. In other words, when we are interested in what the test-takers can do, and under what circumstances they can do it.

Although I prefer to avoid calling such tests performance tests (because the term already has a variety of different meanings), tests whose construct has been defined in this way will meet McNamara's (1996) definition of a **weak performance test**, namely when 'the capacity to perform the task is not the focus of assessment. Rather the purpose of the task is to elicit a language sample so that second language proficiency . . . may be assessed' (McNamara, 1996:44).

There are two steps involved in such a procedure. Firstly, we have to come up with a suitable list of target-language use tasks that the listener should be able to perform. Secondly, it is necessary to produce a set of test tasks that somehow replicate these real-world tasks. Bachman and Palmer (1996) suggest a list of task characteristics that can be used to compare test tasks with real-world tasks. This is given in Table 4.2. These task characteristics will be discussed in more detail in Chapter 5.

The underlying theoretical notion is that of authenticity. Bachman (1991) argued that authenticity was of two types: **situational authenticity**, which is the extent to which the test tasks are perceived to share the characteristics of the target-language use tasks; and **interactional authenticity** which is the extent to which the test tasks engage the same abilities as the target-language use tasks. Later Bachman and Palmer (1996) argued that the interaction between the language user and the task, that is the ability that is engaged, should not be considered an aspect of authenticity, and interactional authenticity was renamed **interactiveness**.

Table 4.2. *A framework for defining listening task characteristics*

Characteristics of the setting: the physical circumstances under which the listening takes place.

> **Physical characteristics:** the actual place, background noise, live or recorded etc.

> **Participants:** the people around, including test administrators.

> **Time of task:** time of day, whether the listeners are fresh or fatigued.

Characteristics of the test rubric: the characteristics that provide the structure for the test, and how the test-takers are to proceed. These have to be made explicit in the test, but are usually implicit in language use.

> **Instructions:** instructions, details or procedures, as well as purpose of listening, including the language used, and whether they are oral or written.

> **Structure:** structure of the test, how the parts of the test are put together, including the number of listening passages, whether the passages are repeated, their order, the number of items per passage etc.

> **Time allotment:** the time allowed for each task.

> **Scoring method:** how the tasks are scored including criteria for correctness, steps used for scoring or rating, and how the item scores are combined into the test score.

Characteristics of the input: the listening passages and other accompanying material.

> **Format:** whether passages are spoken or recorded, their length etc.

> **Language of input:** including phonology, grammar, lexis, textual, functional and sociolinguistic knowledge.

> **Topical knowledge:** the cultural, schematic or general world knowledge necessary to understand the passages.

Characteristics of the expected response: the response expected from the test-taker to the task.

> **Format:** selected or constructed, the length, the form it will take, time available.

> **Language of expected response:** for constructed responses whether in the L1 or the L2, criteria for correctness etc.

Relationship between the input and response:

> **Reactivity:** whether the listening is reciprocal, non-reciprocal or adaptive.

> **Scope:** the range of listening material that must be processed.

> **Directness of relationship:** the degree to which the response can be based primarily on the language of the passage, or whether it is necessary to use information from the context, or apply background knowledge.

Adapted from Bachman and Palmer, 1996

Bachman and Palmer argue that authenticity, by which they mean situational authenticity, is important to 'demonstrate how performance on a given language test is related to language use in specific situations in other than the language test itself' (Bachman and Palmer, 1996:43), and further that authenticity is examined by comparing the characteristics of test tasks and target-language use tasks. They suggest that 'the key to designing tests that . . . is to include, in the test, tasks whose distinguishing characteristics correspond to those of the TLU tasks' (Bachman and Palmer, 1996:45).

A task-based approach to construct definition addresses the major problem of the competence-based approach, namely the difficulty of determining which abilities are required for performance on both target-language use tasks and test tasks. Instead we just replicate the target-language use tasks as closely as we can, and then assume that the abilities required to perform one will be the same as the other.

However, there are drawbacks. Firstly, the target-language use situation is often ill-defined. For example, what is the target-language use domain for a general proficiency test – all possible situations? And even if we have a more specific target, such as academic language use, the target language will vary according to the field of study, the type of study and so forth. It is often not clear which tasks we should choose. Secondly, even if we decide which tasks are important, it is not possible to accurately replicate target-language use tasks, simply because the testing situation is different from the real-world communicative situation – it is a test. We need to ensure, therefore, that the test task replicates the most critical aspects of the target-language use task, and the obvious way to do that is to compare the competencies they both require. And that brings us back to the difficulty of determining which competencies particular tasks require.

Defining a construct based on the interaction between competence and task

When making test tasks, the important thing is not that the test task is similar to the target-language use task, but that the interaction between the test-taker and the test task is similar to the interaction between the language user and the task in the target-language use situation. In other words, they should require similar competencies.

This suggests using both traits and tasks as a basis for construct definition. This approach is most appropriate when we think that the consistencies in listening performance are partly due to some underlying knowledge and ability, partly due to situational factors, and partly due to the interaction between them. In other words, we see performance in terms of underlying language competence, but this is influenced by contextual factors. Given the work reviewed in Chapters 1 and 2, this is probably a theoretically more defensible position than either the competence-based or task-based approach.

Using both competence and tasks has practical advantages too. We can get the best of both approaches, and hope that the strengths of each will compensate for the weaknesses of the other. To do this, it may be sufficient just to produce lists of relevant abilities and lists of the most important target-language use tasks, and then go ahead and develop test tasks that require both. We may, however, want to be more systematic and try a matrix-based approach. The idea is very simple. A two-dimensional matrix is produced with the components of language competence in the rows, and the most important tasks in the columns. This defines the construct, and the test-developer creates the test by sampling from this matrix.

An illustrative example of a matrix approach to construct definition is given in Table 4.3. Let us assume that the target-language use situation is a college or school. We talk to experts, read the research literature, and so forth, and determine the listening tasks students need to perform. For the sake of discussion, let us assume that these are lectures, student presentations and assignments, and let us further assume that there are three different types of each. So we now have nine tasks in our hypothetical target-language use situation. Of course, in the real world we are likely to have many more tasks.

In the rows we have the components of language competence which we think are important, and we can then determine which competencies each of the tasks is likely to need. Some aspects of language, like vocabulary or grammar, are present in every language task, but we are only interested in cases where they are particularly crucial to task completion. When a particular competence is critical to comprehension – such as unusual vocabulary, complex syntax, the necessity of understanding discourse markers or the significance of cultural references – we mark this in the box. The completed matrix provides a definition of the construct we need to assess.

Table 4.3. *A matrix for defining a construct of academic listening*

	Most important tasks								
	Formal lectures			Student presentations			Instructions/ assignments		
	#1	#2	#3	#1	#2	#3	#1	#2	#3
Language competency required									
Grammatical knowledge:									
phonological modification	x		x	x	x				x
stress/intonation	x		x	x	x				x
spoken vocabulary/slang	x			x	x				x
oral syntax	x			x	x				x
repetitions and false starts	x			x	x	x			x
Discourse knowledge:									x
discourse markers		x	x	x				x	
rhetorical schemata		x	x	x				x	
story grammars			x	x				x	
asides/jokes	x			x			x	x	
separating main points/detail	x	x	x	x		x		x	
Pragmatic knowledge:									
basic functions conveying ideas							x	x	
manipulating, learning or creative	x	x						x	
indirect meanings/hints	x		x		x		x	x	
pragmatic implications	x	x			x		x	x	x
text-based inferences		x					x	x	
Sociolinguistic knowledge:									
appropriacy of linguistic forms	x					x		x	x
informal	x					x			x
idiomatic expressions	x					x		x	x
local dialect	x					x			x
cultural references	x					x			x
figures of speech						x			x

Defining the construct in terms of both competence and task does lead to some conceptual difficulties because the underlying assumptions of the two approaches are different. The competence-based approach makes the assumption that it is the competence or ability that determines performance, and this exists independent of the context, whereas the task-based approach makes the assumption that it is the context which determines the performance (see Chapelle, 1998). However, in most practical test-development situations, these conceptual difficulties will be of minor importance, and I believe an approach that uses both competence and task has much to recommend it. For most test-development projects, this will be the best practical approach.

The target-language use situation

The target-language use situation is a very important and powerful notion. It refers to those specific situations in which the test-taker will use the language. The aim of the test is to determine whether the test-taker can perform in that specific situation. It is the language-use domain to which the test results should generalise.

If we know the target-language use situation, we can use that to determine which aspects of language competence should be on the test. We determine which type of speakers, which accents, the degree of phonological modification, the vocabulary, grammar and the type of discourse structures we need to include in our test. We can also consider the main language functions, communicative intentions, the type of inferencing, the pragmatic implications and the sociolinguistically appropriate language. We can then select listening texts which require similar competencies. We can also determine what are the most common tasks, and what cognitive skills and metacognitive strategies are required. We can construct test tasks that require similar abilities – tasks that have interactive authenticity.

Whichever approach we take to construct definition, it is advisable to look carefully at the target-language use situation. As a general strategy, it is always useful to try to replicate as many aspects of the target-language use situation as possible. The better the test replicates the important characteristics of the target-language use situation, the more likely it is to tell us about performance in that domain.

However, test-development projects vary, and in some cases we will know the target-language use situation well, and in others we will not. For example, in a test of specific purposes (see Douglas, 2000) we usually know what the target-language use situation is – a tour guide in Geneva, or a nurse in a general hospital, for example. We can then carry out research, called a **needs analysis**, to determine the listening necessary in that target-language situation, and this can be used as the basis of construct definition and test design.

In other cases, the target-language use situation may be very broad and ill-defined. The TOEIC is designed to test general English ability in the context of the global work place, but there are many different work places throughout the world, and the English in a multinational corporation in Texas will be very different from that in a Malaysian/ Japanese joint venture in Singapore. Consider also IELTS, which is used to determine whether students are ready to study at an English-medium university: obviously the listening required to study history at a British university will be quite different from that required to study engineering at an Australian university. In such cases, test-developers will have to make do with an approximate idea of the domain. Often it is possible to use general knowledge: many of us could probably make a fair guess at much of the English that would be necessary in most work places, even if we do not know it precisely. We can also talk to colleagues, or look at text books, but the best thing to do is to talk to people who know the domain, especially people who operate in it. Test-developers can then come up with a set of knowledge, skills and abilities, along with ideas about texts and tasks, that seem most common, or most typical, of the listening in the target-language use domain. It is in partially defined domains such as these where the dual approach of defining constructs in terms of both competencies and tasks seems most useful.

To summarise, when there is no clear target-language use situation, there are no criteria to determine the appropriacy or authenticity of test tasks and a competency-based approach to construct definition is the only real possibility. So in the case of a general test of listening proficiency, for example, we could define the construct by sampling across all the components of the framework in Table 4.1, in the proportions that seem most appropriate. When the target-language use situation is more clearly defined, it becomes easier to use tasks as a basis for construct definition and test design; and when the target-language use situation is very clear and explicit, we may prefer to define our construct entirely in terms of the tasks from that situation.

A default listening construct

The purpose of the test, as well as the target-language use situation, should determine the appropriate construct, and in some cases consideration of the resources available will also influence that decision. There are no hard-and-fast rules about what is an appropriate listening construct, but the issues are complex, and some general advice and guidance may not go amiss. In the absence of good reasons to do otherwise, these are my recommendations regarding the listening construct.

- It is important to put the emphasis on assessing those language skills that are unique to listening, because they cannot be tested elsewhere. Thus, I think listening tests ought to require fast, automatic, on-line processing of texts that have the linguistic characteristics of typical spoken language.

- It is crucial that the listener be required to understand the basic linguistic information in a variety of texts, on a variety of topics. Thus it is important to ensure that grammatical knowledge is covered in a manner appropriate for listening comprehension.

- Discourse skills are important, and wherever appropriate, tasks should require listeners to process more than just short utterances – or at least some of them should. Additionally, including longer texts will also tend to engage aspects of pragmatic knowledge and strategic competence.

- It is important to go beyond literal meaning and include the understanding of inferred meanings. These should be included as long as they are based on linguistic clues, or other clear evidence from the text.

- Knowledge-dependent interpretations are also important in listening, but all test-takers should share that knowledge. If the test-takers are a clearly defined group, then it seems appropriate to create tasks which depend on knowledge they all share. If not, it is better to depend on knowledge that has been provided earlier in the text.

- Finally, as a general principle, we should attempt to include anything that is dependent on linguistic knowledge, and we should attempt to exclude anything that is dependent on general cognitive abilities. Often it is not possible to differentiate between these, but I think this is a good guideline to keep in mind. Thus, inferences based on intelligence or common sense should be avoided, but inferences based on subtle textual cues could be included.

Together these recommendations describe a set of abilities that can be used to form a **default listening construct**. This is the construct I would recommend in cases where there are no strong reasons to do otherwise. I believe this forms the best compromise between theoretical rigour, practical utility and return on work invested.

Here is a more formal definition of my default listening construct. It is the ability:

- to process extended samples of realistic spoken language, automatically and in real time,
- to understand the linguistic information that is unequivocally included in the text, and
- to make whatever inferences are unambiguously implicated by the content of the passage.

This is linguistic processing, not in the narrow sense of phonology, vocabulary and syntax alone, but in a much more expanded sense that includes all the linguistic devices speakers use to convey meaning – stress, intonation, tone of voice, subtle word-choice, discourse structure, and so on. While this does not capture all aspects of the language competence in the framework in Table 4.1, I think it does capture the important ones, and avoids most of the problems of context-dependent interpretations. What is lacking is sociolinguistic knowledge.

This is a competency-based construct definition; it says nothing about the context. It is a richer, more realistic construct than that operationalised by most integrative tests, but clearly not as good as the communicative testing ideal. In terms of the two-stage view of listening, it falls between the two: better than just a basic linguistic understanding of the text, in that it does require going beyond local literal meanings, but not including the full range of implied meanings.

If we know the target-language use situation, we can easily improve on this default construct simply by including as many as possible of the characteristics of that situation in the test. The language used, the type of texts, the context of the situation, the sociolinguistic variables associated with that, the pragmatic inferences likely to be made and, most importantly, the tasks we require test-takers to perform – all these can be used to improve the default construct. For example, in the case of a test of academic English, test-takers could be required to understand lectures, homework assignments or a class schedule; whereas a test of business English could ask test-takers to understand telephone inquiries, voice-mail messages, or a business presentation. If we start with the default construct, and then use texts and tasks from a target-language use situation, most of the remaining aspects of language competence, pragmatic and sociolinguistic knowledge, will be included, as well as many aspects of strategic competence.

Even when there is no clear target-language use situation, we can still try to use realistic texts. We can choose a selection of tasks that are typical of common communicative situations: for example, following directions, listening to announcements, understanding explanations, listening to narratives, discussions and so on. Although there are no clear criteria to evaluate the authenticity of the tasks, we all have a fair idea of what most people would listen to in a typical day. A well chosen selection of such texts and tasks can broaden and enrich our construct, even when there is no clear target-language use situation. Thus, if we have tests which provide a good measure of the core linguistic skills, and if we use a variety of realistic tasks, we will have a good basic design for a general test of listening comprehension.

Conclusion

In this chapter I have looked at testing purposes, and shown that there are a number of different purposes for assessing listening. I also discussed some of the constraints that determine what we can test and what we cannot test. Then I discussed different ways of defining our construct: competence-based and task-based, and I argued that both have advantages. I recommended taking an interactive perspective and defining the construct in terms of both the underlying competence and target-language use tasks. I illustrated this by means of a matrix design for construct definition. Finally, in this chapter, I have attempted to define a default listening construct that could be used as a basis of test design.

In the next chapter, I will examine test tasks, and in Chapter 6, I will talk about how to provide suitable texts.

CHAPTER FIVE

....

Creating tasks

Introduction

In Chapter 4 I discussed the definition of a suitable listening construct. The next step in test construction is to operationalise that construct through a series of tasks to be carried out by the test-taker; not just any tasks, but tasks that are dependent on comprehension of the text, and whose successful completion requires the knowledge, skills and abilities we included in the construct definition. Then, from performance on these tasks, we can make inferences about how well test-takers have mastered the construct.

Most tests use a number of different task-types to operationalise the construct. The test specifications should lay out in detail what these various tasks should be, and each individual task may only operationalise part of the construct, but taken together the tasks need to represent the whole construct. To the extent that they do, the test will have construct validity.

In this chapter, I will discuss tasks from a variety of perspectives; it will be organised into four main sections:

i an overview of listening task characteristics;

ii the interaction between the task and the test-taker;

iii the use of comprehension questions;

iv evaluating and modifying tasks.

Chapter 6 will deal with issues related to constructing and delivering spoken texts; in this chapter discussion of texts will therefore be kept to a minimum.

Task characteristics

The framework of task characteristics given in Table 4.2 (p. 107) is intended to function as a checklist for comparing test tasks with target-language use tasks. It is a means of investigating task authenticity, as well as an aid to the development of new tasks (see Bachman and Palmer, 1996). In this section, I will discuss the components of the framework and consider how they apply to listening.

Characteristics of the setting

The circumstances in which a test is given can have a crucial effect on performance, and in the case of listening tests the most important characteristics of the setting must be those that affect the quality of the listening experience.

Physical characteristics

The physical situation is particularly important. It is necessary to ensure good acoustics and minimal background noise so test-takers can hear clearly and comfortably.

In some cases, the listening material will be presented by a live speaker which involves training speakers and making sure their presentations are as standardised as possible; but in most cases recorded sound will be provided, in which case the equipment is crucial. The recordings need to be clear, with a minimum of background hiss. The player needs to be of reasonably good quality, powerful enough to drive room speakers, and the playback heads need to be clean. Most importantly, the speakers need to be large enough to fill the whole listening space comfortably above the level of background noise, and without sound distortion. The same technical requirements apply if the recorded text is delivered via radio. In the case of video presentation or TV broadcast, it is important to provide listeners with an adequate view of the picture, with equal visual quality.

Language laboratories and computers usually deliver sound through individual headphones. This brings the sound right to the listener's ear, and can improve sound quality by reducing the effect of background noise. However, the headphones must be good enough for the job; poor headphones are just as bad as poor speakers.

Participants

Test administrators need to be efficient and know what they are doing. In the case of listening, this means they should understand any audio equipment being used. They should ensure that it is being used properly, and be prepared to modify sound levels so that everyone can hear comfortably. If headphones are being used, administrators need to be able to deal with defective ones.

Administrators must also ensure quiet, while the texts are being played: both by being quiet themselves and by keeping others quiet – especially those outside the room. This is not always easy, but high levels of noise can completely ruin a listening test administration.

Administrators who provide live texts to the listeners need to make sure they know what to do, and that they have practised and prepared themselves in the manner laid out in the instructions. They need to pay particular attention to any pauses inserted in the script.

Time of task

Generally, the time of the test administration will not be important, as long as the test-takers are not suffering fatigue. However, in some situations certain times may be preferable. Schools are noisy places when the students are all leaving, rush hours can lead to high levels of street noise, as can road works or street markets. Weekends, or evenings, might be much quieter, although administering tests at such times may not be possible.

Characteristics of the test rubric

The test rubric includes those characteristics of the test that provide structure to the test and the tasks. These have to be made explicit in the test, but are usually implicit in target-language use. However, the test rubric can provide a rationale for the activity and can function in an analogous way to the listening purpose in target-language use situations (Alderson, 2000). Test-developers can often increase the authenticity of the task, if they can structure the test rubric in such a way as to replicate the effects of a real-world listening purpose.

Instructions

As Brindley (1998) notes, it is important that test-takers are provided with clear, simple and explicit instructions on how to do the tasks. The penalty for misunderstanding one question is one item incorrect, but the penalty for misunderstanding one simple instruction could be many items incorrect – a penalty usually far out of proportion to the mistake made. Give instructions in the native language where possible, or if a second language is used, try to ensure that the language of the instructions is easier than the level the test aims to measure. Use clear examples, and if possible prepare the test-takers with sample items before they take the test.

In standardised tests it is likely that most test-takers will already know the instructions, and many of them will not pay attention to them again. If the instructions change, many test-takers may not notice, and the administration could go badly wrong. If reading or listening to the instructions is crucial, ensure that all test-takers are fully aware of this.

Test structure

The test specifications will specify the nature of the tasks, how many there are, and how they are organised and ordered. It is traditional to order test items with the easiest items coming first and harder items later. This ensures that lower-ability test-takers encounter all the easier items, which gives them the best chance of showing their true ability level. In the case of a **testlet**, that is a listening passage that has a number of items attached, it may not be possible to order the individual items according to difficulty, and the testlet must be treated as a whole unit.

Real-world listening always takes place within a context, and it is sometimes possible to turn the test itself into a context by organising the tasks around a theme. This creates a known situation that can be used to test context-embedded interpretations, sociolinguistic competence and inferences based on knowledge that has already been provided. For example, we could ask test-takers to imagine they were visiting England for a vacation, and then we could build a coherent set of tasks around that theme. Test-takers could listen to descriptions of hotel rooms; follow directions; listen to train timetables, theatre or concert times; listen to descriptions of places of interest or famous people; or they could listen to strangers talking about their work, their hobby or their views on social issues. The list is almost endless. After listening, test-takers could answer questions, fill in information grids or make decisions based on a specified context.

The theme does of course need to be relevant to the testing purpose. For example, in a test of business English, the theme could be a request from a colleague for information about a new product. Firstly, the listener could hear a message on a voice-mail asking for general information, followed by listening to a presentation about the new product, and then a talk on plans for product promotion. Such themes can easily be used to test integrated skills (Alderson, 2000). The listener could then be asked to read something about the new product, perhaps write a summary of the presentation, or record a spoken reply on the colleague's voice-mail.

There is much to recommend a thematic approach to test design, but the danger is that it will restrict the range of topics and text types, or advantage test-takers who have background knowledge relevant to the theme. When we develop a test, we want a sample of the competences and tasks in the construct definition. The greater and more varied the sample, the more likely it is to represent the construct fairly, and the smaller or narrower the sample the more likely it is to underrepresent the construct. Test-developers need to weigh the advantages of a thematic test design against the dangers of construct underrepresentation.

Time allotment

In most testing situations there is a predetermined time allotment, and the test administrators must keep track of time. In the case of listening, the timing of the test is usually determined by the sequence of texts and tasks. Often there will be one recording that includes all the listening texts, the instructions, questions, response pauses and so forth, and this recording will control the test; the administrator just presses the button and waits. It is easy to standardise administrations in this way.

Not all listening tests are controlled by one recording; sometimes there will be a number of recordings, and in other cases there may be a live presentation. In all cases, the test-developer will have to sequence the texts and tasks, and ensure there is enough time allowed for all the activities. For example, if we require test-takers to respond by making a simple mark on an answer sheet, five seconds' response time per item may be enough, but if we require them to write a sentence in response, then one minute may be necessary. Test-developers are well advised to practise the timing of activities, and trialling the whole procedure is advisable.

From the listeners' perspective, what this means is that they are not usually in control of their own speed of working. On a reading test, the test-taker can usually respond at a rate they feel comfortable with, and if they need more time for a difficult item, they can take it. This is not possible on many listening tests, and some test-takers may feel this is a disruption of their preferred way of working, and some may feel frustrated or even resentful as a result. However, some computer-based tests do allow the listener more freedom to decide when to move on to the next passage.

Scoring method

Scores are what give meaning to test performance, and our aim in test development is to ensure scores are meaningful in terms of the construct we have defined.

It is important that tasks are scorable; by that I mean that it must be possible to say, based on the listening passage, that certain responses are definitely correct and others are definitely incorrect. Given the nature of comprehension, the need to determine that one interpretation is correct and another is not correct can be problematic. When we insist on one particular understanding of a text, there must be no doubt that this was what the speaker intended. This is one reason why I have suggested in Chapter 4 that the default construct should test only those things for which there is clear and unequivocal linguistic evidence in the text. Although we would like to know whether listeners have understood the range of possible interpretations, any aspect of comprehension that is open to alternative interpretations is very difficult to assess.

When we require test-takers to construct responses, what they produce may be quite exhaustive or cursory, unequivocally correct or doubtful, indicate complete comprehension or only partial comprehension. It is important that the criteria for scoring these are clearly determined and consistently applied. For example, if a question asks why something happened, we would have to determine whether it is enough just to give the main point, or whether a full explanation is necessary. If there are two reasons in the text, do both need to be given in the response, is one required and the other optional, or is either good enough? One way of avoiding such problems is to use selected responses. The advantage is that they can constrain the responses available to the test-taker, who can be asked to choose between the correct response and alternatives that are definitely incorrect. This makes scoring much easier.

It is widely believed in educational testing that it is easier to write constructed response items but harder to score them, and conversely, it is harder to write selected response items but easier to score them. We write items once, but score them for each test-taker, therefore constructed response items will require less total work when testing volumes are small, and selected response items will require less total work when volumes are high.

Another important scoring issue is the extent to which the scoring criteria are made explicit to the test-taker. It is vital that test-takers know what constitutes a sufficient response. With open-ended responses they need to be told not only what is expected, but how much is expected, so that if they have understood the text well, they will be in no doubt about the adequacy of their reply. With multiple-choice tasks, there is less room for ambiguity, but instructions may need to ask for the best option, or the most appropriate response, rather than the correct one.

It is also important that test-takers know the relative value of each task in the test they are taking: how many points or what proportion of the total test each task is worth. This helps them to structure their time and efforts.

Characteristics of the input

The input into a listening task obviously consists of the listening text, but it will also include the instructions, questions and any materials required by the task. Much of the content of this section is dealt with in far more detail in Chapter 6.

Format

The input will be a sample of spoken language, and the length is important. Longer texts will tend to require discourse skills, whereas shorter texts will tend to focus more on localised grammatical characteristics. Listening to long texts can be tiring. Furthermore, when texts are even a little challenging to listeners, small difficulties can accrue in longer texts, until listeners lose the thread, get completely lost and just give up (Buck, 1990). It is certainly more difficult to maintain concentration if the content is boring or the presentation is bad. Interesting texts are much better. If the texts are challenging, it may be better to keep them shorter. If the specifications call for longer texts, it is often better to choose relatively easier texts. If the text is both longer and challenging, try to choose texts with an obvious structure, so that if listeners do lose the thread, they can get back into it relatively easily.

It is becoming increasingly common to present listening texts in video format. This is because visual information supplements the audio information, and this is a more realistic replication of real-world listening. It is important to make certain that the video complements the audio text, rather than conflicts with it, and that successful task completion still depends on processing the audio input. However, there can be problems: watching the video, reading the text, listening and writing responses all at the same time may be too complex, and many test-takers give up watching the video – which rather defeats the purpose (Alderson *et al.*, 1995).

The task will not only require a spoken text, but may also require written information, questions, pictures, diagrams, a grid to be filled in or a transcript of part of the text. In order to minimise construct-irrelevant variance, it is important that these are not a source of difficulty. Written language should be as simple and clear as possible – as should any pictures, diagrams and grids that are used. There are cultural differences in how things are conventionally represented in pictorial or diagrammatic form, and test-developers should ensure that test-takers understand clearly what is represented, and what they are supposed to do with it.

Language of input

The language of the input will be determined largely by the construct that has been defined. We need to ensure that the texts include the linguistic characteristics called for by the construct definition – aspects of grammatical, discourse, pragmatic and sociolinguistic knowledge. But that is not enough. It is also important that the test tasks engage the listener in *using* those competencies. For example, if the construct includes facility with a certain accent, it is relatively easy to check that the texts use that accent. Stress patterns and intonation are subtler, and it is not as easy to ensure that successful task completion requires understanding them. If the construct calls for discourse knowledge, just providing a longer text with comprehension questions may not actually engage the discourse characteristics; it might be possible to respond based on grammatical knowledge applied to short sections of the text.

Topical knowledge

Comprehension is an inferential process and the information that forms the basis for the inference is often outside the text. In some cases this may be part of the construct definition: for example, in a test of French for academic purposes we can assume that test-takers will know something about the French university system. In a test of German for business, we can assume that test-takers would recognise a German telephone number, or know how a fax machine works. This is construct-relevant knowledge. However, in other cases comprehension may require construct-irrelevant knowledge. There is ample theoretical evidence that background knowledge is important in listening comprehension, and there is research evidence to suggest that it does affect test performance (Chiang and Dunkel, 1992; Long, 1990; Schmidt-Rinehart, 1994). However, the relationship between background knowledge and test performance is complex and varies from one test to another, and probably from one topic to another (Jenson and Hansen, 1995).

There are three ways to ensure that test-takers have the background knowledge necessary: (a) use tasks that depend on knowledge that everyone has, (b) use tasks that depend on knowledge that no one has, or (c) use tasks that depend on knowledge that has been provided in the test.

Characteristics of the expected response

Responses can be provided in a wide variety of ways, but as discussed in Chapter 4, in all listening tests the response will be a potential source of construct-irrelevant variance.

Format

The format of the response can vary considerably. With selected responses it may amount to little more than a mark on a score sheet, or making a simple addition or alteration to a drawing or diagram. Constructed responses, however, vary greatly; these may require just writing one word in the case of a gap-filling test, or one or more sentences in the case of comprehension questions. A longer response could require writing a short summary of a text such as a lecture – this is not uncommon in research studies. It is also possible to have spoken responses, in sentence-repetition tasks for example, and listeners could be required to summarise what they have understood by speaking in their native language. Other response formats are drawing pictures or creating diagrams.

Language of expected response

In the case of constructed responses the language of the response is important. These could be given in either the target language or the test-takers' native language, and could be either written or spoken.

In the case of second-language responses, the main issue is whether the response will be evaluated for correctness, appropriacy and so forth, and whether those judgements will affect the score. In a listening test, it seems reasonable not to penalise mistakes if the response is intelligible and clear. After all, we want to know whether test-takers have understood a text, not whether they can produce correct language. Serious mistakes in the response will be penalised automatically, because when they are bad enough to interfere with the meaning, the response will be scored incorrect because it cannot be understood.

Task interactiveness

Looking at task characteristics is very useful, but it puts emphasis on the observable characteristics of tasks, whereas what we are really interested in is the knowledge and abilities that enable the test-takers to carry out that task. This brings us to the notion of **interactiveness**. This refers to 'ways in which the test-taker's areas of language knowledge, metacognitive strategies, topical knowledge, and affective schemata are engaged by the test task' (Bachman and Palmer, 1996:25). If the competence and knowledge engaged by the test task are those required by the construct definition, then the task has **interactional authenticity** in Bachman's (1991) terms, or minimal construct underrepresentation in Messick's (1989) terms. Put simply, it means the test is testing the construct it was intended to test. Interactiveness is important because it gets to the heart of construct validity.

We need to look at interactiveness from two perspectives: firstly, to see whether successful completion of the test task is dependent on comprehension of the text, and secondly, whether the knowledge, skills and abilities required to comprehend the passage represent the knowledge, skills and abilities in the construct definition.

Passage dependency

Passage dependency is the notion that successful completion of the task is dependent on comprehension of the text. It is central to comprehension testing. This is very basic and seems obvious, but a number of researchers have looked at multiple-choice reading tests and found that test-takers could usually score far better than chance even if they have not read the passage (Preston, 1964; Wendell *et al.*, 1967; Connor and Read 1978).

Test tasks may lack passage dependency for two reasons. Firstly, all test tasks provide some information to the test-taker, and this will usually give some clue to the content of the passage, which clever test-takers may use to help them respond. This is clearly the case with traditional multiple-choice items, but is also likely to happen with gap-filling tasks on written summaries, and can happen on information grids when part of the information is already given.

Secondly, tasks may lack passage dependency because test-takers might be able to use their background knowledge or intelligence to respond. Many things in life are predictable, and spoken texts are no different. Comprehension questions can often be answered by using common sense. For example in the case of a series of pictures that must be arranged in order based on a narrative, it may be possible to make sense of them without the narrative. In the case of multiple-choice options, a little thought will often suggest which options are more likely and which are less likely.

In Chapter 3 I noted that comprehension tasks must be designed in such a way that they provide clear evidence of comprehension. The only way to be sure the meaning has been processed is by using responses that require the semantic content to be expressed in a different form from the input. So for example, just pulling a phrase out of a text and repeating it does not provide sufficient evidence that the meaning has been processed, whereas matching the phrase to a picture, or matching it to a synonymous phrase does.

As test-developers, we should never underestimate the resourcefulness of test-takers in finding ways to compensate for a lack of comprehension. It is often difficult to ensure that our tasks are passage dependent, and that they provide clear evidence that the meaning has been processed.

Construct-relevant variance

We design tasks based on our construct definition, and different tasks will be appropriate for different constructs. For example, if we want to test a narrow view of listening – understanding short utterances on a literal level – we will look for a task that we believe requires this ability. Dictation or statement evaluation are possible choices.

Let us assume next that we want to assess a slightly broader construct: grammatical knowledge plus discourse knowledge, but not pragmatic or sociolinguistic knowledge. In this case we would have to find a longer text in which information was spread throughout the text, with plenty of references from one part of the text to another, and where the rhetorical structure was important. Alternatively, we could find a text with many oral discourse features, where the unplanned nature of the discourse resulted in repetitions, repairs or rephrasing of various parts. We then need to devise tasks that would engage the test-taker in understanding these aspects of the discourse. Neither the dictation nor the statement evaluation task would likely be suitable. Comprehension questions, statement completion tasks or gap-filling tasks could be used; the important issue is whether they engage the knowledge, skills and abilities of interest.

We could adopt an even wider view of listening. We may want to test grammatical, discourse and pragmatic competence, or the entire range of linguistic competence in the Chapter 4 framework. The procedure is the same: we first find texts whose comprehension requires these abilities, and then we devise tasks that engage them. Finally, in high-ability or first-language testing situations, we may want to go beyond the framework and test listening in the sense of understanding what the speaker felt about what she was saying. We would find a suitable text, or maybe a variety of short texts, in which the speaker's feelings are made evident by the tone of voice and the choice of words. We could then present listeners with a list of words describing emotions – angry, doubtful, fearful, embarrassed etc – and ask them to select the words that seemed most appropriate to the speaker's feelings. This is all easy in principle, but in practice it is difficult to determine exactly what sub-skills are required by particular tasks.

Construct-irrelevant variance

Whatever task we devise will require skills other than listening skills. In the case of the dictation, test-takers need to be able to write English; short-answer questions will require some reading and a little writing; and multiple-choice items usually require quite a lot of reading. As noted above, what is important is not that we get rid of these construct-irrelevant skills – that is not always possible – but to choose those that do not add any variance to item difficulty.

If we have a group of test-takers who are not literate, such as young children, tasks that require writing will not be appropriate. Test-takers who come from a first-language group which uses a different writing system, say Chinese students taking an English test, may be disadvantaged compared to test-takers who use the Roman alphabet in their own language, say French students. In the case of a test of Japanese as a second language, the same Chinese students, however, would likely be greatly advantaged compared to the French students, because both Chinese and Japanese use Chinese characters.

Multiple-choice items are another example. Many people believe that performance can be improved by the use of appropriate test-taking strategies, and there is evidence that practice does improve performance on multiple-choice items (Powers and Rock, 1999). Multiple-choice items are used widely in some countries, and virtually never in others. If we use them in multi-cultural situations, we may find some test-takers disadvantaged through lack of familiarity.

Task processing

Tasks are designed to engage particular aspects of language knowledge, but how do we know what knowledge, skills and abilities they require? The short answer is that we are never sure (Buck, 1991). Given the complexity of listening processes we can never be sure exactly which abilities particular tasks are engaging. Such labels as *vocabulary item* or *grammar test* rarely indicate more than the test-developers' intention. The reality will usually be far more complicated.

The necessary information

One useful way of focusing on what particular tasks are measuring is to identify the **necessary information**. This is the information in the text that the test-taker must understand in order to be sure the task has been done correctly. It is more than just the basis for a good guess; it is the information that would tell us whether the guess was correct. For some tasks, the necessary information may be one short statement, in others it may be a number of statements scattered throughout the passage, and in others it may be a whole section of text. Sometimes the necessary information is repeated in a passage, and sometimes it only appears once.

Once we have identified the necessary information, we can then assume that any knowledge, skills or abilities that are engaged in understanding this are likely to be important in task performance. Usually that is what the task will be assessing. Other abilities may also be involved, and there may be alternative ways an item might be processed, but the necessary information is usually the best and easiest way of developing hypotheses about what test tasks measure.

An example of how items are processed

I think it is always a good idea to examine illustrative items and attempt to understand how they may be functioning. The examples are taken from Buck (1991) and Buck (1994). Imagine a narrative about a woman who has been burgled many times, and she goes to a man called Dagbovie for help. The assumption up to this point is that Dagbovie is some sort of private investigator, but the story heads in a new direction when the narrator states, 'Dagbovie was a sort of animist or witch-doctor who had some special power to understand these strange events.' This was the necessary information that was targeted by two short-answer questions: Q1: 'What was Dagbovie?', and Q2: 'Why could Dagbovie understand strange events?' The words 'animist' and 'witch-doctor' are quite low-frequency vocabulary, and these items were intended to test vocabulary knowledge. The expected response to Q1 was 'an animist' or 'a witch-doctor', and to Q2 'because he had some special power'.

Six test-takers were selected and asked to discuss their listening and their test responses. The two highest ability test-takers responded correctly to both these items, and the four lowest ability test-takers responded incorrectly. This suggests these were both good items, because they discriminated well between listeners of different ability levels.

Now let us examine what happened. Firstly, regarding those four who got the item wrong, three of them heard the word 'witch-doctor' and inferred that Dagbovie was a doctor. Furthermore, two of them misheard the word 'animist' as 'analyst', presumably an inference based on the acoustic form of 'animist' and perhaps due to some association with *doctor*. These two then inferred that Dagbovie was some sort of psychoanalyst. In other words, they did not understand the vocabulary being tested, and so they used their inferencing skills to compensate, and made very sensible inferences given what they knew – but they were wrong.

Now let us look at the two test-takers who responded correctly to these two questions. Can we assume they knew the vocabulary being tested? One responded that Dagbovie was *'someone with supernatural powers'*. In her discussion she explained that although she had correctly processed the words *'animist'* and *'witch-doctor'* she had no idea what they meant. She had answered correctly because she had understood the second part of this section that Dagbovie had some special power, and had made an inference that this was supernatural power. The other test-taker responded to Q1 with *'animist'*. The word was not in her vocabulary, but she inferred the meaning from the context.

Just like those who answered incorrectly, the two test-takers who answered correctly did not know the words *'animist'* or *'witch-doctor'* either, and they also used their inferencing skills to compensate for their lack of linguistic knowledge. Unlike the weaker listeners, however, their inferences were correct, presumably because they were processing the text efficiently, understanding it well, and they had more information on which to infer the meaning of the vocabulary items from the context.

To summarise, from the six test-takers we find three different reactions to Q1. The first group of two test-takers heard the isolated word *'doctor'* from *'witch-doctor'* and assumed that Dagbovie was a doctor. The second group of two test-takers misheard or inferred that Dagbovie was some sort of analyst, presumably based on hearing the word *'animist'*. The third group did not understand the vocabulary items but inferred what they meant from the content and their general knowledge.

Thus, if we consider the sub-skills involved in answering Q1, we must include at least the following:

- lexical knowledge
- the ability to isolate and recognise known words in an unprocessed stream of speech
- the ability to infer the form of words through phonological knowledge
- the ability to process clearly stated information
- the ability to ignore irrelevant information
- the ability to infer the meaning of words from context

- knowledge about the world in general
- and general knowledge about Africa.

If we now come to consider the sub-skills involved in answering the next question, Q2, we have to include all those which were involved in Q1, plus ideas about what constitutes a reasonable answer, clever guessing and more inferencing based on world knowledge, but also based on the inferences already made.

Looking at the relationship between answers to the two questions, it is easy to see how the comprehension and inferences made in one section, or in response to one question, could then in turn influence later sections. Thus, there is a cumulative effect, such that interpretations of later parts of the text, or test tasks coming later in the passage, can be influenced by a greater weight of personal, and perhaps idiosyncratic, inference than earlier items.

It is clear that we need to be very careful in labelling items in terms of the knowledge, skills and abilities we design them to measure. Processing language, as opposed to static linguistic knowledge, will always require a whole range of linguistic knowledge and processing skills, including phonology, vocabulary, syntax, discourse variables as well as inferencing ability. When the test-takers have difficulty comprehending, as will happen when we probe the limits of their knowledge in a testing situation, then processing becomes even more complex, and the result is a rich inter-linking of language skills with background knowledge, inference and speculation.

This does not mean we should give up designing tasks to address particular aspects of language competence. When creating tasks it helps to have some systematic scheme for item construction, and targeting particular components of language competence – such as knowledge of vocabulary, grammar, discourse etc – is one useful way of doing that. We are simply emphasising the things we think are important, but we must realise that the actual task processing will likely be quite different from what we intend. In the case of listening comprehension, task interactiveness is a complex and little understood process.

Targeting particular constructs

It would be very convenient to be able to offer a list of tasks suitable for each particular competence, or each definition of the listening construct, but as we have seen, task processing is often complex and unpredictable. Nevertheless, some tasks are more suitable for one purpose than another, and some suggestions can be made.

For example, although sound discrimination items are certainly not adequate tests of listening comprehension, they may still be perfectly good tests of knowledge of the sound system. There are plenty of situations in which language teachers will find their students having problems with the sounds of the target language, and they may want to devise tests that focus on these troublesome areas. Table 5.1 has a wide selection of tasks that are intended to do that.

Table 5.1. *Techniques for testing knowledge of the sound system*

Minimal pairs with decontextualised words

- Test-takers listen to two (or three) words and indicate whether they are the same or different.
- Test-takers listen to two (or three) words and indicate whether they rhyme.
- Test-takers listen to one word first, followed by a number of other words, and indicate which of these is the same as the first word.
- Test-takers listen to a number of words, some in the target language and some not, and indicate how many words are in the target language.
- Test-takers listen to two (or three) words and indicate which has the meaning expressed in a picture.

Minimal pairs with words in an utterance

- Test-takers listen to a sentence and choose which of two (or three) pictures indicates a word in the sentence.
- Test-takers listen to a statement, followed by two possible responses (which differ in only one word), and choose which response is appropriate.

Recognising grammatical structures

- Test-takers listen to a sentence and indicate whether the verb (or noun) was singular or plural.
- Test-takers listen to a sentence and indicate whether a particular word was masculine, feminine or neuter.
- Test-takers listen to a sentence and indicate whether the verb was in the past, present or future tense.

Recognising intonation patterns

- Test-takers listen to an utterance and choose one of three curved lines to indicate the intonation curve of the utterance.

Recognising stress

- Test-takers listen to an utterance, and then read three transcriptions of it in which capital letters indicate heavy stress; they choose the one which indicates the stress of the utterance they listen to.

Adapted from Valette (1977)

Another definition of the listening construct is understanding explicitly stated information, or understanding the passage on a literal semantic level. It is relatively easy to assess this, and Table 5.2 lists a number of suitable tasks.

It is much more difficult to find tasks which are primarily suitable for testing a broader listening construct or going beyond literal meanings. Probably the most common way of testing these skills is by asking comprehension questions. These are discussed in detail in the next section. However some tasks do suggest themselves, and these are given in Table 5.3.

The tasks in Table 5.3 do not automatically test listening in the wider sense, but they have the potential to do so. It is up to the test-developer to use them to test such skills as understanding gist, inferences, implied meanings, contextual implications and so forth.

Comprehension questions

Probably the most common tasks used to assess listening are comprehension questions. The idea is simple: a text is presented to test-takers, who are then asked to answer questions designed to measure how well they have understood the content. This is a common procedure; comprehension questions can be used with a variety of text-types, and they can be used to test a wide range of knowledge, skills and abilities. Furthermore, they appear easy to devise, although as we shall see, there can be problems.

Some general points

Before looking at particular question types, it is useful to consider some general points. The first issue concerns the type of information that should be targeted. Shohamy and Inbar (1991) looked at three types of questions: global questions, which required test-takers to synthesise information or draw conclusions, local questions, which required test-takers to locate details or understand individual words, and trivial questions, which required test-takers to understand precise but irrelevant details not related to the main topic. They found that the global questions were harder than the local questions, but that the trivial questions behaved in an unpredictable manner

Table 5.2. *Tasks for testing understanding of literal meanings*

Body movement tasks

- Test-takers are given commands to move various body parts (raise your right hand, go to the door etc.).

- Simon says: test-takers are given commands to move various body parts (e.g. raise your right hand, go to the door etc.) and only do so if the command is preceded by 'Simon says'.

- Test-takers are told to draw a certain object (e.g. draw a rose, draw a circle if you are a girl etc.).

Retention tasks

- Test-takers listen to two utterances and indicate whether they were the same or different.

- Test-takers listen to an utterance and write it down.

Picture tasks

- Test-takers listen to a statement, and then look at a number of pictures and indicate which represents the statement.

- Test-takers look at a picture and listen to a number of statements, and then choose which is relevant to the picture.

- Test-takers are given a pile of about ten pictures and listen to a series of utterances; they have to choose a picture of the object mentioned in each utterance.

- Test-takers are shown a complex picture with many things happening in it, they hear a series of statements about the picture and indicate whether these are true or false.

- Test-takers look at four pictures labelled A, B, C and D, and listen to a series of utterances (e.g. it is raining, the man is wearing a suit) and indicate which picture each utterance applies to.

- Test-takers look at five small pictures, listen to four short utterances, and select the picture being described in each utterance.

- Test-takers see a series of simple diagrams (e.g. lines, squares, rectangles, circles etc. arranged in a variety of patterns), listen to statements describing these, and indicate which diagram is being described.

Conversation tasks

- Test-takers listen to a statement followed by a response, and indicate A if the response was appropriate, and B if it was not.

- Test-takers listen to a question followed by three possible responses, and indicate which was the most appropriate.

- Test-takers listen to a statement followed by three possible continuations, and select the one that would continue the conversation best.

- Test-takers listen to a short dialogue (usually persons A, B and A again), and then listen to a short question about it, to which they choose one of three (or four) options (usually written in a booklet).

Self-evident comprehension tasks

- Test-takers are given a series of statements and asked to indicate whether they are true or false (e.g. the snow is white, Paris is in Spain).

- Test-takers listen to statements made about some sort of visual (or object), and indicate whether they are true or false.

- Test-takers are given arithmetic calculations and indicate whether they are right or wrong (e.g. three plus three is seven).

Adapted from Valette (1977) and Heaton (1990)

Table 5.3. *Tasks for going beyond local literal meanings*

Understanding gist

- Test-takers listen to recordings from the radio, and indicate what type of programme they are listening to (e.g. news, sports, weather, fashion etc.).
- Test-takers listen to a description of a person, place or thing they are all familiar with, and write down its name, or what it is (perhaps in their native language).

General passage comprehension

- Test-takers listen to a monologue or dialogue, and then answer a number of multiple-choice questions (either spoken or written questions).
- Test-takers listen to a monologue or dialogue, and then answer a number of short-answer comprehension questions on it.
- Test-takers listen to a short talk or lecture, read a number of statements and select which are correct given the talk.
- Test-takers listen to a short talk or lecture and answer comprehension questions on it.
- Test-takers listen to a short talk or lecture, and then read a short summary of it in which some words or phrases have been deleted and replaced with blanks; they fill in the blanks with content appropriate to the talk.

Information transfer tasks

- Test-takers are given a map and a starting point, they follow directions on the map, and then indicate the destination (the instructions can be extremely complex and as an example Heaton (1990) recommends listening to a description of a robbery and then following the police chase, periodically indicating where the robbers are).
- Test-takers listen to an announcement of some information (e.g. a timetable or result of a competition) and fill in the information in a grid.
- Test-takers are given a goal (e.g. arrive in Paris before midnight, solve a problem), they listen to an announcement or explanation, find the information necessary to complete their goal, and then do the task.
- Test-takers listen to a person on the telephone and take a message according to the speaker's instructions.
- Test-takers look at a picture (e.g. a street scene, a room) and draw in objects or other details according to instructions (draw a table and two chairs in front of the café; draw a vase of flowers on top of the table); this can be expanded into a narrative (or dialogue).
- Test-takers see a series of pictures and listen to a talk or discussion and then classify the pictures based on that (e.g. a set of children's drawings representing different developmental stages, which need to be put in order based on a talk about child development).

Adapted from Valette (1977) and Heaton (1990)

and 'served no meaningful purpose in an evaluation tool' (Shohamy and Inbar, 1991:37). This research suggests that questions need to focus on the key information in the text, not irrelevant detail.

Another important issue is whether the questions should be provided before listening or after. In virtually all real-world listening situations, listeners know why they are listening and what information they need to get from the text. If we ask test-takers to listen to a text with no specified purpose, and after listening give them questions that require understanding anything and everything, we are asking them to do something very unnatural. Hence, most scholars recommend giving test-takers the questions before listening (Berne, 1995; Brindley, 1998; Buck, 1990). However, research on the effects of question preview is rather mixed. Buck (1990) made two versions of a test, one with item preview and one without preview, and gave them to two groups of test-takers. Although test-takers clearly felt that question preview aided comprehension, results showed that it did not make a significant difference to item difficulty. However, question preview did make a considerable difference to item discrimination, suggesting that preview does affect item processing, but in ways not yet understood. Berne (1995) found that question preview led to significant improvements in test performance compared to the effects of other pre-listening activities, whereas Sherman (1997) found that preview did not significantly improve performance. Wu (1998) found that preview of multiple-choice questions facilitated processing for the more advanced listeners, but not for the less advanced.

It is very difficult to make firm recommendations about question preview, but it does seem to have a positive psychological value for test-takers, and conversely the uncertainty of not knowing why they are listening has a negative psychological effect (Buck 1990; Sherman, 1997). Another problem is that a list of questions often makes little sense out of context, and it is not until listeners hear the passage that the questions start to seem relevant (Sherman, 1997). Question preview may not motivate listening as much as test-developers hope. Sherman (1997) found that the most powerful improvement in performance came from showing the questions after listeners had heard the passage once, but before they heard it a second time.

There is some evidence to suggest that if a listening passage is intrinsically interesting, there is no need to motivate the listening with questions – listeners will simply listen out of interest (Buck,

1990). If the questions then focus on the main topic, or the central thread of the discourse, good listeners will have the information necessary to respond, in which case question preview may not be necessary. If, however, the test-developer doubts whether the passage is intrinsically interesting, or doubts whether the questions focus on the main points of interest, then providing question preview seems the most prudent course of action.

There are some conventions about the use of comprehension questions. It seems to be widely accepted that questions will ask for information in the same order in which it occurs in the passage (Thompson, 1995), and also that once an item of information has been used in one question, it will not be used again in another (Buck, 1990). Test-developers who break these conventions may confuse test-takers, which could lead to unreliable performance.

In many testing situations, especially testing academic listening, test-takers want to take notes while listening. Whether this is allowed or not will depend on the definition of the listening construct and target-language use situation. Hale and Courtney (1994) found that allowing students to take notes during listening did not significantly improve their performance on the TOEFL listening test, and urging them to take notes significantly impaired their performance.

Finally, there is the issue of question spacing. It is important to leave enough time for test-takers to respond to each question, before going on to the next. This is especially problematic when test-takers are asked to complete a task at the same time they are listening – especially when filling in information grids, but this also happens with short-answer questions or multiple-choice questions. As Brindley (1998) notes, it is very important that questions are spaced out so that test-takers will not be responding to one question at the same time as they need to be listening to the information necessary for the next one.

Short-answer questions

Comprehension questions are relatively simple to write if we allow test-takers to construct the responses themselves. If we design the questions so that the answers will be short, scoring should be reasonably fast. Such questions have much to recommend them, and are particularly suitable for testing the understanding of clearly stated information. We can illustrate the process by attaching questions to a passage from Chapter 2 where the young man talks about a tennis tournament.

Example 5.1

Test-takers hear:

> *and i got there, and it turned out i was only the second person signed up for the entire tournament. and so there_ the people who ran it were like 'do you even want to bother playing the tournament?' and i was like_ 'let's it a great opportunity because if i win then i've won a tournament only with one match. so i can beat one guy, and even if i don't, like who cares.' so_ and_ cuz you get points for when you finish. so a runner-up gets the points anyway. so i was kind of hoping that the other guy i was gonna playing against was gonna dropout, and just give me the trophy. but he didn't. so anyway we went out and played, and we didn't even start_ we started like way after_ because i got there for a seven o'clock match. we didn't start playing until like ten at night.*

Test-takers read:

> Q1. How many people turned up to play?
> Q2. Did the speaker want to play?
> Q3. Why was he not very worried about losing?
> Q4. How late were they in starting the match?

Sometimes short-answer questions can be presented in a sentence-completion format. Example 5.2 gives sample items from the December 1998 listening paper of the Cambridge First Certificate (reviewed in Chapter 8).

Example 5.2

> 9. Emily's childhood and background were not very _____
> 10. Unlike her brothers, she was educated _____
> 11. With her tutor, she travelled around _____
> 12. She then produced _____

These sentence-completion items could just as easily be presented as short-answer comprehension questions. However, the fact that these items are easy to produce, does not mean that it is easy to produce good ones. Like all test items, there are pitfalls, and items need to be pre-tested and bad ones need to be identified and either deleted or re-written.

Marking

Allowing test-takers the freedom to construct their own responses means that we need to make decisions about which responses will be marked correct and which will not. This is the most difficult aspect of using open-ended questions. In the case of items that ask for a simple fact, scoring is not usually so difficult. For example if the passage says, *'the train left at ten o'clock'*, and the question asks, *'What time did the train leave?'*, there is little chance of ambiguity.

The way to make marking easy is to write items that have unambiguous responses. This is often quite possible, and many texts will allow plenty of such items. However, the result may be questions that focus on superficial understanding of clearly stated information, and as test-developers, we are often trying to assess comprehension at a subtler level. As we probe deeper, however, it becomes more difficult to determine what should constitute a correct response. There are two potential problems: firstly, determining what constitutes a reasonable interpretation of the text, and secondly, what constitutes a sufficient response to the question.

Evaluating responses

Imagine a test about a burglar who *'was stealing something very small'*, and then a question asks, *'What was taken?'* The obvious answer would seem to be *'something small'*. So how should we score the answer *'something trivial'* given by a person who assumed that something small meant something of no value? Is this a correct response or not? What about a response *'nothing of value'*? When we know that some small things could actually be quite valuable, it is not easy to determine which should be accepted as correct and which not.

There is also the problem of deciding what is sufficient information to constitute a full response. Imagine that the same text continues by saying that the woman tried many things to stop the burglaries – putting bars over the windows and hiring a guard. If the question asks, *'What did she do about her problem?'*, what is the correct response? Is it enough to say she tried to stop the burglaries, or do we insist that the test-takers say how she tried to stop them? After all, we could guess that she would try to stop them, without listening to the text. And how will the test-takers know their response is good enough? These are difficult decisions that should only be made in the context of the testing situation.

A strategy for determining correct responses

The fact is that comprehension is not a simple dichotomy, and **dichotomous scoring** (i.e. scoring each item as being either correct or incorrect) of free-response questions turns a complex continuum into a simple dichotomy. The scorer has to make a whole series of decisions about which responses are acceptable, and which are not.

How can we decide? With sufficient resources the test can be administered to a group of competent listeners and their responses used as a basis for judging the acceptability of responses; but many of us will not have sufficient resources to trial our items in this way. In that case, when scoring the items, keep a record of the responses: note which are definitely right, which are definitely wrong, and which are borderline. Keep a note of the papers which have the borderline decisions. As you continue scoring you will come to understand better how the test-takers are interacting with the task and what the question is measuring, and as a result you will probably develop a better idea of exactly which of the borderline cases should be accepted as correct and which should not. Then go back and re-mark the borderline responses. Slowly a reasonably consistent marking scheme should emerge, even though there may still be some inconsistencies. This is not an ideal way of scoring, but in the real world of limited resources, we cannot always pre-test everything as we would like.

Shortage of time

In any test, listeners need to know how much time they have to respond, and this is particularly important with short-answer questions, because there is usually only time for short answers. If test-takers give answers which are too long, they may spend too much time on one question, and could miss the next question, or even the next listening passage. A useful strategy is to restrict the response to no more than three words, for example, although this is not always practicable.

Sometimes test-takers take a long time over a question because they are thinking about the response, but generally, if test-takers have understood the passage, thinking time will be short compared to the time taken to write the response. So when test-takers are spending extra time thinking of a response, it is usually because they have not understood the text well enough to respond. If individual test-takers want extra time to think about their responses, assume their comprehension is lacking, and find some way to force them to move on.

Longer responses

Sometimes we may want to ask comprehension questions that require longer responses. For example, if we asked why something happened, we might get two or three sentences in response. When responses are longer and more complex, we will have to develop some sort of rating scale to evaluate their suitability.

Developing a rating scale involves deciding what responses test-takers are likely to produce, how these should be evaluated relative to each other, and how many marks should be awarded for each. Having developed a scale, the job has only just begun. It is then necessary to try it out on a sample of tasks, preferably with a number of raters. Then all raters must practise using the scale until they can all apply it consistently. Developing a reasonable rating scale is not usually difficult, but it does require time and effort to develop it properly (McNamara, 1996).

Multiple-choice questions

Selected responses can be of many types, but the most common is the multiple-choice item with three, four or even five options. Constructing these items is a high-level professional skill, which takes considerable time and training to do well. All items ought to be pre-tested before being used in any high-stakes assessment, but this is particularly the case with multiple-choice items. They are complex and unpredictable, and after pre-testing expect to throw away, or seriously modify, a large proportion of your multiple-choice items, perhaps even all of them. Most people are very disappointed with their first attempts to write multiple-choice items.

Multiple-choice items are difficult to write because of their complexity. Many scholars believe that they have a strong method effect (Brindley, 1998) and that they make considerable processing demands on the test-taker (Hanson and Jensen, 1994). They can force test-takers to re-adjust their interpretation if it does not agree with the options (Nissan, DeVincenzi and Tang, 1996). Wu (1998) found that they favoured more advanced listeners, and that misinterpretations of the options led to test-takers selecting the wrong options, and conversely, test-takers selecting the correct options for the wrong reasons.

If the test-takers are all from the same L1 background, giving the questions in the first language works very well, and is probably the best way of ensuring that listening test scores are not contaminated with other skills. However, in many cases test-takers will be from different first-language backgrounds, and it will be necessary to give questions in the L2. The most common way is to provide written questions, and so multiple-choice listening tests are tests of reading as much as listening – which often may not be a bad thing.

There are two basic formats for presenting the questions. In Example 5.3 below the stem is in the form of a question, followed by alternative responses.

Example 5.3

Test-takers read:
> *When did she get back home from her sister's house?*
>   (a) *Just before six o'clock.*
>   (b) *Late in the afternoon.*
>   (c) *About tea time.*
>   (d) *At exactly half-past nine.*

An alternative is the sentence-completion format, where the stem is an incomplete sentence, and the options are alternative completions. Example 5.4 gives the same item in this format.

Example 5.4

> She got back home from her sister's house
>   (a) *just before six o'clock.*
>   (b) *late in the afternoon.*
>   (c) *about tea time.*
>   (d) *at exactly half-past nine.*

Example 5.5 is a typical multiple-choice comprehension question, taken from a TOEIC sample test (TOEIC MT-93, 1993). Test-takers hear a short dialogue, and then respond to a comprehension question based on the dialogue.

Example 5.5

Test-takers hear:

 Female: *is Carlos really quitting?*
 Male: *yes he's tired of the restaurant business. he wants to try something entirely different.*
 Female: *that leaves his sister Rosa to run it alone.*

They read:

 Why is Carlos changing his job?
   (a) *He is lonely.*
   (b) *He is moving to another city.*
   (c) *He has lost interest.*
   (d) *He is ill.*

This item requires understanding a number of short utterances on a literal semantic level. The test-taker must equate the meaning of *'he has lost interest'* with *'he's tired of the restaurant business. He wants to try something entirely different'*. The two expressions mean the same thing, but they are not simple synonyms. Example 5.6 is from the Test of English as a Foreign Language website (http://www.toefl.org/lc-pq.html).

Example 5.6

Test-takers hear:

 Male: *do you mind if i turn the television off?*
 Female: *well i'm in the middle of watching a program.*
 Narrator: *what does the woman imply?*

They read:

   (a) *The man should watch the program too.*
   (b) *The man should leave the television on.*
   (c) *The program will be over soon.*
   (d) *She'll watch television later.*

This example is different for two reasons. Firstly, the question is presented aurally (note that it helps if the narrator's voice is noticeably different from the speakers'). Secondly, the question is given after the text has been heard, so test-takers will not know what to listen for before they hear the text (when the questions are written in the test book, test-takers can often take a quick peek before listening).

Another interesting point about Example 5.6 is that the woman does not explicitly refuse the man's request, so the listener must go beyond understanding the literal words and make a pragmatic inference in order to understand that the woman is actually refusing permission to switch off the television. Although this is an easy inference to make, the test-taker has to understand the inferred meaning by taking into account the communicative situation.

In the next example, also from the TOEIC sample test (TOEIC MT-93, 1993), test-takers hear a short talk, and then answer comprehension questions.

Example 5.7

Test-takers hear:
> *welcome to our semiannual sales meeting everyone. after lunch and a brief business meeting, a team from our research and development department will join us and demonstrate our newest products. each of you will have chance to try samples from our new line and ask questions of the team. now please help yourselves to the delicious buffet that has been set up in the adjoining dining room.*

They read:
> Q1: *Who is attending the meeting?*
>   (a) *Sales personnel.*
>   (b) *Food service staff.*
>   (c) *Bank executives.*
>   (d) *Factory workers.*
> Q2: *What will the people do first?*
>   (a) *Try out some new products.*
>   (b) *Eat a meal.*
>   (c) *Visit the research department.*
>   (d) *Discuss salaries.*

These two items are clearly testing comprehension. The questions are printed in the test book, and so test-takers may have time to scan the items first, which means they should be able to listen for specific information, rather than just generally trying to understand everything. Q1 *'Who is attending the meeting?'* requires understanding a very short piece of explicitly stated information, *'welcome to our semiannual sales meeting'*, or perhaps it is enough just to catch the expression *'sales meeting'*. Q2 *'What will the people do first?'* requires test-takers to understand that the expression *'now please help yourselves to the delicious buffet that has been set up in the adjoining dining room'* is an instruction to go and eat. Again not a difficult inference, but a pragmatic inference, nevertheless.

It is outside the scope of this book to go into details of how to write good multiple-choice items (see Popham, 1989), but a few words of advice might help. Make sure the question is about something on which there could be plausible alternatives. It is often the case that there is one obvious distractor, which is definitely wrong, but which seems likely to attract students who do not understand. It is much harder to find the second and third distractors. An option that no one chooses is worthless. When looking for alternative options, think of other information similar to that in the correct option, or try words that sound similar. Something that would appear plausible to a person who did not hear the text will often work.

Make sure that the form of the question does not give away the correct option. Check that all the options fit the stem, and that the correct one is not longer, nor different in any way. Make sure that neither the stem nor the options are ambiguous, and check that none of the incorrect options could be considered correct. Take care that the answer cannot be provided from background knowledge or basic reasoning.

Although they are complex and difficult to make, multiple-choice items can be used to test a variety of listening sub-skills: from understanding at the most explicit literal level, through combining information from different parts of the text, making pragmatic inferences, understanding implicit meanings, to summarising and synthesising extensive sections of test.

True/false questions

There is another type of selected option question that is very popular, the true/false format. This is very simple: after presenting a text, one or more statements are given, and test-takers have to decide whether each statement is true or false. Example 5.8 illustrates the format with a series of true/false questions from the December 1998 CCSE.

Example 5.8

After listening to the statements, test-takers mark whether they are true or false.

	True	False
1 Barry never sleeps more than 5 hours.	☐	☐
2 He wishes he could sleep longer.	☐	☐
3 He thinks vegetarians may need more sleep.	☐	☐
4 His fitness is not affected by his sleeping pattern.	☐	☐

There is some disagreement about the utility of this question type (Brindley, 1998). Burger and Doherty (1992) claim that they are not suitable for testing listening because listeners normally focus on what is said, not on what is not said, and as there is no text for them to refer back to, listeners have no means of checking false statements.

The other major problem with true/false questions is that test-takers can get half the questions correct by random guessing. This is also a problem with three- or four-option multiple-choice questions. There are a number of ways of dealing with guessing. Firstly, it is possible to reduce the effects of random guessing by including more items on the test – the more items there are, the less effect each individual guess has on the total score. A second problem arises when some test-takers are guessing and others are not. It is important to tell test-takers that they should guess, so that they are all pursuing the same strategy.

There is another advantage to having test-takers guess. Many guesses are not purely random guesses at all. Even when they do not know the correct answer, test-takers often have some comprehension of the point being tested, and so they are inclined to favour one response over another, perhaps without even knowing why. In such cases, the guess is based on some degree of partial comprehension which is relevant information about the construct being measured.

Inference questions

During the course of the previous chapters, I have continually claimed that inference is at the core of language processing. Thus, it is important to assess inferencing ability, and many scholars recommend questions that go beyond literal meanings (Boyle and Suen, 1994; Burger and Doherty, 1992; Thompson, 1995; Weir, 1993). Inference questions can, however, be difficult to make because the answers are not explicitly stated in the text.

It is important to distinguish between two types of inferences in test tasks. The first is inferences about what the speaker means. These are usually construct-relevant inferences. The second are inferences about what the test-developer expects, and what the best test-taking strategy is. These are usually construct-irrelevant inferences, and we should try to keep them out of our tests.

The main problem with inference items is that it is often very difficult to say with certainty that any inference is completely wrong. After all, we are free to infer what we want. There are other problems. It must be possible to get the item wrong – items which ask for personal reactions or predictions about future events clearly cannot be marked wrong, for example. Also, questions must be passage dependent, in the sense that they require something which can only be inferred by understanding the passage. It is often possible to use common sense or general knowledge to infer a reasonable reply. Furthermore, inferences are based on background knowledge, and it is important to make sure that the knowledge is shared by all test-takers.

Many of these problems can be avoided by using multiple-choice items. Even if the correct response is not the best possible inference, as long as the other options are clearly less preferable, it should be obvious which is the correct response. Make sure to ask test-takers to choose the *best* option, rather than asking them to choose the *correct* option.

The sort of information that can usually be addressed by inference questions is:

- asking for the main idea, or gist, of the text, or a section of the text;
- asking about anything which is not clearly stated, but that is clearly and deliberately indicated by the speaker, using choice of words or tone of voice – the connotations of words is a particularly rich source of inferences;
- asking about any pragmatic implication, or logical entailment, that follows on from what the speaker said;
- asking the meaning of indirect speech acts.

Inferencing is involved at all levels of language processing, even explicitly stated information. Once we attempt to test pragmatic or sociolinguistic knowledge, which involves interpreting meaning in terms of a wider communicative context, then inferencing becomes even more important. Good listening tests will generally include inference items. It takes time and trouble to make them, but they are too important to exclude.

Evaluating and modifying test-tasks

Creating test tasks is a complex skill, and there are many ways they can go wrong: for example, there may be no correct answer, there may be two answers, or it might be possible to answer correctly without understanding the passage. The best way to avoid such problems is to give the tasks to a small number of potential test-takers, or colleagues, ask them to complete the task, and then solicit their feedback. This will usually reveal any obvious problems.

This will not provide information about the difficulty of the task, nor whether it is measuring the right construct. In order to do that, it is necessary to pre-test the items on a sample of test-takers similar to the target population, and then subject the results to item analysis. This pre-testing will show whether the tasks are of the right difficulty level, and whether they discriminate well between test-takers who have different abilities on the construct. After pre-testing, it is usually worthwhile trying to modify problematic tasks so they can be used. In the case of poor discrimination this can be problematic – in some cases it is very clear what is wrong, whereas in others it may not be clear at all.

In the case of difficulty, it is often possible to modify tasks to make them easier or harder. This can be done by modifying the text, or by modifying the task. In the following sections, variables that affect text difficulty and variables that affect task difficulty are examined, in order that task difficulty can be better evaluated, or in order to make test tasks more suitable for the target test-takers.

Text characteristics that affect difficulty

The following list is put together from a number of different sources, including Anderson and Lynch (1988), Brown (1995b), Freedle and Kostin (1996, 1999), Buck *et al.* (1997), Buck and Tatsuoka (1998).

Linguistic characteristics
- Texts with slower speech rates tend to be easier than texts with faster speech rates.
- Texts with longer pauses between idea units tend to be easier than texts with shorter pauses between idea units, or no pauses at all.
- Texts with more familiar pronunciation tend to be easier than texts with less familiar pronunciation.

- Texts with natural intonation patterns tend to be easier than texts with unnatural or unusual intonation patterns.
- Texts with more high-frequency vocabulary (i.e. common words) tend to be easier than texts with more low-frequency vocabulary.
- Texts with less complex grammar tend to be easier than texts with more complex grammar.
- Texts with idea units or clauses strung together tend to be easier than texts with ideas units or clauses embedded within other clauses.
- Texts with simple pronoun referencing tend to be easier than texts with more complex pronoun referencing.

Explicitness

- Texts in which the ideas are explicitly stated tend to be easier than texts with less explicit ideas.
- Texts with more redundancy tend to be easier than texts with less redundancy (but not if the listeners fail to realise that the information is redundant).

Organisation

- Texts which have events described in a linear or temporal order tend to be easier than texts which have non-linear structure.
- Texts which have main points stated clearly before examples tend to be easier than texts with illustrative examples coming before the point being made.

Content

- Texts with topics more familiar to the listener tend to be easier than texts with less familiar topics.
- Texts with fewer things or people to be distinguished tend to be easier than texts with more things to be distinguished.
- Texts in which the important protagonists or objects are more easily distinguished tend to be easier than texts where they are harder to distinguish.
- Texts where relationships between the elements are fixed tend to be easier than texts where relationships are changing.
- Texts with concrete content tend to be easier than texts with abstract content.

Context

- Texts with visual or other support which supplements the content tend to be easier than texts with visual or other information that conflicts with the content.

Task characteristics that affect difficulty

Probably the simplest way to make tasks easier is to allow listeners to hear the text twice (Berne, 1995). However, playing the text a second time may significantly change the nature of the listening construct, and such a decision should probably be made as part of the process of construct definition, rather than as part of task revision. Tasks can be made even easier by giving the questions or the task in the interval between the two hearings (Sherman, 1997). Below are some general guidelines taken from a variety of sources.

- Tasks that require processing less information tend to be easier than tasks which require processing more information.
- Tasks that require processing information from just one location in the text tend to be easier than tasks which require integrating information scattered throughout the text.
- Tasks that require recalling exact content tend to be easier than tasks which require extracting the gist, or making a summary.
- Tasks that require simply selecting information tend to be easier than tasks which require separating fact from opinion.
- Tasks that require information that is relevant to the main theme tend to be easier than tasks which ask for irrelevant detail.
- Tasks that require immediate responses tend to be easier than tasks which require a delayed response.

Research on variables that affect difficulty

We can see many of these characteristics in action in a study by Freedle and Kostin (1996, 1999). They examined 337 TOEFL multiple-choice listening items, which asked comprehension questions on short monologues, in order to examine which item characteristics were related to difficulty.

They found that questions which required understanding explicit statements were easier when:

- the necessary information was repeated;
- the correct option contained more words used in the necessary information than the incorrect options did;
- the correct option contained more words used in the text than the incorrect options did;
- the incorrect options contained more complex grammar than the correct options did;
- there were relatively more topic shifts in the passage;
- the text was on a non-academic topic;

and they were harder when:

- the passage had relatively more text coming before the necessary information;
- the question had relatively more referentials (such as pronouns).

In the case of the items which required the test-taker to make inferences, they found items were easier when:

- the necessary information came at the beginning of the passage;
- the correct option contained more words used in the text than the incorrect options did;
- the topic was arts, or social science;

and they were harder when:

- the necessary information was not repeated;
- the necessary information came in the middle of the text;
- the rhetorical structure of the passage involved a comparison.

Finally, items which asked for the identification of the main idea were easier when:

- the topic was a non-academic topic;
- the correct option contained more words from the text than the incorrect options did;

and they were harder when:

- the rhetorical structure of the passage was problem solution.

A number of things are clear from this study: the topic affected difficulty, as did the rhetorical structure, but the two most important determinants of difficulty were the location of the necessary information, and the degree of lexical overlap. When the necessary information came near the beginning of the text, or when it was repeated, the item tended to be easier. **Lexical overlap** is when words used in the passage are found in the question or in the options. Lexical overlap between the correct option and the text, especially the necessary information, is the best predictor of easy items. Similarly, lexical overlap between the text and the incorrect options is the best predictor of difficult items. Presumably, this is because test-takers tend to select options which contain words they recognise from the passage.

Conclusion

Having defined a listening construct, the next step is to operationalise that in terms of tasks. All tasks have their particular strengths and weaknesses, and tend to engage different skills: some assess one set of skills and some another; some advantage one group of test-takers, and some another. By using a variety of different task types, the test is far more likely to provide a balanced assessment, and it will usually be a fairer test (Brindley, 1998).

In this chapter I have discussed tasks from a variety of perspectives; firstly, in terms of the Bachman and Palmer (1996) schedule of task characteristics. Then I argued that the most important characteristic of tasks is the knowledge, skills and abilities they engage in the test-taker, and I discussed at length various aspects of task interactiveness. The point was made that although we would like to create tasks to address particular sub-skills of listening, task performance is essentially unpredictable. Nevertheless, certain tasks were examined as being suitable for testing certain aspects of listening. I also discussed comprehension questions in detail, and considered how to make texts and tasks easier or harder.

In the next chapter I will discuss texts; how to select them, or create them, and how to present them to the test-taker.

CHAPTER SIX

....

Providing suitable texts

Introduction

All listening tasks present a sample of spoken language to the test-taker, and this is the one characteristic all listening tests share. Once we start providing spoken texts, however, we have a number of practical issues to address. We need to understand the nature of spoken language, and we need the equipment and some expertise to present the text to the test-taker. There are two main issues we need to consider, and they form the two sections of this chapter:

i   providing suitable texts;

ii ensuring good quality sound.

Providing suitable texts

Selecting listening materials is more complicated than selecting reading materials. Written language is by its nature preserved, and most of us have a large selection of books, periodicals and other materials easily available, and if we cannot find anything appropriate, we can easily write something. When selecting listening materials, we still have the same choice between using an existing text or creating our own. However, spoken language is much harder to preserve than written language, and most of us do not have a selection easily available. Creating recordings is also more technical and requires more equipment than creating written texts.

Finding pre-recorded texts

We hear recorded material all the time: we listen to radio and television recordings, and we hear announcements and recorded messages. Language teachers will hear recordings of teaching materials, and many of us will have access to the large amount of recorded material on the Internet. It would be very convenient to use some of these materials.

Broadcasting companies

Many broadcasting companies have extensive archives of recorded material, and some will make these available, usually for a fee. The problem is identifying what is suitable. We need to listen to the recordings first, and most companies will not allow us to rummage through their archives. Furthermore, most broadcasts are meant for native speakers and many may be too difficult for second-language learners.

Although it is not easy finding suitable pre-recorded materials from recording companies, it is a good idea to be on the lookout for suitable materials and then make a note of the particulars – date, time, name of speaker etc. Then it is easier to approach the company with the exact details.

The Internet

More and more audio materials are becoming available over the World-Wide Web. News, radio broadcasts and much else is kept in archives that can often be searched. Some of this is free, and some is not. The good thing is that it is often possible to listen to it first, at leisure, to find out exactly how suitable it is.

But there are problems. The Internet is nothing more than access to other people's computers, and sites are continually revised – materials available today, may not be available tomorrow. Sound quality is another problem. Audio files are huge, and usually it is not possible to transfer the data fast enough to listen to the file in its full quality except with an expensive high-speed connection, so we usually have to listen to a lower quality file. Although it may be possible to download the file to your own computer, and then listen to it later, this may take 10 or 20 minutes for a one-minute recording (depending on file format, sound quality, size of modem connection etc.). Furthermore, most Internet sites will not allow you to download their files, they only want you to listen to them online.

Teaching materials

One source of suitable pre-recorded texts are teaching materials. Published listening materials are often very well made; they are at appropriate difficulty levels, and on suitable topics. Most teachers will have a collection of old text books, and many schools have a resource centre or a library of materials. These may be suitable for low-stakes assessments, or teacher-made tests, but security could be a serious problem.

Security

If you use materials that are publicly available, there is always a possibility that test-takers will also have access to those materials. This may not matter in a low-stakes testing situation, but if the stakes are high it is imperative to use secure materials – materials that you feel confident have not been heard by any of the test-takers. This is especially problematic when the test will be administered on more than one occasion, as there is a danger that test-takers will identify the piece, and later test-takers will be able to find a copy, and practise it before the test.

Copyright

If you want to use materials made by someone else, or you want to record someone else, copyright is something you need to take very seriously. If a recording has been published, it belongs to someone who owns the copyright, and if it has not been published, the copyright will usually belong to the speaker. Making recordings takes time and money, and recordings are valuable assets. Most publishers regard copyright violation as theft, and the law agrees with them. You must approach the copyright owner and ask for permission to use the recording, and you will have to meet any conditions or charges they impose.

Teachers often take copyright material to use in the privacy of their own class-room without asking permission, and many feel that this is permissible as long as they do it for the benefit of their students. Although this situation is somewhat ambiguous, teachers who do this are taking a risk, although the chance of being caught is very small. Sometimes teachers may take teaching materials which they have every right to use for teaching, but then use them to make a test. Copyright may be a problem here, and a phone call to the publisher is the obvious solution, although getting permission can be a troublesome and time-consuming process. Outside the classroom things are much simpler. Legally you should get permission, and if your test is in any way a commercial venture, failing to get formal permission will likely land you in court, and you could suffer serious consequences.

Recording off-air

Many teachers and test-developers try to get authentic texts by recording radio broadcasts off-air: for example, the BBC World Service, or the Voice of America for English materials. Sometimes, when visiting Britain, English teachers will record radio stations such as Radio Four. Although radio broadcast material is often scripted and very formal, it is designed to be heard by the general public, as non-participant listeners, and it is also possible to find some very useful spontaneous speech, and even interactive discussions. Some of this material is very good, and makes both good teaching material and texts suitable for testing. When recording from the radio, it is important to find a station with good reception, and then make the recording by attaching a cable directly from the radio output to the recorder input – recording with a microphone in front of the radio speaker is likely to result in far lower quality.

Some teachers also record TV stations, such as the English news station, CNN. It is important to realise that if this is recorded with an audio recorder, the video picture will be lost. This will usually make the text harder to understand, of course, but at times it may actually make it easier by removing distracting visual information which the TV editor has included simply because he needed to have a picture of some sort. Again, record directly from the television output to the recorder input.

Such off-air recordings are a valuable source of materials for teachers, especially in situations where they do not have access to native speakers of the language. However, it must be stressed that copyright is a serious consideration, and permission must be obtained to use most off-air recordings.

Recording live target-language use situations

Finding suitable pre-recorded materials is not always easy, and one obvious alternative is to find target-language use situations where people are listening, and record what they are listening to.

The biggest advantage of recording live listening situations is authenticity. I have argued that we need to ensure that our listening texts have the characteristics of target-language texts, and what better way to ensure this than to actually record target-language use situations! Other scholars have made similar arguments – Hughes (1989), for example, stresses the importance of using samples of authentic speech. The practical problems, though, are considerable.

Getting permission

You need to get permission to record people. Secretly recording someone is considered unethical by most people, and is illegal in some places. Even if it is not illegal, you will not legally be able to use the recording without permission from the copyright owner – usually the speaker.

When people know they are being recorded, they often modify what they say. This probably will not make much difference when the speaker has a definite purpose, such as in an academic lecture or a presentation – the communicative purpose will determine the content, and if the speaker is a little more careful, or omits some frivolous comments, this is not likely to have a significant impact on the authenticity of the text.

In less constrained situations, speakers may modify what they say, and how they say it, because they are being recorded. There are two ways to get round this. Firstly, it may be acceptable to record people and then ask their permission afterwards. If permission is not granted, the recording can be destroyed. It is important to be very careful: people can get very angry when they realise that they have been secretly recorded. Secondly, it is worth remembering that although speakers may be very self-conscious when they are first recorded, after a while, many relax and forget about the microphone. Sometimes, if you wait a while, speakers can provide very natural speech samples.

The effect of context and content on comprehensibility

When I argue that we should use authentic listening texts, I mean that texts should have the characteristics of target-language speech, not that we need to actually take the texts from the target-language situation. That is not always a good idea. The context has a huge influence on the content of spoken texts, and when taken out of their context, they may not always make sense.

Speakers modify what they say depending on the listeners' knowledge of the topic and the purpose of the communicative event. For example, most lectures are given to students who already know something about the topic, and such lectures will not be suitable for a general audience. Business presentations are usually carefully targeted at listeners who have a specific purpose for listening, and who have a certain amount of knowledge of the topic. Meetings are not usually between strangers, but between people who share knowledge of their organisation, as well as a common corporate culture. Participants also share the same room, and other aspects of the situation. A simple reference to some visual characteristic of the room, or one of the participants, would not be comprehensible to anyone not there. The listener will be in the role of overhearer, and can often miss important parts of the communication because they lack this shared knowledge and understanding.

This is made worse when only part of the original speech event is used. Lectures, meetings or presentations may last an hour or longer, but test-developers usually only present a few minutes of text. Listening intently to understand a decontextualised and truncated sample of live speech is something that is very different from what happens in the target-language use situation. Far from being an authentic activity, this is very inauthentic indeed.

Ensuring good quality sound

Many people think that you can record live events by just leaving a cheap portable tape recorder in the middle of the room. This may be good enough to make a record of what was said, but the recording will not usually be clear enough for use in a test. We need to provide a recording that listeners can hear clearly and comfortably.

There are a number of practical difficulties recording many live speech events, but the biggest problem is background noise. For example, fifty people in a lecture hall make a great deal of noise: coughing, talking, shuffling books, moving in their seats, entering and leaving the room and so forth. Projectors, neon lights and air-conditioners all hum at times. The level of background noise tends to be higher in interactive situations, such as seminars or group discussions, and highest in public places, such as restaurants. The human ear has a tremendous capacity to filter out these extraneous sounds, and focus on the sound source of interest, but microphones do not. When we listen to recordings, these extraneous noises will be very apparent, and the recording may not seem very authentic at all.

To exclude background noise, microphones need to be very close to the speaker. In many situations, however, speakers do not keep still: presenters and lecturers often move around a room, waiters walk around a table, and people far from the microphone may ask questions or intervene in some way.

All these problems can be dealt with. Speakers can be given personal microphones, or lecturers can be told not to move from the podium. In small meetings or seminars, for example, it is often possible to put everyone around one large table, with a good quality multi-directional microphone in the middle, and then ask people to sit forward when they speak. You should remember that most of these recording procedures will be intrusive: they require active intervention in the speech event, and coordination and cooperation with the main participants. This intervention will necessarily change the event to some extent.

Recording your own texts

Because suitable pre-recorded material cannot easily be found, and recording live situations can be problematic, most test-developers will probably want to create their own listening texts. This is not so difficult, even for the beginner with no experience of recording.

The necessary equipment

All the equipment you really need is a recording machine with a microphone. Make sure it is a portable recorder. If at all possible, get a digital recorder – for this purpose it is far superior to analog cassette recorders. A piece of audio processing software is useful, but not vital.

There are two realistic options for digital recorders: digital audio tape (DAT) or mini-disk. DAT is now the standard in the recording industry, and this is without doubt the best option if quality is the prime consideration. DAT is the same quality as a CD. There are a number of machines available, but they are expenive. Mini-disks are a much cheaper option. These compress the sound and so they can fit a great deal of recorded material onto one small disk, but at the cost of a loss of audio quality. The quality is not as good as DAT, but is still far better than an audio-cassette recorder, and is quite adequate for most listening tests. They are small, easy to use, they allow simple editing, and they are rather cheap.

The microphone is important, and in most cases good ones are worth the extra money – get the best you can. It is not necessary to use a stereo microphone, monaural is good enough for making voice recordings. There are three types of microphones that you might consider, depending on the situation you will record. Firstly, a small clip-on microphone for the speaker's lapel; these are small, unobtrusive, very portable, and especially good for speakers who move around while talking. The second type is a large-diaphragm condensor microphone with a table stand; these provide by far the best quality sound, and are ideal for recording one person sitting at a table, but they are not as portable, although they can be carried around with care. Finally, a flat omni-directional table microphone is good for recording a group of people sitting around a table.

This equipment should be easily available, and none of it is difficult to use. An hour's practice should be all that is necessary to become quite familiar with it. Most importantly, the sound quality will be quite sufficient for making good listening tests.

Finding suitable speakers

The next thing is to find people to record. There are professionals who make audio recordings for a living, but good ones can be very expensive. They usually have rich, authoritative voices, with clear enunciation, and many standardised tests and professionally produced listening materials use such professionals. However, they speak quite differently from how most people generally speak. I usually prefer to use ordinary people. It is cheaper, and often more realistic. If the budget is available, it may be a good idea to use professionals to read scripted materials or the instructions. They will do a far better job than most amateurs, and the resulting test will probably sound far more professional.

The best speakers for any test are speakers typical of the target-language use situation. This would usually mean native speakers, but in the case of a test of English for international communication, it may be appropriate to use non-native speakers. One useful resource is to contact a local university. Most universities will have students, especially graduate students, who need a little part-time work to support themselves. Another possible source of speakers are retired people.

In some cases, there may be no standard English speakers available, and then the test-developer may have to make a difficult decision: whether it is appropriate to use speakers with a strong regional accent, or even non-native speakers. The answer depends entirely on the purpose of the test, and the context in which it is used. English is a world language, which comes in many different versions, and is used in many different situations. Often a little variety will be a good thing: a mild Australian or Scottish accent may be quite appropriate on a general proficiency test, even if test-takers have not heard these accents before. However, a strong accent would be a problem. For a test of English in Japan, a high-ability Japanese speaker of English may be quite acceptable. In India, where English is used as a native language, a speaker of Indian English may be preferable. To a considerable extent, it depends on what test users are prepared to accept. From a measurement perspective, the most important thing when using an unfamiliar accent is that it is equally unfamiliar to all.

If you have to use accents that are unfamiliar to the test-takers, it is wise to use a number of different speakers, with as wide a variety of accents as possible. Then, listeners who have trouble with one speaker may do better with another.

A practical dilemma

A serious practical dilemma underlies all efforts to construct realistic spoken texts. We start with test specifications that lay out the knowledge, skills and abilities we want to test. Typical examples would be: knowledge of specific vocabulary or grammatical points, understanding certain functions, the ability to understand certain discourse markers. In order to test these, we need to have spoken texts that contain these features, in such a way that we can write items to assess them. Thus, we need to control the content of the texts to ensure that we can meet the test specifications.

Experience shows that if we write a script and ask someone to read it aloud, we will not get realistic spoken language. It is virtually impossible to write spoken language, and very difficult for someone to speak it naturally even if we did. Scripted language generally lacks hesitations, false starts or self-corrections; the unplanned, inefficient, rambling discourse style typical of most spoken texts is usually replaced by planned text that wastes few words. The interaction between interlocutors is often very unnatural, as it usually lacks the interruptions, overlap and unfinished statements of spoken language. Experience shows time and again that the vast majority of speakers can only produce genuine spoken language – that is speak with the oral characteristics typical of spoken texts – when they are speaking spontaneously.

This is a dilemma: we want to control the content to meet the test specifications, and yet we need to leave the speakers free to speak spontaneously in order to get realistic oral texts. These are two mutually conflicting requirements. There is no simple solution to this dilemma, although we can work around it to some extent.

Semi-scripted texts

If fully scripted texts are unlikely to produce suitable listening passages, one common solution is to use **semi-scripted texts**. This is when we decide the content in advance, but only the ideas, not the words. Speakers then speak freely expressing these ideas in whatever way comes naturally.

An example of a semi-script is given below. This is for a role play, used in the construction of a test of English for Tourism. It is a discussion between a difficult hotel guest, and a member of the hotel desk staff. The guest (A) has a British accent, and the staff member (B) has an American accent.

> A: Complaint: Wanted a plaza suite, with the Central Park view. Unhappy with the view.
> B: It has some view.
> A: Contradicts.
> B: Tries to find another suite.
> A: 2nd complaint: only one living area.
> B: Looks at reservations. Offers a room on 9th floor. Apologises.
> A: Finds it low. View.
> B: Another look at reservations on the 11th floor. Finds a room with a view of the park.
> A: Does it have satellite BBC TV?
> B: It hasn't.
> A: He asked on the phone. Special match he wants to see. Threatens to move.
> B: Leaves to speak with the manager.
> B: Offers the presidential suite.
> A: Concerned about the price.
> B: No extra charge.
> A: Wants to check the room.

(With thanks to Eva Barta for her kind permission to use this.)

The results of semi-scripting vary. Sometimes the technique produces quite natural texts, and at other times it does not. Usually, the result is a compromise. Often the speech will have more oral characteristics than fully scripted texts: the pronunciation will be more natural, there are often some hesitations, and the discourse is often structured more like oral text. But there can be considerable artificiality: sometimes speakers try to make their speech more oral by deliberately adding hesitations and such like, which works well at times, but at other times it can be very artificial.

If the test specifications require that something quite specific needs to be included in the text – a certain function, or a particular phrase, for example – the test-developer needs to work with the speaker to ensure that this is included. It may be necessary to practise the required part, perhaps even scripting it, but the rest can be left as free and unscripted as possible.

There are ways to make semi-scripted texts more natural. The first is simply to wait until the speaker becomes relaxed. Speakers who are not used to making recordings tend to be rather nervous and tense at first. But after a while, most people relax and their speech becomes more natural. It is often a good idea to start by asking the speaker to make some warm-up recordings that probably will not be used. Then after a while, when they are less self-conscious about being recorded, give them the recording you want for the test.

The second way to make semi-scripted texts more natural is to allow the speaker more freedom. Generally, the more freedom they have to be spontaneous, the more likely they are to use realistic speech. For example, a speaker told to describe the members of her family one after another is likely to be far more natural and spontaneous than a speaker who has been given a detailed list of things they have to say.

Although realistic texts are important, not every text needs to be authentic. A piece of scripted language, even if it lacks some of the important characteristics of speech, can still assess important listening skills. The important thing is that the test, as a whole, measures all aspects of the construct. When we want to target specific knowledge or abilities, however – certain vocabulary, certain tenses or particular inferencing skills – there is probably no alternative to scripting the texts to some extent.

Making monologues

Monologues are probably the easiest type of passage to make. After a few moments' thought, most people can talk about something in their lives. Then, once people start talking about what interests them, they will often provide lots of useful listening material. Especially when the specifications are rather vague – for example a passage about daily schedules, shopping or food – we can simply ask whoever happens to be available to describe their own schedule, explain why they like shopping or talk about their mother's cooking. Monologues can also be role plays: for example, a speaker can be asked to record a railway announcement, a voice-mail message, or a news item. In which case, they are likely to be semi-scripted or even fully scripted.

Monologues are the best place to start creating your own texts. However, although making monologues is very convenient, there are two drawbacks. The first drawback is that the speaker is talking to a disembodied recording machine. This means they lack normal back-channelling and listener feedback, and that often results in the discourse being a little unnatural; ending is especially difficult, because the listener lacks a speaker to hand over the next speaking turn to. It helps if the person operating the recording equipment can provide visual feedback, through facial expression, attitude and so forth, but it is important to do so silently. Also, warn the speaker that you will be silent. Some speakers are better able to make good monologues than others, and it may be necessary to try more than one speaker in order to get a good result.

The second drawback with monologues is that they do not contain many features associated with interactive discourse. Much listening is in interactive situations, and speakers usually use a variety of linguistic conventions as they interact with a listener who is present (McCarthy, 1998). Although I have deliberately restricted this book to testing non-collaborative listening – that is listening in situations where the listener does not help to construct the discourse – this type of listening can still include listening to interactive discourse, either as an overhearer, or as a non-speaking participant in a group discussion.

Making interactive texts

There are three main ways to get interactive discourse, and each one has advantages and disadvantages: free discussions, interviews and role plays. They can all be completely spontaneous, semi-scripted, scripted or any combination of these. It is very important to ensure that the speakers can be easily distinguished. With video it is easy to see who is speaking – at least if the video is well made – but when the texts will be played in an audio-only format, many voices can sound similar, and this creates confusion in the listener. One common solution is to use one male and one female voice, or if the speakers are the same gender, to use speakers who have different accents. If not, make sure that the voices are easily distinguished.

Free discussion involves putting two (or more) people together and asking them to have a discussion on a particular topic – talking from their own experience on topics they know about will work best. If the test-developer needs to be more specific about the test content, then the speakers will have to be told what to say, or how to say it, but if possible, decide the content not the words. If it is necessary to practise the actual words, it is usually a good idea to record the practice sessions, just in case the main session does not go as well.

Free discussion will often put the listener in the position of an overhearer of a conversation that was intended largely for the participants. Two-way interactions are social interactions, and there is usually some interactional language used to establish and maintain the social relationship between the participants, and such language usually has little information content. It is probably sensible to leave this in the text to preserve the authenticity of the interaction, but it is usually not a good idea to base questions, or test-tasks, on interactional language. These should usually be based on transactional language: i.e. language intended to convey information, rather than maintain relationships. Furthermore, when the participants are known to each other, they will take their shared experience and knowledge into account as they interact, and this can make comprehension difficult for an overhearer.

Interviews can eliminate the problems that arise due to the test-taker being in the position of an overhearer (Hendrickx, 1977). Interviews are one of the few natural conversational interactions conducted for the benefit of non-participants.

They also have other useful advantages: the text is divided into short coherent sections, with natural breaks, and this is ideal for making short test tasks. The question and answer format is particularly convenient for asking a series of comprehension questions, but be aware of the length of the responses. It can happen that interviewees talk for too long in response to each question and turn the interview into a series of monologues. In some cases, that may not be a bad thing, because using interviews to generate texts does not mean we have to use the interview in the test, and a response to a question may be quite capable of standing on its own, as a short independent text. A series of speaker monologues will, however, lack the characteristics of typical interactive discourse.

Interviews can also be used to make semi-scripted texts more realistic. The interviewer can prepare questions that elicit the topic or language of interest, without the interviewee knowing this in advance. The questions will be planned, but the responses will be spontaneous.

Role plays are appropriate when the test-developer wants to include an identifiable situation. They are especially suitable for service interactions, but also such as asking and receiving a set of directions, explaining how things work, or even holding a discussion.

Speakers have to act out, or role play, the situation, and the best people to do this are those who have experience of the target situation themselves. They know the content, they know the appropriate language, and they can often just *ad lib* and produce an appropriate text with little or no preparation.

However, it is not always possible to find people who know the target situation. In that case, select the most suitable speakers in terms of gender and age etc. Some preparation and practice will usually be necessary, and that will mean scripted or semi-scripted texts.

Making academic texts

Much interest in second-language listening has been concerned with listening in an academic setting (Chiang and Dunkel, 1992; Flowerdew, 1994; Hanson and Jensen, 1994; Jenson and Hansen, 1995), and hence one common testing purpose is to assess academic listening skills. This usually means listening to lectures or presentations on academic topics in a college or university. This is specific-purpose testing (Douglas, 2000), and it is therefore important that the language of the texts has the characteristics of authentic target-language use academic texts. This might be an ideal situation for recording live speech events, if it is practically possible.

There is one compromise solution that works very well. Graduate students usually know a great deal about their field (and are often looking for a little part-time work). I have often asked them to give short, five- or ten-minute talks about their discipline, targeted to listeners who are non-experts. Many can do such talks with very little preparation: they know their subject well, and they are used to talking about it. They tend to slip naturally into the usage and discourse patterns of their discipline, but are still able to minimise technical jargon and target the talk to the listener with little specialised background knowledge. Often they will be able to provide a number of short talks on different aspects of their field.

Authentic texts vs. authentic tasks

In the sections above, I emphasised the importance of encouraging speakers to talk naturally. However, natural speech is often too difficult for lower-ability listeners to understand. As a test-developer wanting to make tests for low-ability listeners, there are two alternative solutions to this, and both of them preserve some aspect of authenticity and sacrifice some other aspect. Firstly, it is possible to give listeners challenging realistic texts, but then give them tasks which require only superficial processing of the content. This preserves the situational authenticity of the text, in that it still has the characteristics of typical target-language use texts, but it does sacrifice the interactional authenticity, in that it does not require the abilities normally applied to such texts. The alternative is to give test-takers simpler texts, but then give them tasks which require them to process the content in a reasonably realistic manner. This sacrifices the situational authenticity of the text, in that it is no longer a realistic target-language use text, but it does preserve the interactional authenticity in that the abilities required to process the text will be similar to those in the target-language use situation.

Test-developers should make this trade-off depending on the purpose of the test, and the context of use. In some cases, such as special purposes testing, there will be a stronger reason to use genuine texts, and in other cases, such as proficiency tests, there may be a stronger reason to use texts the test-takers must be able to process in a realistic manner. However, I tend to give more importance to authentic processing than to authentic texts, especially in the case of lower-ability listeners. This is because I believe automatic, real-time processing is at the core of listening ability, and I do not want to sacrifice that in order to use more authentic texts.

Making texts for lower-ability learners

However, when we make our own texts, it may be possible to have reasonably realistic texts that are also suitable for low-ability learners. Here are some simple guidelines to produce easier texts.

- **Topics:** Choose simple topics which the listener is likely to be familiar with: family, daily schedule, work, hobbies, vacations, leisure activities, likes and dislikes and so on.

- **Content:** Ask speakers to stick to rather simple ideas, which are not conceptually complex.

- **Speech rate:** Ask speakers to speak a little more slowly, but not unnaturally so. More importantly, ask them to pause more between their utterances.

- **Vocabulary:** Ask speakers to avoid using slang and less frequent vocabulary. If they do have to use words that they think might be unknown, ask them to provide an explanation.

- **Grammar:** Ask them to use more simple statements, with fewer embedded clauses.

- **The addressee:** Lastly ask speakers to imagine that they are addressing their remarks to a foreign visitor, sitting in front of them, who does not understand English very well.

My experience is that some speakers are better than others at speaking naturally for lower-ability listeners: some produce very easy texts, that seem very natural, whereas others produce more or less the same as they would normally. Although the language might become a little unnatural, and the content trite and uninteresting, if the test-takers are struggling to understand, the task is unlikely to be boring to the listener. If you cannot get suitable texts through this method, then there is probably no alternative to writing very easy texts and having these read aloud.

Playing the recording more than once

Another problematic testing issue is how many times listeners should hear the text. In many listening tests, test-takers are allowed to hear the text twice. Arguments for and against this are complex, and there are good arguments on each side. As always, test-developers need to consider this in the light of the purpose of the test, and the testing situation.

What seems to be clear is that playing the text a second time will make the test task much easier (Berne, 1995; Cervantes and Gainer, 1992). As noted in Chapter 5, giving the task after the first listening, but before the repetition, makes the task easier still (Sherman, 1997). Playing the text twice is a useful way of making difficult tasks easier for lower-ability test-takers.

However, in terms of both the situational and interactional authenticity of the language, playing the text just once seems the obvious thing to do. In virtually all real-world listening situations we hear the text once, and only once, and fast, automatic processing of language is a basic listening ability that we need to test. If listeners fail to catch something, this is what happens in most target-language use situations, and the ability to make inferences to bridge comprehension gaps is a fundamentally important listening skill. Furthermore, hearing and processing a text a second time may utilise different comprehension skills from the first time – we really do not know.

The problem is that in most target-language use situations it is not so vital that the listener understands exactly what is said, and comprehension is normally much more approximate than we realise. When it is important that we understand precisely, we often have a chance to ask clarification questions and negotiate the meaning in some way. The testing situation is unnatural in demanding that the listener comprehend with a much greater degree of precision than is normal. In other words, in preserving the situational authenticity by giving the text only once, we are sacrificing interactional authenticity by asking listeners to understand more precisely than in the target-language use situation. Given this, playing the text a second time does not appear such an unnatural thing to do. Furthermore, in many testing situations there is a room full of people, possibly with inadequate sound quality, and there is always a chance of some noise disturbing the listener just at exactly the wrong moment. Others will argue that playing the recording only once places an undue psychological stress on the test-taker. As a result, many test users demand that the recording be played twice.

Furthermore, in most target-language use situations, there are some texts that are meant to be heard more than once. Pre-recorded announcements, certain information texts, voice-mail messages and so on. Often these are texts in which it is important to get the detail correct – timetables or schedules are good examples. A good compromise is found in the Finnish National Language Certificates (see Chapter 8): when tasks require listening for details, the text is played twice, but when tasks require understanding the main idea, the text is played once.

If texts are to be played only once, repeating or re-phrasing important points is often a good idea. This makes it less likely that test-takers will miss an important point, and it should generally aid comprehension. However, too much additional redundancy can become very unnatural.

When making decisions on this issue, test-developers need to take into account the construct they want to measure, the characteristics of the testing situation, and the quality of the audio the test-takers will hear. I tend to prefer giving the text just once, where that is feasible, because I feel that automaticity is such an important part of the listening construct; but other testers disagree.

Providing video

Traditionally most listening tests have used audio recordings, but recently video has become increasingly available, and video presentation of the listening text is an obvious possibility. Eventually, as multi-media technology develops, video is likely to become the norm. However, that day is far away, and providing video still requires serious compromises.

The advantages of video seem obvious. In many target-language use situations, the listening text is accompanied by visual information, which can have a significant impact on the interpretation (Kellerman, 1990). Seeing the situation and the participants tends to call up relevant schema. If visual information would be available in a target-language use situation, making it available in the test situation is likely to improve both situational and interactional authenticity. As Gruber notes, 'there are features of the process, or setting, of how the language is being used which cannot be separated from its meaning' (Gruber, 1997:339). Another advantage of video is to bring assessment into alignment with current pedagogical practice where video is being increasingly used (Lynch and Davidson, 1994). It also provides listeners with a focus for their attention as they are listening.

Brindley warns that 'video media in language testing remains largely unexplored' (1998:10), and we do not really know much about how it affects performance (Gruber, 1997). My own instinct is that visual information is more important in interactional language use, where the emphasis is on the relationship between the participants, but less important in transactional language use where the emphasis is on the content. In most cases, language tests are assessing transactional language use. Furthermore, we are usually interested in the test-takers' language ability, rather than the ability to understand subtle visual information. As noted in Chapter 2, the research indicates that people differ quite considerably in their ability to utilise visual information (Burgoon, 1994). There are good reasons to keep the emphasis on the audio information.

Whatever we decide is appropriate from a construct perspective, there are some serious practical constraints with video. Most importantly, providing video, or other forms of multi-media, is more time consuming, and hence more expensive than audio-only presentations (Gruber, 1997). Although analogue video recorders are common in some countries, editing and processing analogue recordings requires expensive equipment and advanced technical skills. Digital recorders are also available, and editing and processing software is not very expensive, but digital video takes truly enormous amounts of computer storage and processing capacity.

Another problem with video recordings is that the audio quality will usually suffer. Most built-in video camera microphones are small, of relatively poor quality, and are usually held too far from the speaker. An external microphone is better, placed near the speaker's mouth. The problem is that if you place the microphone in front of the speaker's face, it will cover the face and spoil the picture. The microphone must therefore be placed some distance away, or a small clip-on microphone can be used. Small microphones tend to provide lower-quality sound, so make sure you use a good one. However, a small reduction in sound quality may be a worthwhile sacrifice for the additional authenticity, although in a test of listening, I believe good sound quality should be the main priority.

There is one possible compromise, which is being used on the TOEFL computer-based test: the listener is not presented with a video, but with a still photograph of the participants speaking. This has the advantage of showing the scene, in order to activate relevant knowledge schema, and provides the test-takers with a focus of attention, but without the considerable resources necessary to present a full motion video. The picture need not be of the actual speakers, but could be of different people posing for the picture.

Conducting a recording session

It is really impossible to give complete instructions on how to conduct a recording session as test specifications, participants, equipment and all other factors will vary. I intend to describe a hypothetical, but typical, session in which I ask a colleague to record three different passages for a listening test. This example illustrates how to make an audio recording, but the basic idea, especially how you handle the speaker and get them to provide the text, would be essentially the same whether making an audio or a video recording.

In this hypothetical situation, the test specifications call for two listening sections, one a scripted dictation, and the second an 'authentic' passage on the topic of vacations, on which there will be some comprehension questions. For the authentic passage I am going to make two recordings, one semi-scripted and one quite spontaneous.

Preparation

I have decided to use the dining room in my house. It has a carpet and curtains, which are closed. The acoustics are reasonable, with very little echo. It is a weekday afternoon when everyone is at work, and the local children are at school. The room has a table, with two chairs on opposite sides, facing each other. I have a microphone on a stand on the table, in front of where the speaker will sit. I will sit opposite the speaker, with the tape recorder on the table in front of me. I am comfortable using this recording equipment because I spent an hour or more yesterday practising how to use it. The speaker is inexperienced, and the table is covered with a heavy cloth so that if he accidentally bangs the table top, it will not sound too loud. There are no pens or small items near him, so there is nothing for him to fidget with if he gets nervous. The kitchen door is closed, and we will not be able to hear the fridge if it comes on, and the heater and air-conditioner are off.

My friend comes and I sit him down in his seat. He is polite and clearly a little nervous. The microphone is quite large, on a stand on the table near him, and he is very aware of it. I offer him a drink of juice or coffee, and we just relax and chat for a while. We talk about the weather and his work, and I also explain about the test I am making. He asks suspiciously if the microphone is turned on, and I reassure him that it is off. I promise I will tell him whenever I am recording, and I assure him I will not record anything without his knowledge and consent.

Recording a scripted text

When I feel he is more at ease, I show him the script for the dictation. I want him to be familiar with it, so I ask him to read it twice. I check that he understands it. Then I suggest we try recording it, and he agrees, nervously. Firstly, I check the recording level on the tape recorder. I ask him to get comfortable and sit in the position in which he will speak – I suggest sitting slightly forward, with just a little tension. I move the microphone and adjust it to within about six inches (15 centimetres) of his mouth. He looks as though he expects it to bite him! I ask him not to move back and forth too much, but to try to keep the same distance from the microphone. I warn him not to crackle the paper he is reading from, and not to bang the microphone or the table. (If this were a video recording, I would put his head and shoulders in the picture, and ask him not to wave his arms about, but tell him to feel free to animate his face.)

Then I put the machine in Record/Pause mode, and ask him to start reading, in the way he intends to do it, while I check the recording level. I set it as high as I can without any distortion. I assure him that we are not recording yet. I have a pair of headphones plugged into the recorder, and I listen to his voice through these as I set the recording level. I let him go on reading longer than I need, to give him more practice and get him used to the situation. I know that people are usually nervous at first, and also that they usually relax after a while. After I have finished, I tell him that it sounds great, and I tell him he has a good recording voice. That reassures him, and he relaxes a little.

Then I switch the tape-recorder to Record, and give him a signal to start. He begins reading. I just watch the recording level, making a few minor adjustments, and listen to him through my headphones. I try to appear confident. He is very nervous and not reading too well. He reads it far too quickly. He finishes, and I switch off the recorder. He is clearly not very happy, but I tell him it was great, and quite good enough. We talk a minute or two and then I suggest that we should try again, just to make sure. He agrees. I ask him to read the text silently again before we start. He does and I pretend to adjust the machine. By now he knows the passage very well. I ask him to read much slower this time, then we make the recording. This time it is much better. He knows the passage better, and he is more at ease, and he reads slowly but confidently. This one is quite good enough. We then play it back to make sure it is recorded properly, and I reassure him that it sounds good, and is exactly what I wanted.

Recording a semi-scripted text

I am now thinking about the second recording, the vacation. This is going to be more difficult. I need to plan as I go along. I start asking him questions about his vacations. How many weeks a year does he have, where does he go, who with etc. By talking in this way, I am doing a number of things. I am probing into his vacations to find anything interesting, I am getting him to recall his memories about his vacations, and I am putting him at ease. The microphone is still there, but he is far less aware of it. I react to what he says with questions and comments, and I tell him a little bit about my vacations, just enough so that he does not feel that he is being interrogated. After about 10 minutes I have two ideas for recordings.

The plan for the first vacation recording is to get him to talk about his vacations in general: how many weeks he gets every year, when he goes, where he goes, who with, what he does, what accommodation they get, and most importantly, why he chooses such vacations. I think that such a text would provide some specific details that could be used to assess the ability to understand clearly stated information. Then, when he explains why he chooses such vacations, there should be something suitable to ask summary or inference questions. I explain my plan, and ask him if he feels comfortable talking about this and he agrees. I tell him I want him to talk for about two to three minutes, knowing full well that most people will then talk for about three to four minutes (although occasionally some people talk less). We then make some brief notes together: just a few words, or short points, to remind him of the topics, and lay out their order. Note that I do not ask him to practise it, and at no time in the conversation did he give me the whole story, although he has talked about various parts of it.

When he has made his notes, I remind him to address me when he is talking, I check the controls, and set the tape recorder going. Then I give him a signal to begin. While he is talking I remain silent, but in all other respects, especially with my facial expressions, I give him the impression that I am listening attentively to what he says, and so we get a good recording of a reasonably natural piece of spoken discourse.

Recording an unscripted text

After a quick check to make sure I recorded it correctly, I am now ready for the second vacation passage. During our conversations he had mentioned that he once went to Hawaii, and really enjoyed it. He still looks back on this as a high point in his life, and I want him to talk about that. I believe people are most interesting when they talk about what interests them most. I am not very concerned about the exact content, and I am happy to let his own interest determine what he says. I am concerned, though, that he will ramble on too long. Some people do. I tell him that I want him to talk for about three minutes, but I expect four to five minutes. I show him a gesture I have that indicates that it is time for him to stop, not stop abruptly, but just wind down naturally. I know that some speakers have difficulty ending a monologue; it is unnatural and they sometimes just keep going because they do not know how to stop. I warn him about this. I tell him that the best ending is a summary that brings it all together, on a falling intonation. I also tell him that if he cannot do that, it does not matter, and I reassure him that ending with a trite statement such as 'and that was my holiday in Hawaii' is perfectly fine.

We set the machine to Record and again I act the part of the interested listener. I look at him, smile, nod and respond – but silently. He does a good job, as most people do, but some parts are better than others. He has a good introduction, with an amusing incident, in the middle he gets a little unfocused, but he then picks up the interest again when he talks about his efforts to learn surfing. He makes some nice comments about the journey home, and he suddenly realises that he has nothing more to say – he has actually finished without realising it. There is a long pause, he looks at me in panic, I smile, switch off the recorder and assure him it is great. Despite sounding just a little bit unnatural, it is a good piece of spoken text, with virtually all the characteristics typical of spoken language, and is quite adequate for my purpose.

Now he is into his stride; he is relaxed and talking freely. I remember that the students taking the test may want some practice materials, and I may have to make another test next year. So I ask him to talk about his family, and we do a short two-minute recording of him discussing the members of his family. It is a little bit easier than the other passages, but very useful. We follow this with four minutes on his passion, playing football. He speaks quickly, throws in a little slang, and adds a few asides as he is speaking. This is very natural, although perhaps more challenging than the other passages.

The whole process has taken a little over an hour and I have everything I need for my test construction, and some spare recordings for backup, or for practice materials. The sound quality is good enough, and although a dog barked during one of the recordings, it does not interfere with the intelligibility, and I tell myself that it adds a little authenticity.

This is a very typical recording session. I believe that with a little care and a little practice anyone can conduct such a session and can get quite usable spoken texts.

The impertinent interviewer technique

The above discussion has assumed that there would be a friend, a colleague or perhaps a paid speaker, who would cooperate to create the texts. However, it is quite possible to record complete strangers. The basic idea is simple: decide who you would like to interview, ask to interview them, and then go round to their office or home with your recording equipment and record one long interview with them. The great advantage of this technique is that the language is usually spontaneous and varied, and the topics real. The disadvantage is that the recordings will contain unusable material, and will need extensive editing.

The first task is to identify potential speakers. In the case of testing for specific purposes, you may have very clear requirements – a businessman or a nurse, for example. You might just want to find interesting people in the community – perhaps someone with an unusual job or an interesting hobby, or perhaps a well known local personality. The next step is to contact the potential speaker. Although it may seem impertinent to ask complete strangers to give you their precious time for nothing, it is surprising how often people will agree. The initial request is important. Make it clear that you are interested in their work (or hobbies or whatever); most people enjoy talking about their jobs or hobbies, and often have no one who will listen to them. They will likely be concerned whether they can provide anything of interest, so reassure them that you do not want them to talk about anything extraordinary, just what they do – and perhaps give them examples, such as their daily schedule or their company structure. Make sure you tell them how long it will take, and be prepared to stick to that; although in practice most interviewees are happy to talk longer once they find they are enjoying the interview.

It seems to help if the recording is being made for a non-profit, educational purpose. One Hungarian test-developer approached 82 Londoners for an interview, including many busy professionals – and she was refused only twice! Most of us will not have such success, but if you are reassuring and the prospective interviewee feels your enthusiasm, and if you agree to meet at a time and place convenient to the interviewee, success rates should be worthwhile. Even when people refuse, they sometimes pass you on to an associate who can help you.

The next step is to prepare for the interview, and this is crucial to success. Find out all you can about the interviewee; especially what makes them unique and what interests you about them. If you are going to meet the mayor of a local town, for example, do some research about how she was elected, or current projects she is dealing with, or just find out about the local town. If you go to meet a circus clown, read a book about clowns or circuses, and prepare a list of relevant questions. If you are meeting a leading businessman, find out about his company, what it does, how successful it is. If you can find any relevant literature or pamphlets in advance, do so. As you prepare, keep the test specifications in mind, and work out a strategy for the interview, with a detailed list of questions, follow-up questions, and so forth. If you need to make short-answer questions then prepare to ask a number of short questions; if you need longer descriptive monologues, then prepare questions that will result in longer responses.

You need to have portable equipment, with a good microphone – a clip-on microphone would be best. Be pleasant, polite and efficient. Be prepared to explain what you are doing, and agree to meet any conditions the interviewee may have. Make sure that you have permission to use the interview materials, and perhaps ask the speaker to sign a statement allowing you to use it. Always respect any requests for confidentiality, or restrictions on use. Do not waste any time during the interview. Once the preliminaries are finished, switch the tape recorder on, and leave it on for the rest of the interview. If you are well prepared, in half an hour it is possible to get a considerable amount of recorded information.

During the interview, the most important thing is to be flexible. Take notes while you are listening, and be prepared to abandon your plans if something more interesting comes up. Sometimes your plans may not work. For example, you may prepare a list of questions on a particular topic, and then find that the interviewee knows nothing about that, and has quite different expertise; or perhaps a businessman may find his work boring, and may want to talk about his hobby, stamp collecting. If so, follow the speaker's inclination. Just be aware of the test specifications; remember, they are your target. If you need a grid-filling task, for example, look around for an organisation chart or a schedule of events, and ask the speaker if you can have a copy. Then if you can, ask him to describe the chart or schedule, and you will have the raw material for the grid-filling task. In some cases you will find you can involve the interviewee in your plan to construct a specific test task, and in other cases you will find you cannot. It all depends on the interviewee.

When the recording is finished, you will find there are some parts of it that are not usable. All the interaction, such as the interviewer's questions and explanations, will probably need to be deleted or put aside for other purposes. Much of what the interviewee says may not make sense out of context, although there is a lot that can be done to create context through the test rubric. Material that is not suitable for use in the test can often be used as sample test materials or for test preparation. Teachers may be able to use some in their lessons.

Ensuring good sound quality

Getting a suitable text is only the first part of the process – it then has to be administered to the test-takers. This is crucial. If the sound quality is poor, test-takers will have difficulty hearing and understanding. In such cases their performance may not represent their actual ability. This is a very common problem with listening tests.

The problem can be in two different forms. In the first case, the sound is just poor, and all the test-takers have difficulty understanding it. This may affect the validity of the test as a measure of listening comprehension, but the test is fair in the sense that everyone is suffering the same. The second case is when the sound is poor for some of the test-takers, but not for others. This can happen when the acoustics are poor in some parts of the room, but not others, when external noise is worse in some parts than others, or when the speakers are not powerful enough to fill the entire room. This is more an issue of reliability than validity, but it is a blatantly unfair situation.

Live sound

The easiest way to present a spoken text is to put a person in front of the test-takers and let her speak to them. This has two huge advantages. The first is that it is very easy to do – busy teachers, short of time, who want to administer a quick and simple class listening test can easily do this. They do not even need another interlocutor, they can just speak to the class themselves. The second advantage is that it requires no technical equipment. Many teachers do not have the necessary equipment to make good recordings, and in other situations play-back equipment may not be available.

However, using a live speaker has disadvantages, and for most testing situations these disadvantages will outweigh the advantages. Firstly, we have seen how spontaneity is very important in providing realistic spoken texts, but if we allow the speaker to speak spontaneously, we do not know in advance exactly what they will say. It is almost impossible to write test items before the text is known. Even if we plan carefully, with detailed notes for a semi-scripted presentation, in the heat of a spontaneous presentation there is no guarantee that the speaker will follow the plan. The obvious solution is to provide the speaker with a written script and strict instructions to follow it. Then it is possible to write a variety of items in advance. Dictation seems a very suitable task when we have scripted texts read aloud, but questions asking for clearly stated information, as well as inferencing questions, are quite possible. However, we now have a written text read aloud, and we have already seen how this would lack many of the important oral characteristics of spoken language.

The second major problem with live texts is that every presentation will be different. Comprehension difficulty varies enormously depending on a variety of speaker characteristics: speech rate, clarity of pronunciation, stress, intonation, accent and so forth. Test-takers who get a faster speaker, for example, will be disadvantaged compared to those with a slower speaker. Those who get a speaker who reads well, and emphasises the important points, will be advantaged against those who have a boring monotone speaker. Standardised instructions and training can have some impact, but it is impossible to control for all these speaker differences. Such a test can never be fully standardised.

Security is another problem. It is important that as few people as possible know the test content in advance. Normally, in a high-stakes assessment, we want the recordings to come straight from a sealed package into the player, so that no one will know the test content in advance. If, however, we use a live presentation, speakers will have to know the text in advance to practise it, and this is a serious security threat.

A national test in Sri Lanka used live speakers to give a dictation. Speakers were trained in how to pace themselves, and how to leave the pauses for test-takers to take notes, and they were required to practise before each reading. Researchers who investigated the project during the first year found that the procedure worked well, with acceptable levels of reliability (Alderson *et al.*, 1987).

Although there are considerable disadvantages to providing live speech, it is better to have a live speaker who can be heard and understood than a recording that cannot be heard; and in situations where the alternative to a live speaker is no listening test at all, many educators would prefer the live speaker.

Recorded sound

In most testing situations recorded sound will be used. With sufficient care it is possible for any amateur to make reasonable recordings, but if you have the resources, or if this is a high-stakes assessment, you may want to have recordings professionally made. It will be expensive, but should provide better quality than most of us could make ourselves.

When making recordings, care and attention to detail are vital. We start with an original sound source, usually a person talking, and our aim is to preserve that sound and reproduce it elsewhere. It is important to grasp one basic idea, namely that whatever we do with that sound – record it, amplify it, edit it, copy it, play it back or whatever – will usually reduce the quality of the sound in some way.

Some things we do will reduce the sound quality a lot, and others only a little, but it is the cumulative effect of all these processes that turns a good, clear, spoken voice into a noisy, crackly, muddy recording. Our job, as sound engineers, is to do everything we can, to attend to every little detail, in order to preserve the sound quality. The aim when recording and processing sound is not so much to make good sound as to avoid making bad sound. All the money spent on expensive recording studios or on high-end audio equipment has this one simple aim, to preserve the original sound and reproduce it faithfully.

Sound recording is a technical and highly skilled profession, and as amateurs, it is unrealistic to think that we can provide top quality. However, our aim is only to make clear voice recordings, not music, and that is much easier.

The signal-to-noise ratio

The difference between good recordings and bad recordings is considerable. Anyone who has ever compared professional studio recordings with typical home recordings will be shocked at the difference. Even with home recordings, there is a considerable difference between recordings made on good quality equipment and on poor equipment – a $300 microphone really does sound far better than a $15 microphone.

Our aim when making voice recordings is to record the voice with no other noise. The voice is our signal, and we want to make that as clear as possible, but we also want to keep other noises out of the recording. In other words, we want to get a high signal-to-noise ratio.

The way to improve the signal-to-noise ratio is to record the signal as loud as possible, and reduce the noise as much as possible. There is no one simple way to do this, but rather we need to attend to details, each of which in itself is not so important, but which have an incremental effect.

Increasing the signal

Firstly, we need to get the source, the speaker's voice, as near to the microphone as possible. Read the instructions for the microphone and follow those, but as a general rule, six or eight inches (15–20 cm) is a good distance. If we get too close, say two or three inches (5–8 cm), a good microphone will pick up explosive puffs of breath from the sounds /p/ and /b/. These pops can be loud and sound bad, although you can buy a small screen to put in front of the microphone to shield it from such pops.

Secondly, set the recording level as high as possible. There are many different ways to record sound, analogue tape recorders, digital tape recorders, mini-disks or directly onto a computer hard disk, and you should read the instructions for whichever medium you use. If the recording level is set too high, the sound will become distorted – set it as high as possible without distortion. Analogue tape recordings do not sound too bad if the level is set a little too high, but with digital recorders it is vital not to exceed the maximum recording level, otherwise you will get a sharp crackling noise that will spoil the recordings.

Reducing the noise

Keeping the noise-level low is vital. Firstly, exclude as much background noise as possible. Choose a quiet place, and close all the doors and windows. Draw the curtains. Listen for distant traffic, the hum of voices, television or music next door, people walking, doors closing, dogs barking and so on. Perhaps choose a time of day when the place is deserted, such as a weekend or late at night. Take care especially with electronic equipment which often makes a continual background noise: fridges and air-conditioners switch on and off, many computers have an internal fan which hums continually, and some neon lights have a low buzz. These sounds will add noise to your recordings.

The second source of noise is from the equipment you use. Everything has the potential to add a little noise. Cheap microphones add noise to the recordings, as do poor-quality recording machines; good-quality ones add much less. If you turn the amplification up too high, then you will get some hiss. If you use tapes, poor-quality tapes will add more noise than good-quality ones. Always use the best equipment you can get.

Processing recorded sound

Processing recorded sound is a technical skill, and traditionally audio-engineers needed racks of expensive hardware to process their analogue recordings. For the amateur it was unthinkable to buy the equipment and develop the expertise to use it. With the advent of more powerful personal computers and digital processing technology, things have changed. For a price similar to the cost of a word processor, and for a similar amount of learning time, the amateur can control a piece of software that will do very sophisticated audio processing. The great advantage of digital processing is that when you copy it, or edit it, you do not lose any quality at all. The copy is exactly the same as the original.

Most computers with multi-media capability, especially those set up to play games, will usually have the necessary hardware for adequate sound processing. If not, you may have to buy a sound card to add to your computer.

Editing recordings

First load the recording into the computer. Sound files are huge: CD-quality stereo sound, music or voice (i.e. 16 bits, sampled 44,100 times a second, on two channels) occupies 10 megabytes of storage per minute of sound. For voice, 16 bits sampled 22,050 times a second on one mono channel is quite good enough, but this still requires 2.5 megabytes per minute of recording. Make sure you have sufficient storage space. You may want to buy a new hard disk if you are going to process a lot of audio. After loading the audio file into the audio-processing software, it will show you a waveform of the recorded sound. This waveform is what you work with. You can zoom in to look at the waveform for just one word, or zoom out to see the whole recording. You can copy and cut and paste the recording by manipulating the wave form.

First, listen to the whole recording and decide what you want to keep and what you want to delete. Usually, the first editing task is to determine the length. Find where the speaker starts and delete everything before then, perhaps leaving half a second of silence before the voice actually comes in. Do the same at the end.

Now look for any serious problems. If there are any unnaturally long pauses, or if the recording went wrong, or if there are any unwanted noises – a telephone ringing, people interrupting or the speaker saying something inappropriate – try to cut it out. You can delete it just like deleting a word in a word processor. If you want to delete something, but do not want to shorten the recording, you can replace it with silence. Just copy a piece of silence from anywhere on the tape, a pause where the speaker is silent, then replace the noise with it. It should sound very natural. Alternatively, you can just highlight the unwanted noise, and reduce the volume until it is very low. However, when the unwanted noise occurs at the same time the speaker is actually saying something that you want to keep, there is little you can do, because if you cut out the unwanted noise, you will cut out the speaker.

For most purposes, this will be sufficient editing, but you can still clean up the recording even more. Listen more carefully to the speaker and look at the waveform. Many speakers have a variety of lip smacks, and mouth clicks that we never notice, because the ear filters them out, but they can sound quite loud on a recording. On the waveform they often look like very short, high spikes, especially just before the speaker starts speaking again after a short pause. You can cut these out. Often amateur speakers breathe badly. As they get excited and speak faster they often gulp huge breaths between words. It is some-times a good idea to reduce the volume of these breaths, so that they sound more like a natural breathing and less like they are gasping for air. If you improve the recording in this way, it will sound better.

This is all the editing that is necessary. Notice I have only recom-mended editing things that were due to the recording situation. My advice is never to attempt to clean up the oral feature of the language: leave all the hesitations, false starts, mistakes and disfluencies just as they are.

Slowing recordings down

Earlier we discussed how to make realistic texts for lower-level listen-ers. There is a lot of evidence to indicate that texts with slower speech rates are easier, and we can use our audio-processing software to slow down our recordings. This is almost certain to make the text easier, as long as the natural qualities of the spoken text are preserved.

The first thing is to decide whether a recording is suitable. I tend to look for passages that have most of the characteristics of easier texts, namely a reasonably simple content, and not much use of low-fre-quency vocabulary or complex syntax. I also look for speakers who tend to speak quickly, but with pauses between their utterances. I have found that passages with no inter-clausal pauses tend to sound very unnatural and monotone when they are slowed down. Before starting work, make a copy of your file, put the original somewhere safe, and work on the copy.

Most audio-processing software will have a facility to lengthen a recording without changing the pitch – whatever you do, you must not change the pitch. Lengthening the recording makes it slower. I tend to be conservative: I do not lengthen the passage by much – up to 10 per cent longer seems about the maximum lengthening before the voice begins to sound unnatural. The voice will sound slightly different from the original, so listen carefully to it and check it does still sound natural. This might be enough to make it easier, but I sometimes also lengthen some of the silent pauses. Note, I do not add new pauses, I just lengthen those that occur naturally. I choose pauses that occur at syntactic boundaries, or where the intonation of the speaker clearly indicates there is a pause, and I copy a short section of silent pause into the middle of that pause, to make it longer. I do not add very much; pauses of, say, half a second may become three-quarters of a second, or even a second. I check to make sure it still sounds natural. If it does not, I use the Undo command. In this way I try to lengthen a number of pauses throughout the text. The key is to keep checking both the individual changes and the overall text to make sure that it still sounds natural.

It is my experience that many recorded passages can be lengthened by 10 per cent quite easily, and up to 20 per cent with care, and still sound natural. I doubt if anyone would notice that my passages had been modified in any way. Although this is a somewhat experimental technique, I believe it is worth trying.

Signal processing

After editing the recording, we can process the sound to make it better. Although we can never make a bad recording into a good one, we can improve the clarity of the voice and make it easier to hear. Basically there are two types of processing: modifying the volume, and emphasising certain frequencies. To do this well takes professional skill, but with an ordinary software package and a little bit of practice, the following should be possible. Do them carefully in the following order, and remember: too little is probably better than too much.

Noise-gating: Many recordings have a low level of constant background noise. When the speaker is talking it is not noticeable, but it can be very obvious during silent pauses. Noise-gating is a way of dealing with this. Sounds above a certain volume-level are left untouched so the voice is unaffected, but when the volume drops to a certain level, i.e. just above the level of the background noise, a gate is closed and no sound gets through. This eliminates much of the noticeable hiss in the pauses between the speech, but it will not eliminate the hiss when the speaker is speaking.

Equalisation: Equalisation (or EQ) changes the tone of the signal, rather like the base and treble controls on a home stereo. This is done by increasing the volume of certain frequencies, and reducing the volume of other frequencies. Using EQ, you can emphasise the frequencies of the voice, especially between 1kHz to 4kHz. Just turn them up a little, maybe about three decibels. You can also reduce the frequencies of the unwanted noise, especially very low frequencies below 60Hz, and very high frequencies above about 10kHz. These have very little effect on the voice. Do not overdo it, however, or your recording will start to sound like a poor-quality AM radio.

Compression: We want to turn up the signal as loud as we can, but we cannot turn it up above the level of the highest volume peak. With digital audio, if we increase the volume above the maximum level, it will sound very bad. So we use a two-stage process to increase the overall signal level. The first stage is compression, which reduces the difference between the loudest and quietest sounds by turning down the louder ones – the louder they are, the more the volume is reduced. This makes the high peaks lower.

Normalisation: We then normalise the sound. Normalisation turns up the volume of the whole recording as high as possible until the peaks are near the maximum. This results in a much higher average signal level than if we had not first compressed the file. Normalisation gives the sound a more audible punch, or presence, and makes it much easier to hear. This should be left until last, because once the file has been normalised, we should not attempt to modify it again.

Making a master test recording

Complete listening tests can be presented in a number of ways. A person could stand in front of the test-takers, hand out a test booklet, and then run the test by explaining the instructions and reciting the listening texts, or playing various recordings. But in most tests, there is a test booklet and one recording. The recording will usually provide all the listening texts, and may also provide instructions. In some cases the test is run entirely by a recording, which provides all the instructions, the actual listening texts, pauses for responses and so forth. The person running the test just hands out the materials, starts the recording and then does nothing until the test is finished. This recording will often be on an audio cassette, but it could be a video tape, a CD, a mini-disk, or a computer program.

Combining the various recordings and different voices onto one longer master recording is quite easy with digital recordings, but is very difficult with analogue cassette tape.

Combining digital recordings

If you are going to build a master recording, the sensible advice is to do it on a computer with digital software. You start with a plan of the whole recording, but it does not need to be accurate, because you can change your mind as you are working. First, you input all the recordings into the computer, and save them on a disk. Then you can start building your master from wherever you like – you do not need to start at the beginning. Just build an audio file by cutting and pasting parts from other files. You can insert things, copy or move them, delete them, add or lengthen pauses, change the volume of particular parts, and then save it to a disk anytime you want. No matter how many times you move it or copy it, the sound quality remains exactly the same.

When you have finished you can copy it onto a tape, or any other medium that you choose. Then, if you do not like it, you can come back and work on it again until you get it right. It is not difficult to put together a complete test in this way.

Combining analogue cassette tape

It is possible for the amateur to build a master tape by editing analogue tape, but if you decide to try it, be prepared for one of the most frustrating tasks you will ever do. Cutting and splicing tape is for professionals – as amateurs we can only reasonably expect to record onto a tape, and hope we get it right. Analogue tape is a linear medium, and if you make a mistake, you will have to delete all the recording from that point and start again. Most of us will start over again more than once.

Firstly, you must design the master tapescript. That means you make a plan of everything that will go onto the tape, including every single word, every speaker, the exact length of the response pauses and so forth. Secondly, you need two tape recorders (preferably good quality), a microphone, the necessary wires and connectors to record from one machine to another, and a pair of headphones to monitor the recording process. You will need copies of the recordings, and spare tapes. Do not forget to clean the playback and recording heads on the machines.

You then start building the tape. If anything is pre-recorded you copy it from one machine to another, if not you use a microphone to record onto the tape, and for the pauses record silence. Keep the recording level as high as you can, at a constant level, and try to keep the noise level low. Continually check what you have done; if you catch an error as soon as you have made it, you can re-record over it. Take care when you do re-record that the original recording is completely erased, and take care not to record over anything you want to keep. After quite some time, you will have a master tape that represents hours of work. Take care of it. When you have finished recording, *always* remove the copy protection tab from the back of the tape so that you cannot record over it. Then make a copy for test use, and store the master tape somewhere safe.

With analogue tape it is particularly important that you keep the recording quality as high as possible. Your master tape will contain a copy of your original recording, and you then make a copy for the administration (your master tape is too valuable to use). With analogue tape, every time you make a copy, the quality drops. Your test-takers will hear a copy of a copy of your original recording, and it takes considerable attention to detail to maintain the quality of that.

Playing recordings

It is no use making good recordings and then playing them on inadequate equipment. If you go to the cupboard and take out an old portable cassette player, with a tiny speaker and a small internal amplifier, you will not be able to fill a large room with intelligible sound – especially a room full of people fidgeting, coughing and shuffling their papers. This happens time and again in serious testing situations. There are high-stakes assessments where the listening passages are recorded in a professional studio, by professional actors, but then played to test-takers through totally inadequate equipment with high levels of background noise. Similarly, in the case of computer-based tests, the same high-quality recordings are converted to a small file size to reduce storage space, with a considerable loss of sound quality, and are then played over small computer speakers. The result is sound that is very difficult to understand.

To fill any room with sound you need to have a reasonable player with a moderately powerful amplifier. Studio quality is not necessary, but it should be something at least like an ordinary home stereo system. You also need to have a pair of speakers designed to fill a room of that size.

If the equipment is not powerful enough and you turn the volume higher, the sound will become distorted. The amplifier should be able to fill the room easily on about half volume. Ideally you should feel that if you turned the volume up, you would cause a nuisance to people in other parts of the building, or even outside. Then adjust the volume so that you can sit anywhere in the room and comfortably hear the recording. Remember when the room is full of people, the sound level will most likely need to be increased.

Avoid having people sit right in front of the speakers – it might be too loud for comfort. Make sure the windows are closed to cut out background noise, and draw the curtains if you can. Traffic noise or building work outside can be a serious problem for test-takers sitting near the window. If the heat is unbearable, you may have to choose between an uncomfortable environment, or a noisy testing situation – a difficult decision. It is usually a good idea to put a large sign outside the room, asking people in the vicinity to be quiet.

In some testing situations, such as in language laboratories or with computer-based tests, listeners are given headphones. They bring the sound right to the listener's ear, which can reduce the effect of background noise. However, just providing headphones is not enough, they must be good enough for the job: good headphones have a clear sound, and preferably they should cover the whole ear to exclude other sounds. Some cheap computer headphones are of poor quality and can be much worse than room speakers. It is always a good idea to test the headphones first, and make sure you know how to change the sound level. Also have a few spare sets, just in case some are not working properly.

Room acoustics

The room acoustics will have a considerable impact on the clarity of the sound. In some rooms the recordings will sound clear, and in other rooms the same recording may sound muddy. Although there may not be any choice regarding the room, go and listen to the sound in the room, and if possible, try to select a room with good acoustics.

Determining room acoustics is complex, but bad acoustics are usually due to the sound bouncing around the room too much. Smooth reflecting surfaces are usually the problem: bare wooden floors, large windows, flat smooth walls, all allow the sound to bounce around. This is why gymnasiums often have bad acoustics. Carpets, curtains, wall hangings and soft broken surfaces all help to absorb the sound. Often closing the curtains will help. As a very rough test, go into the room, close the door and shout one short word in a loud voice. If you hear an echo, or if you hear the sound hanging in the room for a while, then the acoustics are likely to be bad. If you shout and the sound dies quickly, with no echo, then the acoustics are likely to be far better.

Conclusion

The centre-piece of any listening test is the text that test-takers listen to. If we wish to ensure the validity of our test, the nature of the texts must be determined by our construct definition. A necessary condition for testing the full range of listening competence is providing spoken texts that require the same knowledge skills and abilities as realistic spoken language. In this chapter, I discussed ways of selecting and constructing suitable spoken texts, as well as ways of ensuring that the sound quality is good enough for listeners to hear clearly and comfortably.

Providing suitable texts is not a simple matter. It takes time, effort and some expertise. However, I believe it is possible, even for test-developers with limited resources, to do a fairly good job – especially with digital technology. Too often, however, among the testing community, the attitude towards providing listening texts has been one of 'anything will do'. It is time to change that attitude. Without good texts, we cannot make good listening tests.

In the next chapter I will discuss how to bring together the work of the last few chapters, and create complete tests.

....

CHAPTER SEVEN

Designing and constructing complete assessments

Introduction

In earlier chapters, I discussed various aspects of test development: Chapter 4 looked at defining the construct, Chapter 5 looked at test tasks, and Chapter 6 looked at texts. In this chapter I will discuss how we bring all this together to construct complete listening tests.

Each testing situation is unique, and there are many different variables that affect test design and construction, so it is impossible to offer any hard and fast rules. I will begin by discussing important aspects of test design, and then illustrate these by discussing three sample test-design projects. Chapter 8 will examine large-scale tests, developed by professionals, and therefore the projects discussed in this chapter will be small scale. The three projects have been chosen to illustrate three common testing purposes, and three different approaches to construct definition: achievement tests, which define their construct by reference to a course of study, general proficiency tests, which define their construct by reference to a theoretical description of the listening ability, and tests of listening for special purposes, which define their construct by reference to a target-language use situation.

This chapter will be divided into five sections:

i   some characteristics of good tests;

ii   a discussion of test specifications;

iii   designing an achievement test for a listening class;

iv   designing a general test of listening proficiency;

v   designing a test of listening for a specified purpose – academic listening.

Properties of a good test

Tests are designed for particular uses, and the most desirable quality of a test must be its usefulness. Bachman and Palmer (1996) have taken this idea and used it as the basis for quality control in test-development. For them, **usefulness** incorporates the test's measurement properties, as well as the social consequences of test use and the practicality of the test for its particular purpose. They suggest that usefulness is a function of six properties: reliability, construct validity, authenticity, interactiveness, impact and practicality.

A test, or any assessment, is a measurement, and as a measurement it must have two properties: reliability and validity. **Reliability** is concerned with how accurately the test measures. Conceptually this is the idea that we would always get the same result testing the same person in the same situation. There are standard ways of estimating test reliability, which are not very difficult to implement, and test-developers should always attempt to do this (see Bachman, 1990, for an introduction to reliability). As a general rule, the more important the decision based on the test, the more reliable the test needs to be.

Construct validity is the most important property of a test, and many of the other aspects of usefulness follow from it. The basic idea of **construct validity** is simple: it is the extent to which the test measures the right construct. Strictly speaking, it is not tests that have validity, but decisions based on tests. Traditionally, reliability has been regarded as a pre-condition to validity, on the grounds that a test cannot measure the right construct if it is not measuring anything at all. Establishing construct validity is not a simple task, but an on-going process of accumulating theoretical and empirical evidence (see Messick, 1994, 1996, for an introduction to validity theory).

Authenticity and **interactiveness** were discussed at length in Chapter 4 in respect to construct definition, and the relative importance of each will depend on how the construct is defined. Many scholars would argue that these are not separate properties, as Bachman and Palmer (1996) suggest, but are important ways of examining construct validity (Messick, 1994, 1996, for example). Whatever we think of that debate, it is important that we consider these qualities as we define and develop our test.

Tests are powerful things, especially when the stakes are high, and they not only have considerable **impact** on the lives of test-takers, but they also have broad social and educational impact. Test-developers need to do what they can to avoid undesirable impact (see *Standards for Educational and Psychological Testing*, 1999).

One type of undesirable impact comes through **bias**, which is when one group of test-takers is advantaged, or disadvantaged, by the test. Technically, bias is when a test is differentially valid for different groups of test-takers. Bias can occur in listening tests when background knowledge is necessary for comprehension or task completion, and one group of test-takers has more of that knowledge. Bias can also arise if the content could upset certain groups to the extent that it affects their performance: racist or other such offensive remarks can have this effect. Another possible source of bias arises if the speaker has an accent more familiar to one group than another.

Tests will often have an effect on classroom teaching: this is referred to as **washback**. Learners may study for the test, teachers may teach to the test, or test-preparation courses may be offered (Alderson and Wall, 1993; Wall, 1997). If these lead to beneficial language-learning activities the test is said to have positive washback, and if the effect is not beneficial, then the test is said to have negative washback. As test-developers we should try to ensure that the washback is beneficial.

The last of Bachman and Palmer's properties of usefulness is **practicality**. In Chapter 4, I suggested that in test development, the quality of the final product is largely a result of the amount of time, effort and expertise available. Busy teachers working alone and part-time are unlikely to be able to make tests to the same standard as a group of colleagues, and a group of teachers will not have the same resources as a well endowed testing institution. As test-developers, it is important to ensure that there are sufficient resources available to make a test of the right quality, and as test-evaluators, it may be unfair to judge the quality of a teacher-made test by the same standards as one made by a large testing corporation. The test must also be practical for the situation in which it will be administered: it is no good using open-ended questions if there are no trained raters available to score them.

Finally, I would like to add another property to the list of what makes tests useful: the **efficiency** with which the test gathers informa-

tion. Testing time is limited, and we need to collect as much information as possible in that time. For example, a dictation of 150 words
can easily be administered in about 20 minutes, which is about seven
units of information per minute. Statement evaluation items can be
presented quite quickly, at about three or four a minute. Short-
answer questions will provide fewer units of information, maybe
about two a minute, and multiple-choice comprehension questions
can be administered at about one a minute. However, not all units of
information are of equal value. Quality is also important. One word
written correctly in a dictation does not give us as much useful
information as one statement understood correctly, and a comprehension question which requires processing and synthesising a
number of pieces of information scattered throughout a text obviously
provides even more information about the listener's ability.

The appropriate balance between the different properties of usefulness must be evaluated in terms of the particular test-development
project. However, in my view the different properties of usefulness
are not of equal importance: if a test has no reliability it will not
measure anything at all, and if a test does not have construct validity
it will not measure the construct we want to measure (although if we
are lucky, it may be measuring a similar construct). These two measurement properties, reliability and validity, are at the heart of test
quality and test usefulness.

Test specifications

In test design, when we make decisions about the construct, the tasks
and the texts, we are creating the test specifications. The test specifications are the overall design of the test – the plan that proceeds from
a test purpose to a completed test. They are usually in the form of a
written document which provides 'the official statement about what
the test tests, and how it tests it' (Alderson *et al.*, 1995:9). Often these
are kept confidential, especially when new versions are likely to be
developed. They are often accompanied by public guidelines about
what the test covers, what the scores mean and how test-takers
should study.

Even in the simplest situations, it is a good idea to make an explicit
written statement of test specifications. At the very least this statement should contain:

1 a statement of the purpose of the test;

2 a statement or description of the listening construct to be assessed;

3 details of how that construct will be operationalised in actual test items, including number of items, characteristics of tasks, texts, layout and so forth.

Of course the bulk of these specifications would be taken up with details of the layout of the test, and how the items will be constructed.

The level of detail of the specifications will vary depending on the purpose of the test, who will use it and so forth. They tend to be more detailed when the stakes are higher, when the test has more than one form, when there are more people working on it, and when new forms will be made at a later time. At the most detailed level, Alderson *et al.* (1995:9) suggest three main target groups for specifications: item writers, test validators and test users. They provide a separate list of what test specifications should contain for each group. These are summarised in Table 7.1.

In the case of a test being developed for the first time, design of the test will tend to proceed cyclically (Alderson, 2000). The test-developer will usually draft a set of specifications, and start developing and trying out tasks. Then as the test-developer learns more about the test tasks, and how they relate to the construct, the specifications will usually be revised, and then reviewed and revised again a number of times. It is a subjective process in which the test-developer must use knowledge and judgement to develop a test of the most appropriate construct, in the most efficient manner.

In the case of a test-developer making a new version of an established test, the process is very different. The test specifications will function somewhat like a recipe, and the test-developer must follow the specifications and create a test which is as similar as possible to previous versions of the test.

Designing a test of listening achievement

For the sake of illustration, let us assume that we wish to develop a test to determine how well students have mastered the listening content of a course of study. The purpose is to determine class grades, so the stakes are relatively low, and the resources available are

Table 7.1. *Details of test specifications*

Specifications for item writers

> **Purpose of the test:** placement, progress, achievement, proficiency, or diagnostic test
>
> **Test-takers:** age, proficiency, L1, cultural background, education etc.
>
> **Main sub-sections of the text:** how many sections, how long
>
> **Target-language use situation:** and whether this will be simulated in the test
>
> **Text types:** source, topics, functions, nature of the language, level of formality or orality, instructions on how they will be selected; how the texts will be presented, recorded, live etc.
>
> **Language competence:** components of language ability: vocabulary, grammar, discourse structure, main ideas, specific detail, inference, following instructions
>
> **Language elements:** a list of structures, vocabulary, notions, functions, speech acts
>
> **Type of tasks:** discrete-point, integrative, authentic, objectively scorable
>
> **Number of items in each section:** relative weighting in final score, details of scoring
>
> **Testing techniques:** multiple-choice, short-answer comprehension questions, gap-filling, statement evaluation etc.
>
> **Rubric:** instructions to the candidate, example items
>
> **Criteria for marking:** what is considered a satisfactory response, and what is not

Specifications for test validators

> Statement of the **purpose of the test**
>
> Description of **theoretical framework** underlying test design
>
> Explicit **definitions of the listening construct** or constructs operationalised
>
> Explanation of why this **operationalisation meets the purpose** of the test

Specifications for test users

> **Characteristics** of the test
>
> **Use** of the test
>
> **Limitations** of the test
>
> Appropriate **population** for the test
>
> Detailed **instructions**
>
> **Example items**
>
> **Content** of the test
>
> Meaning of the **test scores**
>
> Guidance on **suitable preparation**

limited: just one teacher, with little time and little test-specific expertise. This is a reasonably common scenario.

Defining the construct

In this case the construct is defined by the listening activities given in
the class. The course materials consist of a set of texts and tasks, and
these can be regarded as a target-language use situation.

Operationalising the construct

We have a clear set of materials which can form the basis of test
development, and given the lack of resources, it is sensible to keep
things simple. The teacher has two main options: to sample directly
from the course materials, or to use the course materials as a model
to make similar activities.

Sampling the course content

If a random sample of the course materials could be used, the argument for the validity of the test is strong. If the listening passages
have comprehension activities attached to them, such as answering
questions, filling in information grids, matching pictures or whatever,
these might be used as test items almost unchanged. Such a test is
easy to make, and will give a good indication of how well the material
has been understood. However, the drawback is that test-takers may
be able to remember the correct responses from their classwork
without listening to the passage again. This can be avoided by
creating new comprehension tasks for the passages. These could be
very similar to the original tasks, or could be different task types
altogether. However, there is still the problem that some test-takers
may remember the content of the listening passages from class
study.

Sampling course materials in this way is an easy way of making a
test, but memory may be a serious source of construct-irrelevant
variance. Furthermore, such tests do not tell us whether the students
can apply their listening skills to novel listening situations.

Replicating the course content

If new listening activities are needed for the test, there are two ways the teacher can avoid making a completely new test. Firstly, it may be possible to look through old text-books, or use a library resource centre, and find course materials very similar to those studied in class. If the course materials used were relatively standard, this should be possible. A second alternative is to use the course materials as a model and copy those. For example, if there are passages with people introducing themselves, then make recordings of similar people introducing themselves; if there is someone talking about theatres in London, then make a recording of someone talking about cinemas in Birmingham. Then, as far as possible, replicate the comprehension tasks used in the teaching materials. Of course, it is not always possible to copy professionally made materials, but it is sensible to make the test as similar to the class materials as possible.

Improving the test over time

Although pre-testing should be a standard procedure with all new test items, most teachers do not have the time or resources. This is a pity, and as a result the quality of the test may not be as good as it could be. However, if the course is to be repeated and the test used again, the test can be improved over a period of time. After the administration, analyse the test and throw out the items that are too easy or too hard, and keep those that are difficult for the low-achieving students and easy for the high-achievers. Items with poor discrimination may be kept or discarded, depending on the relevance of the content. New items should be developed and included in the test. Then, at the next administration, the test will be far better. If this process is repeated over a number of administrations, the test can be refined to a high standard.

Designing a general proficiency test

For the second illustrative test-development project, let us assume we wish to develop a general test of listening ability, either as part of a battery of tests or as a stand-alone listening test. This would be used in-house, in an organisation such as a school or a business. The test is not tied to any particular course of study, nor intended to target any particular domain of language use.

For the sake of discussion, we will assume the stakes are quite high, and the resources available are reasonably limited – a committee of a few people, working part-time over a few months. I will discuss some of the options available, and propose some possible solutions, but again I should stress that other solutions would also be quite appropriate.

Defining the construct

As there is no identifiable target-language use situation, we will take a competence-based approach to construct definition. Given the high stakes and limited resources, we need an appropriate construct that can be assessed reliably with reasonably limited resources. Generally speaking, all the discussion in earlier chapters suggests that the narrower the construct definition, the easier it is to construct items that will test it well.

One solution would be to restrict the construct to grammatical knowledge. Although this is only one part of listening ability, in second-language listening it certainly accounts for a high proportion of the total variance. It includes sentence-level grammar and basic vocabulary, as well as much of what makes listening unique – the sound system, the phonology, stress, intonation and the need for automatic processing.

If resources allow, a better strategy would be to test the default construct described in Chapter 4. This includes grammatical knowledge, discourse knowledge and quite a lot of pragmatic knowledge, and most of what is unique to listening.

As for the tasks, because there is no clearly identifiable target-language use situation, we have no basis for evaluating the authenticity of our tasks, and so the emphasis will be on finding tasks that test our construct with maximum efficiency.

Operationalising the construct

I will discuss the operationalisation of two different listening constructs: a very narrow grammatical construct, and the default listening construct I defined in Chapter 4.

Assessing grammatical knowledge

Probably the easiest way to assess grammatical knowledge is to construct a number of tasks that require processing short samples of realistic language on a semantic level. We need to ensure that the texts are fast, with typical phonological modification, and that they are processed automatically. It is always a good idea to have a number of different task types, to minimise the effects of one particular test method – three or four is probably sufficient.

Statement evaluation items are a good choice; they are easy to make and they provide clear evidence of comprehension. Test-takers could look at a picture of a complex scene and evaluate statements about the content, or they could listen to pairs of statements and indicate whether they mean the same thing or not.

For a second task type, response evaluation items could be used. Test-takers could be given a series of statements, each one followed by three alternative responses, and choose which is the most appropriate. These could use informal oral language, and it might even be possible to include some indirect speech acts or inferred meanings.

A third task could use longer information texts, with lots of explicit factual content, and require test-takers to fill out information grids. We could construct a text which gives a series of facts – for example a school curriculum, a schedule of events for travel – we can then devise a grid for the information and leave most of the details blank. Listeners listen and fill in the details. Because the emphasis is on detail, I suggest listeners should hear the passage twice.

Then a fourth task type could be a dictation. This is relatively easy to make and provides information about surface-level linguistic processing. The disadvantage with dictations is that they tend to use written language with fewer oral features. This is why it is good to combine them with other texts which have more oral features.

In one hour, with 15 minutes for each section, it would be possible to gather quite a lot of information – probably about 30 statements evaluated, perhaps 25 of the response-evaluation tasks, maybe two information grids, with 10 items each for a total of 20 items, and 100 words on the dictation. This is a total of 175 items. If a wide range of language and topics were used, a test such as this could be very reliable and provide a good measure of grammatical knowledge, on quite a limited budget.

Assessing the default listening construct

However, I have argued that we should try to test a broader listening construct. One suggestion was what I called the default listening construct. To assess that, we need to use longer samples of discourse and devise tasks that require understanding inferred meanings and pragmatic implications. Again a number of different task-types is a good idea.

Although texts need to be longer, we need to balance that with the need for a variety of different texts. Again, we are looking to find items that are easy to make. A good starting point might be texts that contain information which can be put in a grid or diagram of some sort. They could be a little less explicit than in the test of grammatical knowledge alone, although it would not be inappropriate to have one text that provided only explicit information.

Narratives of interesting events are also appropriate. Most narratives lend themselves well to short-answer comprehension questions. They are often easy to summarise, so test-takers could be asked to fill in gaps on a summary of the story. The cause and effect relationships in the narrative can often be used to test discourse processing. Expository texts will also provide variety. Speakers explaining their ideas or views could be used, or an interview with a speaker discussing their opinions or providing exposition on a topic of interest.

Discourse and pragmatic knowledge are important. To test discourse knowledge we want items that require relating information from different parts of the text. A simple way of doing this is to write tasks where the necessary information is scattered over the passage – tasks which require combining or summarising information often assess discourse knowledge. Interviews can be used to test understanding of interactive discourse patterns. Pragmatic knowledge can be assessed by inferences about the main point, the gist, indirect statements, hints, pragmatic implications, indirect speech acts and generally interpreting the tone and attitude of the speaker.

We need to think about how many items are necessary to make a reliable test of the default listening construct. Most professionally made high-stakes proficiency tests, using high-quality pre-tested items, require about two hours of actual testing time, although the listening section will only be between 30 minutes and one hour. If the stakes are high, I would suggest at least an hour's testing time – more if possible.

These tasks will take longer than the short explicit items testing grammatical knowledge, but I would advise 100 items. This is longer than many professionally made listening tests, but professionals are more experienced. A test with 100 items assessing explicit information, discourse processing and some inferencing, on realistic texts, using a mixture of task types should take about 90 minutes to administer. Some would argue that this is too long, and that sufficient information could be acquired in 60 minutes. This may be true, but when important decisions are being made, it is always better to err on the cautious side: it is better to have people grumble that the test was too long, than that the test was not adequate.

Reliability and validity

If the stakes are high, the test must be reliable. It is impossible to say how reliable, or give target figures, because estimates of reliability mean different things depending on the homogeneity of the items, and the ability range of the test-takers. I would like to see internal consistency estimates of .90 or more. One of the main advantages of testing a narrower construct is that it is easier to get high reliabilities, because the test tends to focus on a narrower range of inter-related skills.

Validity will initially be supported by theoretical arguments based on the construct theory, and this can be powerful evidence, but it is very important that validity studies also be carried out. Ideally these should be part of the test development process, but when resources are limited, validity studies are one of the first things to suffer. This is unfortunate. Validity can be explored on an on-going basis while the test is being used, and this should be incorporated into the regular processes of administration and data collection (see Alderson *et al.*, 1995, and Bachman, 1990, for advice on validation).

Designing a test of academic listening

For the third illustrative test-development project, let us assume we wish to develop a test of academic listening, such as would be made by a school to determine whether a student had sufficient language ability for a particular course of study.

The defining characteristic of such a test is that there is a clearly identifiable target-language use situation that can be used as a basis for test design. Specific-purpose testing is complex, and I recommend Douglas (2000) to readers. What I will do here is illustrate how one particular assessment might be designed.

One thing that test-developers need to be aware of is that specific-purpose tests fall along a continuum of specificity. For example, we might want to assess whether students had sufficient listening ability to follow instructions in a particular chemistry laboratory, which would be very specific indeed. Then we could get progressively more general: whether they could follow a course of study in chemistry, whether they could study science, or even whether they could simply study at a university. For this discussion, let us assume that we want to know whether the student is ready to take a course in the chemistry laboratory.

Defining the construct

After determining the target-language use situation, the listening requirements within that situation must be identified. The general procedure, based on Douglas (2000), is as follows:

- Observations and recordings are made of listening activities in the target-language use situation. The participants are then asked to discuss what they think is important and problematic about the listening event.
- Subject specialists – such as language teachers or specialists in chemistry – are then asked to provide information about the listening that takes place in this situation.
- Based on this, a list of target-language use tasks is drawn up.

The list of target-language use tasks is the construct definition. Tasks could be described using the task characteristics in Table 4.2 (p. 107), and should contain enough detail to enable item writers to construct the tasks, and scorers to evaluate performance.

Operationalising the construct

Operationalising the construct is a process of developing a set of test tasks that will reflect the target-language use tasks as closely as possible. The table of task characteristics can be used to make systematic comparisons between the test tasks and the target-language use tasks.

Let us assume that after observing the situation, we discover that there are a certain number of technical terms they must know, and there are three main types of speech event in the chemistry laboratory:

- instructions – on the handling of equipment and chemicals, as well as how to perform the experiments;
- discussion sessions on the course content;
- short talks, or informal lectures, on chemistry and the results of other experiments.

We might decide to develop a set of tasks for each of these. For the instructions, the simplest way would be to bring the test-taker into the lab, and give them instructions and observe whether they can follow them. However, that is very time consuming, so we might devise a series of picture manipulation tasks. We could draw a number of simple pictures or diagrams of a chemistry lab, with typical equipment and common objects. Test-takers can be given instructions to identify certain objects, put them in certain places, move them around and so forth, using typical target-language use instructions. Test-takers could respond by drawing or writing on the pictures.

The second listening task requires understanding discussions. Two task types might be tried. The first one could be statement evaluation tasks to assess whether test-takers can understand the pragmatic and sociolinguistic implications of typical question and response formats. The second could be mini-dialogues – a question, followed by a response and perhaps with a further comment by the first speaker – followed by one or more comprehension questions. These could be used to test comprehension of the chemistry content.

The third listening task requires understanding short talks. In order to test this we can create a series of mini-lectures. This can be done by either recording segments of actual lectures, or by asking lecturers to record short lectures, or lecturettes. Test-takers can be given any task that probes the most important points: comprehension questions, creating diagrams, writing summaries or filling in information grids are all possible.

The relative number of items in each task will depend on the definition of the domain, and the appropriate length of the test will depend upon the stakes, and the resources available. Twenty questions for each of the three speech events might be sufficient, and could be administered in 40 minutes or so.

Reliability and validity

The necessary level of reliability will depend on the stakes. Again expected reliability levels will vary depending on the homogeneity of the tasks and the ability range of the test-takers. Construct validity is largely determined by the closeness of the match between the target-language use tasks and the test tasks.

In principle the process of going from the identification of the target-language use tasks to replicating them in test tasks is linear, but like most test-development projects, it is likely to be cyclical: experts will be consulted, draft task lists will be drawn up, shown to the experts, revised and then evaluated again. It is very important that input from domain experts be involved in all stages. Although the process is likely to be complex and challenging, there is no reason why good tests should not result.

Conclusion

In this chapter I have described how complete assessments of listening comprehension are designed. I firstly made the point that tests need to have certain important characteristics, and I discussed those as part of the idea of usefulness. I placed particular emphasis on the need for construct validity. In the next section I stressed the need for test specifications formally laying out the design of the test. The rest of the chapter was taken up with three illustrative examples of how tests might be designed. These defined their construct in three different ways: based on a course of study, on a theoretical description of listening ability, and on a clearly specified target-language use situation. It is important to understand that these were discussed only for the purpose of illustrating the test design process, and not to offer prescriptions about how particular tests should be constructed.

In the next chapter, I will examine a number of professionally made tests of listening comprehension, in order to provide an illustration and explanation of test construction from a different perspective.

CHAPTER EIGHT

....

Illustrative tests of listening comprehension

Introduction

In Chapter 7, I discussed the development of complete tests of listening comprehension, and illustrated this with three test-development projects. In this chapter I will examine a number of professionally made tests. The purpose is not to provide a comprehensive review of these tests, nor even to provide illustrative examples of how complete tests should be developed, but rather to illustrate how professional test-developers have dealt with the complexities of testing listening.

The tests will be examined as operationalisations of theoretical notions about listening, and they will be reviewed from these two perspectives:

a   the nature of the construct that underlies the test, and

b   the practical issues – the compromises and trade-offs – involved in operationalising that construct in texts and tasks.

After a short descriptive overview of each test, I will discuss a small selection of typical items. Although I have repeatedly made the point that test task performance is very unpredictable, I believe that the 'meaning' of a test is found in the detail of the interaction between the test task and the test-taker, and looking closely at items is very instructive. There is, however, one practical problem: reading a transcript is never the same as listening to a recording. Wherever possible, listening tests are best reviewed by listening to the texts, not reading the transcripts. Unfortunately, this is not possible in a book.

Selecting the tests was not easy. Firstly, I restricted them to English tests. Secondly, I wanted good quality, professionally made tests. These are all excellent tests in their different ways. Thirdly, I wanted to show a variety of approaches to testing listening, including both the US and British traditions, less 'communicative' tests as well as more 'communicative' ones, and a test developed in a foreign-language environment.

Test of English for International Communication

The Test of English for International Communication (TOEIC) was developed by Educational Testing Service (ETS), and is now owned by Chauncey Group International, a subsidiary of ETS.

The TOEIC test is often referred to as a test of business English, but the publishers are very careful not to make such a claim. They state that TOEIC scores indicate how well people can communicate in English in the global workplace. The TOEIC is a huge testing programme, with 1.8 million candidates in 2000 – mainly in Asia. Although the test covers a wide ability range, the target group is probably best described as lower intermediate level, or more precisely the Council of Europe Common European Framework Level B1. The items reviewed here are from a the practice test in the TOEIC Official Test – Preparation Guide (Arbogast *et al.*, 2000).

Overall design

It is fair to say that the TOEIC is a classic multiple-choice language test in the US testing tradition. It is a test of language comprehension, and does not assess productive skills. It has two main sections: Listening, with 100 multiple-choice items, and Reading, also with 100 multiple-choice items. The two sections are reported on separate scales, so the listening test can be regarded as a separate, independent test. The listening section takes about 45 minutes, and has the following four parts:

Part	Task type	No.	Task description
1	statement evaluation	20	test-takers look at a picture, listen to four statements, and select the picture referred to
2	response evaluation	30	test-takers listen to a question followed by three alternative responses, and choose the best one
3	comprehension questions on dialogue	30	test-takers listen to a short dialogue and answer four-option multiple-choice questions
4	comprehension questions on mini-talks	20	test-takers listen to a short mini-talk and answer four-option multiple-choice questions

Texts

The texts are very short. Parts 1 and 2 are simple statements or questions. Part 3 consists of dialogues with the same format: Speaker A, Speaker B, and Speaker A again. Part 4 consists of short mini-talks. They are all in informal, or semi-formal, work-related situations. The bulk of the topics relate to work: office routine, manufacturing, personnel, purchasing, travel and so on. The texts are carefully scripted, and then read in a very slow, deliberate manner with careful pronunciation – the speakers sound more like announcers than actors. The texts have very few oral features: they have little phonological modification, virtually no hesitation phenomena, they do not use word choice or structures typical of spoken language, and the texts are too short to include many discourse features. They are correct, semi-formal written language, read aloud.

Before becoming too critical of the use of written language in large-scale listening tests, it is important to realise why this happens. Basically, large testing programmes need to develop an efficient, cost-effective process for the ongoing production of new versions of their tests. They do this by creating a large pool of standardised items. Test-developers then take their detailed test specifications, and go into the pool to find the right balance of suitable test items. It is far easier, and much cheaper, to store the items – that is, the text with the attached questions – in written form in a simple data-base, and then record the texts after the items have been selected, and the test assembled. It takes a lot of time and energy to select items with the right balance of characteristics, and when recording the texts, test-developers try not to change the characteristics of the item in any way, so they record the texts as carefully as they can. The result of this system is cheap, efficient test construction. The system works very well for reading or grammar tests, for which it was developed, but not so well for listening tests.

The solution, as we saw in Chapter 6, is to start item development with a spoken text, and design the task from that. This is quite feasible with modern technology. Due to increases in computer storage capacity, there is no reason why item pools should not contain the complete task, recorded text and all.

The tasks

The tasks all use the standard three- or four-option multiple-choice format. Parts 1 and 2 can be answered without reading, whereas Parts 3 and 4 require some reading. Given the huge number of candidates, and the need to keep prices low, the test publishers realistically have no alternative but to use machine-scorable responses. Traditionally that meant selected responses, although recent advances in optical scanning devices and natural language processing allow the prospect of machine-scorable constructed responses. However, the TOEIC is administered world-wide, and needs to be scored at a number of local centres, and the use of expensive scanning devices may not be practical.

Even if the test is restricted to selected responses, it might make sense from a measurement perspective to include a wider variety of item formats. However, it is probably too late; test-users tend to be very conservative, and scores need to mean what they have always meant, and so on a practical level, it would be very difficult for the TOEIC programme to change the test format.

Part 1

Test-takers look at a picture and hear four statements. They choose the one that best describes the picture.

Q1. Test-takers look at a picture of two women working at an office desk; one is using a computer keyboard.

They hear:

    (a) the transaction has been completed.

    (b) they're filling out the forms by hand.

    (c) the woman is using the keyboard.

    (d) they're watching a programme on television.

Q11. Test-takers look at a picture of a woman cutting another woman's hair.

They hear:

    (a) her work hours have been cut.

    (b) she's finished clipping out the article.

    (c) there's not much air in this room

    (d) she's giving the person a haircut.

If the four options are understood on a literal linguistic level, they are so different in meaning that matching the statement to the picture should be very obvious. In order to catch test-takers who do not understand well, but who might be able to recognise items of vocabulary, the incorrect options often mention an object that is in the picture, whereas the correct options rarely do. For example, in the picture for Q1, the two women are clearly transacting some business, and there are some forms on the table, and there is a computer screen. Looking at the incorrect options, it is clear that they all have some connection to the picture. This is one way item writers construct incorrect options, and a good test-taking strategy would be to avoid choosing any option that has words which overlap with objects in the picture.

Part 2

Test-takers hear a question, followed by three alternative responses. They choose the best response.

Q21. Test-takers hear:

    M1: *when was Mr. Chen born?*

    M2: *(a) in Hong Kong.*

        (b) since last June.

        (c) in 1958.

Q31. Test-takers hear:

    F: *what are your total production figures for this factory?*

    M: *(a) we produce pharmaceuticals.*

        (b) over 1000 units a week.

        (c) in the shipping department.

As in the previous section, if test-takers understand the meaning on a literal linguistic level, there should be no difficulty choosing the correct option. This response-evaluation format lends itself very well to testing inferences, such as indirect speech acts, pragmatic implications or other aspects of interactive language use, but the TOEIC does not attempt to assess these.

Part 3

Comprehending dialogues: test-takers hear a short conversation between two people, and then read a four-option multiple-choice question and select the best answer.

Q51. Test-takers hear:

> F1: *i left a telephone message on your desk.*
> F2: *oh, did Mr. Murphy's secretary call again?*
> F1: *yes. she said the committee meeting is set for Tuesday.*

Test-takers read:

> Who called and left a message?
>   (a) Mr. Murphy.
>   (b) The operator.
>   (c) Mr. Murphy's secretary.
>   (d) The committee chairperson.

Q61. Test-takers hear:

> M: *i've heard nothing but praise for that new health food restaurant.*
> F: *same here. and i've got a coupon for the salad bar. buy one get one free.*
> M: *i'm always looking to save some money. let's check it out for lunch.*

Test-takers read:

> What are they likely to eat for lunch?
>   (a) Soup.
>   (b) Salad.
>   (c) Sandwiches.
>   (d) Hamburgers.

Q51 is very straightforward, and only requires understanding explicitly stated information; the distractors are things that might be attractive to a listener with partial comprehension. But in Q61 there is no explicit statement that they will eat salad: only her statement that she had a coupon for a cheap salad lunch for two people, which is really an offer, and his reply that he likes to save money, which obviously implies that he will accept her offer and go for the cheap option of the salad bar. This is a simple, and rather elegant, inference item.

Part 4

Test-takers listen to short monologues and answer comprehension questions.

Test-takers hear:

> *it is my pleasure to introduce you to the world-renowned photojournalist Michiko Suzuki. a native of Japan, Ms Suzuki has been working in Australia for the past three years as a staff photographer for the Sydney News Journal. i am very pleased that Ms Suzuki has agreed to join our magazine for six months before she takes her next long-term assignment in Brazil. she'll be working closely with our staff, sharing some of the secrets of her innovative techniques.*

They read:

Q90. What is Ms Suzuki's profession?
   (a) Photographer.
   (b) Magazine editor.
   (c) Advertising director.
   (d) Newspaper publisher.

Q91. Where was Ms Suzuki's most recent assignment?
   (a) Australia.
   (b) Japan.
   (c) Brazil.
   (d) The United States.

The items in this section are assessing the ability to understand explicitly stated information. In Q90, there are two explicit cues regarding her profession: the statement that she is a photojournalist, and the statement that she worked as a staff photographer. Q91 also requires understanding explicitly stated information, namely that '*has been working in . . . for the past three years*' has the same meaning as her '*most recent assignment*'.

Summary

There seems to be little doubt that this test is measuring the ability to understand carefully spoken English, on a literal, local, semantic level. There are few tasks that require inferencing or understanding implications, there are virtually no tasks requiring any discourse processing, and certainly no sociolinguistic processing. Furthermore, the test is not assessing many of the oral characteristics that make spoken language unique: there is very little fast speech, no phonological modification, no hesitation and no negotiation of meaning between the interlocutors.

The test content mainly takes place in a business or work environment, and that does require a small amount of specialist vocabulary: fax machines, managers, staff and so forth, but this is general vocabulary from the domain of office work. The TOEIC is not a test of English for special purposes.

Although the TOEIC is obviously a listening test, in the sense that it requires test-takers to listen and understand, it is not a test of the listening construct, in the sense that it measures what is most characteristic of listening. It mainly requires processing sentences on a literal semantic level, and might be best described as a test of general grammatical competence through the oral mode. While many will feel this too narrow a construct for a test of general listening proficiency, the TOEIC is cheap and reliable, and it measures this narrow construct efficiently and well.

Test of English as a Foreign Language

The Test of English as a Foreign Language (TOEFL) is published by Educational Testing Service (ETS). The test was first developed at the height of the discrete-point testing movement. However, it has been through a number of major revisions, including the move to computer-based delivery, and it is clearly not a discrete-point test. Its prime use is to assess the language skills of non-native applicants to US universities, although the publishers are careful not to call it a test of academic English. It is widely used as a general proficiency test, and the testing programme is large. In 1997–98, a total of 900,000 people registered for the test, although it has since been computerised. The test covers a wide range of ability levels, intermediate to upper intermediate, probably Council of Europe Common European Framework Level B2 to C1. Although the TOEFL reports a total score, which is the score that is intended for most decision-making purposes, the score on the listening section is reported separately to the test-taker.

In this section I will evaluate the practice test downloadable from the TOEFL web-site (ETS, http://www.toefl.org).

Overall design

The computer-based version of the TOEFL has three sections: Listening, Reading and Structure, with the Listening and Structure sections being computer adaptive. This means the number of items is not fixed, but the computer continues selecting and administering items until it has a sufficiently accurate measure of the test-taker's ability. There are two parts to the listening section – short dialogues and longer lecture- or seminar-style texts.

Part	Task type	No.	Task description
1	comprehending short dialogues	n/a	test-takers listen to short dialogues, while looking at a picture of the participants, and then answer multiple-choice questions
2	comprehending lectures	n/a	test-takers listen to simulated lectures or interactive seminars, while looking at pictures of the participants, and then respond to multiple-choice questions

Texts

The texts are clearly carefully scripted, with very few oral features. The speech is a little slow and deliberate, with careful pronunciation. There is little phonological modification. The speakers do not attempt to act or animate the text, but just to read it rather slowly and carefully. The content of the seminar text is explained very carefully, with much rather unnatural redundancy, without natural hesitations and a discourse structure quite inappropriate for that type of speech event. The texts are heard only once.

The sound is digitised, and some form of compression has been used to make the file sizes smaller. Played on good quality equipment, the sound quality varied: the best was just adequate, but the worst sounded rather too 'muddy'. As a native English speaker, I could understand, but second-language listeners, struggling near the limit of their ability, might find the sound quality affects their comprehension. The sound might be much worse on small computer speakers or poor-quality headphones.

Tasks

Given the huge volume of TOEFL test-takers, there really is no alternative to machine-scorable, selected responses, and traditionally the TOEFL has used the four-option multiple-choice format. Obviously the computer-based test also requires machine scoring, but the computer is very versatile, and is capable of administering a variety of different item formats: two new ones are included which were not in the paper-and-pencil version of the test. One new item type requires choosing more than one option to a question, and the other requires moving statements or words into boxes or ordering them into lists. This increased variety of item types will surely reduce the effects of any one test method.

However, from a construct perspective, the greatest innovation of the computer-based test is the introduction of visual support for the texts. This is in the form of still pictures. For example, when a student is asking his teacher a question, as in the first text in Part 2 below, listeners see a picture of a student talking to an older woman. In the case of longer texts, a sequence of pictures is shown, and when the speaker changes, there is a picture of the new speaker. The pictures are designed not to provide information that would help select the correct response – all the relevant information is intended to come from listening to the text – but they do provide background and surely encourage the listeners to activate relevant schema. Furthermore, without the pictures, listeners would be left staring at the blank screen, and this provides a focus for their attention.

However, there can be a problem if the pictures are not entirely appropriate. In the first example from Part 1 below, the picture is of a male student talking to a female student just inside a door. The text makes it plain that she has just come in, and she is complaining about the very strong winds outside. Yet she looks serene and unruffled, with her hair uncovered and perfectly in place – not normally the picture of someone who has just come in from a strong wind. Perhaps this would lead some test-takers to doubt their understanding.

Part 1

Test-takers hear a number of short conversations between two people, each followed by a written multiple-choice question – note that they do not know the questions before listening to the texts.

Test-takers see a male and female student talking to each other just inside a door. They hear:

    M: *how are you*

    F: *okay i guess but the wind is so strong i could hardly make it here from the bus stop*

    M: *thank goodness it isn't a cold day.*

Test-takers hear and read the question, read the options, and reply.

    Q1. What does the man imply?

        (a) The woman should not be out of breath.

        (b) The weather could be worse.

        (c) The bus must have been late.

        (d) He is glad the woman's cold is not severe.

Test-takers see a picture of a male and female student sitting in a lounge. They hear:

    M: *Tina's doing much better in her biology class isn't she*

    F: *yes she's really come a long way.*

Test-takers hear and read the question, read the options, and reply.

    Q2. What does the man say about Tina?

        (a) She has made a lot of progress.

        (b) She was always good in biology

        (c) She travels a long distance to class.

        (d) She has been studying biology for hours.

Q1 requires understanding the pragmatic implication of his statement, but in a way that is clearly constrained by the text. Q2 requires test-takers to understand clearly stated information and then to match that to an option that means the same thing, but in completely different words.

Part 2

This part consists of several talks, seminars or lectures, on a variety of topics. Each one is followed by a number of questions. In the example below, test-takers listen to a group discussion in a linguistics seminar. A voice (the same voice that asks the questions) introduces the situation to orientate the students.

Test-takers see a series of pictures of a group of people around a large table, and then pictures of individuals as they speak. Note that they have not yet seen the questions.

> **Voice:** *listen to a discussion in a linguistics class. the class has been discussing the history of the English language. today the professor will be talking about changes in vocabulary. he'll focus on the English spoken in the British colonies in North America.*

> **M1:** *as you can imagine, colonialisation opens up a wide range of possibilities for expanding the vocabulary of a language. this was certainly the case for the English spoken in Great Britain's North America colonies. so today i want you to try to imagine what the colonists would have encountered upon landing. obviously there'd be a lot of things they didn't have words for. can anyone think of an example. uh yes Denise?*

> **F1:** *well wouldn't they find new animals and plants they hadn't seen before?*

> **M1:** *yes that's a good example. now let's imagine ourselves as colonists encountering a new plant or animal. remember there's no English word for it. what are we gonna do. yes Phil?*

> **M2:** *well you could just ask the people there, uh assuming of course that they speak English . . . which they probably don't.*

> **M1:** *well pointing and saying your word for something usually works pretty well. and the colonists did get words for things from the native North Americans. some names of common animals come to mind, for example, uh the words for moose or skunk. yes Denise?*

> **F1:** *you could also just make up a word.*

> **M1:** *i suppose you could. but apparently not many people did, as far as we know today anyway. what the colonists actually did do was make up combinations of familiar words, for example bullfrog and groundhog. there was another interesting strategy the colonists adopted and that was to take a word for a familiar thing, and apply it to an unfamiliar thing. but of course, the two things had to resemble each other somehow. can anyone think of an example? yes, Phil?*

> **M2:** *well i spent some time in England and i think the robins there are different from the ones here.*

> **M1:** *correct Phil. the two species are related, but not identical. in fact they are different sizes. the same goes for rabbits by the way. the american cotton tail rabbit is a completely different species from the rabbits you find in England, but i guess they must have looked enough like the old ones to the colonists. yet another example you find of this sort is the word corn. i find this example fascinating because corn is a general word used by the british at the time to refer to the principal grain of a region.*

Test-takers hear and read the questions, read the options, and reply.

Q8. Why did the British colonists in North America add new words to English?

    (a) To be independent.

    (b) To start a new language.

    (c) To sound more like native North Americans.

    (d) To name unfamiliar objects.

Q9. What is probably true about robins found in North America?

    (a) They are the same size as the robins found in England.

    (b) They belong to the same species as the robins found in England.

    (c) They resemble the robins found in England.

    (d) They are not called robins by people who live in England.

Q10 How did the words below come into English?
Click on a word. Then click on the empty box in the correct column.

bullfrog	**moose**	**rabbit**
Borrowed from native North Americans	New combinations of familiar English words	New meanings given to familiar English words

Q11. What can be inferred about the word corn?
Click on 2 answers.

    ☐ It was borrowed from the native North Americans.

    ☐ It referred to a different food in North America than it did in England.

    ☐ It was made up by the British colonists in North America.

    ☐ It had been part of the British vocabulary before the British colonists lived in North America.

Regarding the text, not only does the language lack typical oral features, but the interaction is also very unnatural. There is not one wasted word, not one personal touch, nothing to indicate that these are human beings interacting. This is not how people interact, and this discourse lacks situational authenticity as a piece of academic English.

Regarding the questions, we must remember that the test-takers do not know them before they listen, and this obviously has a considerable effect on the skills involved. Test-takers have no clear purpose for listening – except to do well on the test, of course – so we have to assume that they are just trying to understand what the teacher is saying, and remember as much as they can. So to be fair, tasks can only focus on the main points, or anything which falls within the main flow of ideas, and questions on small details or irrelevant asides would probably be unfair, and would likely not work well anyway.

Q8 asks why the colonists needed new words, and as this is the main point underlying the whole discussion, test-takers should have understood this. Q9 asks what is probably true about robins in North America, and although it seems likely that option *(c)* *'They resemble the robins found in England'* is the correct choice, it is not clearly and obviously correct. Many test-takers may want to examine each of the other options, and make comparisons between them, to ensure that they are less desirable, and that involves metacognitive processing skills. Q9 also requires a good understanding of the text, and perhaps also a good memory for all the details about the robin.

Q10 requires understanding a number of pieces of information that are clearly stated in the text; in fact these were all explicit examples given by the teacher. If test-takers have understood well and also remembered well, they should have no difficulty replying. However, does the item require too much memory? The issue is whether everyone who has understood the text would have remembered all these examples. Would it be possible for a test-taker to understand the speaker's main point, automatically and well, but still not re-member the details? I am not sure, and I would like to check the item analysis for this item. The final item, Q11, is similar in that it depends on test-takers remembering all the details about the word *'corn'*. Again it is unclear to me whether this falls within the main flow of ideas, or requires memory for trivial details.

Summary

One of the important characteristics of the TOEFL construct is that in most cases, test-takers do not know why they are listening, and all questions must be answered based on the test-takers' memory of the text. If they misunderstand the purpose of the speaker, or were dis-tracted by the content, they are stuck with their inadequate memory. As an example, I was very engaged by the content of the seminar text. While listening I was not quietly absorbing what the speaker said, but thinking about it, evaluating it, and actively disagreeing with the speaker in some cases. This is what academic listening should be, but I missed some of his points because I was thinking about what he was saying. As a result, I could not answer some of the questions. My failure to answer the questions does not indicate a lack of listening ability – quite the opposite. Perhaps it would be sensible to allow test-takers to see the questions before listening, so they could better focus on the task requirements.

In terms of what the TOEFL items measure, Part 1 not only assesses basic grammatical knowledge, but also assesses the ability to make pragmatic inferences. In the case of the longer texts in Part 2, these will obviously assess important aspects of grammatical knowledge as well as discourse knowledge, and pragmatic knowledge. These are important parts of the listening construct. The test also seems to require some metacognitive processing skills that are associated with the test method, and this may add a little construct-irrelevant variance.

In addition, I think there are a number of significant omissions from the test. Firstly, the oral features of spoken texts – phonology, hesitations and the discourse structures typical of unplanned spoken language – are almost entirely absent. Secondly, although there is a reasonably clear target-language use situation, the English used in US colleges and universities, there is no attempt to test relevant socio-linguistic competence, such as understanding the informal language of US students, nor to require test-takers to relate what they have understood to a context or situation.

The TOEFL is clearly a professionally made test, with some very expertly crafted items. It assesses many important aspects of the listening construct – far more than just grammar and vocabulary – but it does fail to assess many of those aspects of listening comprehension that make listening unique. As a high-stakes test of English in an academic environment, the listening section suffers from obvious construct underrepresentation.

First Certificate in English

The First Certificate in English (FCE) is published by the University of Cambridge Local Examinations Syndicate (UCLES). It is a typical representative of the British language-testing tradition. It is a general English test, and 80 per cent of test-takers take the FCE at the end of a course of English study. The test has come to define the English curriculum for a considerable number of English language schools world-wide. The test is at the intermediate level, approximately Level B2 on the Council of Europe Common European Framework scale. The form discussed here is the December 1998 paper. This is not a stand-alone test, and the listening scores are not reported separately, but are used as one part of a grade describing overall language ability.

Overall design

The test has five sections: Reading, Writing, Use of English, Listening and Speaking. The Listening section lasts about 40 minutes and has four parts:

Part	Task type	No.	Task description
1	comprehension questions on short texts	8	test-takers listen to monologues or interactions, about 30 sec long, and answer three-option multiple-choice questions
2	note taking or blank filling	10	test-takers listen to a monologue or interactions, approximately 3 min long, and complete statements or fill in missing information
3	multiple matching	5	test-takers listen to a series of short monologues or interactions, about 30 sec long, and select a short summary from a list of summary statements
4	comprehension questions on a longer text	7	test-takers listen to a 3 min monologue, or interaction, and then answer multiple-choice questions

Texts

The first thing to note is that the texts are all presented twice. I discussed the arguments for and against this in Chapter 6. Test-users have now come to expect this as standard practice, and UCLES is probably no longer free to change this.

The recordings are carefully planned, user friendly and very professionally made. The texts are fully scripted, and then recorded by professional actors. The speech is quite fast, with some phonological modification, and there are a variety of mild regional accents. The speakers are animated and expressive, and most listeners would probably regard them as reasonably authentic. However, they do not have many false starts or other hesitation phenomena, and the discourse structure is more coherent and has tighter organisation than most spoken discourse. The impression is very much reminiscent of good-quality radio drama.

Tasks

There are only 30 listening items, which would probably not be enough for a high-stakes, stand-alone listening test, but the listening section of the test is not intended to stand on its own. Although there are not many items, each one is based on comprehension of a reasonable amount of text, and so each item tends to provide quite a lot of information.

Three of the four parts use three-option multiple-choice questions. This means that test-takers who guess the correct answer will have a 33 per cent chance of getting the items correct. The simple way to reduce the effect of guessing is to use more items, or to offer more options, and offering a fourth option seems likely to increase the reliability of the test. However, it often proves difficult finding an effective fourth option, and three good options will certainly work as well as three good options plus one poor one. Part 2 does allow test-takers to construct their own responses, although it places tight constraints on what they can produce. The tasks are designed to focus on a wide variety of skills: understanding detail as well as understanding gist, processing explicit information as well as making inferences. The test-takers are given the tasks before they listen, so in all cases they have a clear listening purpose.

Part 1

Test-takers first hear a short statement that sets up the situation, followed by the question and three alternative answers. These are also written in the test-booklet. Then the test-takers hear the text, which is repeated a second time, after which they choose the best answer. Here are the first two items:

Q1. Test-takers hear as well as read the following. They then hear the text:
In a cafe, you overhear this man talk to a friend. Who is the speaker?
   (a) a policeman
   (b) a journalist
   (c) a shop assistant

i was coming out of a book shop about lunchtime when i saw two men run out of the bank carrying a bag. they jumped into a black car which must have been waiting for them. i took down the registration number and car description in my notebook before they disappeared. i was lucky to be in the right place at the right time huh. my boss was really pleased and i got my story on the front page for a change.

The text is repeated. Then test-takers select a response.

Q2. Test-takers hear as well as read the following. They then hear the text:
You hear part of a radio report about an accident. Where did it happen?
   (a) on a bridge
   (b) on an island
   (c) on a road by the sea

and i'm standing here right at the scene and it's much quieter now the heavy lifting machinery has gone. but the thing is that the coast road has been very busy all weekend with lots of people coming over to the island for the day. the main problem now is that they all want to get back to the mainland with their cars and the little ferry can only carry ten at a time. the authorities have said that although the bridge is now clear, no one can drive over until its walls have been declared safe. which wont happen before to-morrow. so it looks like a night on the island for many of them.

The text is repeated. Then test-takers select a response.

These are very interesting items. The answers are not explicitly provided in the text, but require some thought and an inference based on information from more than one place in the text, as well as some background knowledge. In Q1 test-takers have to know what journalists do, for example, and some knowledge of bridges and ferries would help in Q2. However, this seems a reasonable level of background knowledge, given the target test-takers.

Part 2

Test-takers read the questions, listen to the text, and answer the questions. Below is the first half of the talk, with the first four questions:

Test-takers read the following questions.
  9. Emily's childhood and background were not very _____
  10. Unlike her brothers, she was educated _____
  11. With her tutor, she travelled around _____
  12 She then produced _____

Then they listen to the following text.

> in this talk i want to consider the work of Emily Morris, but before we
> study anything written by her it is important to know about her as a
> person i think. she was born in Manchester in eighteen fifty-four and died
> in London in nineteen thirty-four. as for her background, it was not a
> particularly unusual one yet it is most important. she was the only
> daughter of quite rich parents. her father was a tea merchant at a time
> when tea was growing in popularity, and he did well. her mother died
> when she was two. Emily was the youngest child by some eight years. she
> had three brothers. they were all sent away to school as was quite normal
> at that time of course. Emily remained at home, saw very little of them,
> and had a very lonely childhood in many ways. however she had a good
> education at home particularly from one teacher a French woman called
> Sophie Durant. and with her she toured Southern Europe and often
> spoke of this as the most exciting time of her life. from this time came her
> first books, not novels but three travel books. they were published but
> didn't sell well. although they are in fact very good indeed and of course
> have been republished since.

The text is repeated. Then test-takers write their responses.

Such longer texts will obviously require discourse skills, although the
items do not focus on discourse variables *per se*. Q9, Q10 and Q11 ask
for clearly stated information, and test-takers need to be searching for
that as they listen. Q12 requires test-takers to identify something the
speaker produced after her trip to Europe, but they will have no idea
what sort of thing they are searching for – a book, a child or what?
When they hear that she put out three travel books, they have to
realise that this is the information the question is targeting, and that
may not be immediately clear. This item may work well, or not, and it
would be interesting to look at the item analysis.

Part 3

Test-takers hear five people (Speakers 1–5) explaining why they like
going on holiday alone, without family or friends. They must match
each speaker with a summary statement A–F. They read the state-

ments first, then listen to the whole recording twice. The first two speakers are given below.

Test-takers read:

A. sometimes got fed up with other holiday-makers	Speaker 1 _____ (19)
B. enjoyed holidaying alone more than they expected	Speaker 2 _____ (20)
C. preferred to stay in the same hotel as before	Speaker 3 _____ (21)
D. liked meeting a wide variety of people	Speaker 4 _____ (22)
E. like having something in common with other holiday-makers	Speaker 5 _____ (23)
F. found someone to talk to if they wanted to	

Speaker 1
well i think you make more of an effort to see things and do things when you're on your own. and of course you get to know people. the world's full of people who are travelling. people of all backgrounds and ages. last year in Malaysia i met a sixty-five year-old woman who'd just got divorced and had promised herself she would see the world. we still write to each other. that's the sort of thing that makes it worthwhile.

Speaker 2
my colleagues at work seem to think it must be very lonely and i get irritated by that. i mean . . . yes of course there comes a time when you want to have a chat or point out something interesting but you can do that anyway. you're usually so excited about what you are doing that you can't help turning round and saying 'did you see that waterfall?' or whatever to whoever happens to be standing there.

In terms of comprehension, the task requires test-takers to make a summary, or extract the gist, of each monologue. However, selecting the response requires complex processing: comparing their own summary of each speaker with each written summary statement, perhaps revising their own summaries, and then selecting which summary fits which statement best. The texts are relatively easy to understand, but superficially a number of the statements could refer to more than one speaker. For example, the correct response for Speaker 1 is D, she likes meeting a wide variety of people. However, she also found someone to talk to when she wanted to, which means F is a possibility, and if she socialises with other people, she probably likes having things in common with other people, so E needs to be considered. As I listened to the other speakers, some of them fitted the summary statements much better. On the first listening, I made some of the matches, and on the second listening I matched the remaining speakers to the statements. Obviously a variety of meta-cognitive strategies are involved in task completion, and this complex task processing may introduce construct-irrelevant variance.

Part 4

Test-takers hear a reporter talking about a visit to a town. They are given time to read the questions, and then they listen to the text twice. The first half of the text is given below, along with the first three questions.

Test-takers read the following questions.
What does Linda say about . . .

24. the car parks?
    (a) There are not enough of them.
    (b) They are too far from the city centre.
    (c) They are rather small.

25. the shopping area?
    (a) It is too busy.
    (b) It is easy to find one's way around.
    (c) It offers plenty of variety.

26. the park?
    (a) It is as good as people claim.
    (b) It is unsafe for young children.
    (c) It has a lot of strict rules.

Then they listen to the following text:

Announcer: *now here's Linda Watson who's been to Finstowe. Linda did you have a good trip?*

Linda: *well yes i did thank you. i went last Saturday by car and i had a pretty good time, even though it's well into the busy season. i did phone ahead to the tourist office and followed their advice to use one of the car parks on the edge of the city which have regular buses to the centre so it saves queuing into a central car park which can take ages. it is a good system, but you must be prepared to try more than one car park, because they are not big so they fill up fast. but there are six, so you're bound to find a space eventually.*

anyway, having reached the centre i decided first to have a look around the shops in case they got packed out later on. it's no

problem finding where you want to go because they've got the same
sort of shops mostly on the same streets, like there are shoe shops
on New Street, household goods in London Road, clothes in Market
Street and whatever.

The text is repeated. Then they select a response.

This task again requires listeners to listen for specific information in a longer text. However, the information is provided in a synonymous form. For example, in Q24 the correct option says they are *'rather small'* but in the text they are described as *'not big so they fill up fast'*. Q25 also requires matching option (b) *'It is easy to find one's way around'* with the description of why it was easy to get around.

Summary

This is clearly a well designed and professionally crafted test. However, the tasks often require reasoning, and it is not clear to me whether the metacognitive strategies required for task completion should be part of the listening construct, or whether they stray into general cognitive abilities, or intelligence even. The advantage is that this requires the listener to focus cognitive resources on the task, not the language, which means that the processing of the language has to be completely automatic, but is this at the cost of some construct-irrelevant variance?

The texts are reasonably authentic: they are fast, with some phonological modification, and they are long enough for discourse knowledge to be an important variable. Yet they have far fewer oral features than most target-language use texts: I would like to see more hesitations, more spoken grammar and more spoken vocabulary choice. However, on a practical level, it is difficult to use spontaneous texts and still to design tasks that depend on manipulating subtle meanings. There is no specific target-language use situation, although looking at the topics, it is probably fair to call it something like general educated English use.

As for the components of listening ability, this is definitely listening in the wider sense of going beyond the linguistic information to understanding implications or inferred meanings. Basic grammatical knowledge is assessed, and the tasks do require automatic and efficient processing; discourse knowledge also seems to be well covered through the fact that test-takers need to be able to follow longer texts to find the information they need. Many of the questions require inferences, and some require understanding the functions of particular statements, both of which are aspects of pragmatic knowledge. Finally, while sociolinguistic knowledge is certainly difficult to address in a test that has world-wide usage, there are a number of different accents, some figures of speech and perhaps even some idiomatic expressions.

The Finnish National Foreign Language Certificate: English Intermediate Level

The Finnish National Language Certificates are for use in Finland and intended to measure the functional language proficiency of adults in a variety of languages at beginning, intermediate and advanced levels. I will examine the intermediate English test (Mock Examination Two). The scores are reported on a nine-band scale, and the intermediate level is centred at about Level B2 on the Council of Europe Common European Framework scale.

Overall design

The test has five sections: Reading, Writing, Listening, Speaking and finally Structure and Vocabulary. The score on each part is reported separately. The listening section has four parts:

Part	Task type	No.	Task format
1	short-answer questions	7	test-takers listen to a series of short texts, usually dialogues, and write responses to open-ended comprehension questions in Finnish
2	gap-filling	10	test-takers listen to an information text, twice, and then fill in an information grid
3	short-answer questions	7	test-takers listen to a longer text just once, and answer open-ended comprehension question during pauses
4	summaries	4	test-takers listen to a news item twice, then answer summary-style questions

The test covers general daily topics: such as home, family, work, relationships, society, health etc. as well as common functions, such as giving and asking for directions, expressing a point of view, communication management, general social situations etc.

Texts

Generally the texts are not good examples of spoken language, and lack typical oral features. They are scripted, and read by people who do not have good acting skills.

Part 1 consists of interactions between people who are supposed to know each other, but who speak in a slow, rather stilted fashion, with unnaturally clear pronunciation. Sometimes the speakers over-correct their speech by pronouncing sounds that would normally be silent. In Part 2, the speakers are more realistic: recordings of movie times for a cinema are often made by amateurs, so might reasonably have amateurish defects, and playing the text twice is certainly situationally authentic. Parts 3 and 4 were at reasonably normal speeds, although they were quite formal.

Most of the voices appear to be non-native speakers of English, presumably Finnish, but with high levels of competence in English – which seems quite appropriate given the use of the test. The pronunciation, stress and intonation are slightly non-native, but this is hardly noticeable, and falls well within the bounds of standard English.

Tasks

The first thing to note about the tasks is that the questions and the responses are all in Finnish. Presumably the first-language requirements of these tasks are not likely to be challenging to the test-takers, so this will not affect task difficulty. Further, the tasks all require constructed responses, so test-takers will not be involved in the complex metacognitive processes of comparing and evaluating a variety of options. This suggests that the tasks will have comparatively little construct-irrelevant variance arising from test-method effects. Some of the texts are played twice, and these are the ones that ask for details, whereas the texts that are played once ask for main ideas. This is a rather nice solution to the dilemma of whether to play the texts once or twice.

Part 1

Test-takers hear a series of short texts, usually dialogues, and write responses to open-ended comprehension questions in Finnish. They have time to look at the questions, before listening, after which they hear the texts just once. The first three questions are from the second passage.

Test-takers hear:

> *hi it's me, Jane. i just called to let you know that we're all right, but nowhere near your house yet. it's now half-past four and it will take another two hours for us to get there. we got lost in the woods. Markku thought he knew a shortcut, but apparently he didn't, so we spent more than an hour totally lost in the middle of nowhere. but finally we made it back on a dirt road, three kilometres from where we left our car. anyway, we have about twenty litres of blueberries with us, and we'll give you some when we get back. thanks for watching the kids for us, and tell them we're all right and we will be there before seven.*

They read the following questions, and compose a reply, all in Finnish.
  (3) When will the caller come back?
  (4) What has happened?
  (5) What had the caller been doing while away?

Test-takers will listen for the specific information. The questions focus on the main points of the texts. So test-takers who have understood the text should be able to answer easily, even if they did not listen for the specific information. Q5 is interesting. The text does not explicitly say that they had been collecting blueberries in the woods, they could have logically bought them in a store, but the inference would probably be quite obvious to everyone in Finland.

Part 2

In this part, test-takers listen to a recording of movie times at a movie theatre, and fill in the relevant information on a grid. The grid is in English, although the language is very simple. Test-takers look at the questions, and then listen to the recording twice.

Test-takers hear:

> *this is the Arena box office. the box office is open Mondays through Sundays from four P-M to ten P-M. this week's films are. Arena One. Too Far to Go. performances start six-thirty P-M on weekdays, and five-thirty*

P-M and seven-thirty P-M on weekends. Arena Two. The Space Traveller.
performances start at six forty-five P-M on weekdays, and five forty-five
and seven forty-five on weekends. Arena Three. Three Colours Blue with
English subtitles. performances daily at six P-M. Arena Four. The Time of
My Life. performances daily at six-fifteen P-M and eight-fifteen on week-
ends. this weeks Arena Four night performance is The Blade Runner
starting at ten-thirty P-M daily.

They hear the recording immediately again, and then fill in information
on the grid.

Arena 1: Too Far to Go.
Performances: weekdays _____ pm (8)
                weekends 5:30 and _____ pm (9)

Arena 2: The Space Traveller
Performances: weekdays _____ pm (10)
                weekends _____ pm (11) and _____ pm (12)

Arena 3: Three Colours Blue
With English _____ (13)
Performances: _____ (14)

Arena 4: _____ (15)
Performances: daily at 6:15 pm
+ weekends 8:15

Arena _____ night performance: The Blade Runner (16)
This week daily at _____ pm (17)

Seven of the blanks can be filled by entering explicitly stated times,
and the content of the remaining two is also explicitly stated. The
only question that seems likely to cause any problem is Q13, which
seems to require the response 'subtitles'. I could imagine some test-
takers would consider that subtitles are already included in the
concept of an English film and as a result not be sure of what information to put in the blank. However, during the second listening they
will probably realise that there is nothing else that can go into the
blank. It would be interesting to see the item analysis for this item, to
see whether it was working well or not.

Part 3

In this part test-takers listen to a longer text. They are given time to
look at the questions, and then hear the text once. The recording will

stop at some points, and test-takers answer the questions by writing their responses in Finnish. Here are the first two sections of the text.

Test-takers hear:

> *well after fifteen years in the States it always takes me a while to get comfortable speaking Finnish back here. it's pretty frustrating. when i'm in the U-S i often feel like uh my English is not good enough, and then when i'm back here i'm constantly at a loss for words when trying to speak Finnish. that would be pretty frustrating to anyone huh? i've been back here for only a week now, so i'll probably switch over to Finnish in about a week or so. i guess that's what my brain takes, two weeks, to adjust to being here.*

Test-takers read the following questions, and then have about 40 seconds to compose a response.

(18) What does the speaker say about her language in Finland and in the US?

Then test-takers hear:

> *it's been three years since my last visit and it sure feels good to be back. it's always so nice to see relatives. my little cousins have grown up so fast and my grandparents are getting very old. you know it seems like so much has happened. but on the other hand nothing has happened. they still talk about the recession and nothing has come out of it. and there are still people who demand Carelia to Finland. and the Bold and the Beautiful is still so popular. i remember when it started because i was here for my grandma's birthday. it was January twentieth nineteen ninety-two and my grandma became an instant fan of the show.*

Test-takers read the following questions, and then have about 60 seconds to compose their responses.

(19) Mention two things that have not changed while the woman has been away.

(20) What happened to her grandmother on her 80th birthday in 1992?

The tasks in this section seem to require a number of things. Q18 requires a summary of the main point of that section. The information is explicitly stated, but not given in one succinct repeatable statement – it is spread over a number of statements that supplement each other to make the point. Presumably the speaker must understand all these statements, as well as the relationship between them and how they all function to make the point. Clearly this requires discourse competence. Q19 requires listening for specific information, but needs two pieces of information. Q20 is rather interesting: the question appears to test information clearly given in the text, but it asks about the grandmother's 80th birthday, and there is no mention of that, only a birthday. I am not sure whether that will distract test-takers or not, but I certainly had to think consciously about whether the birthday referred to in the text was the 80th birthday in the question.

Part 4

In this part test-takers hear a series of short news items, each one twice. They have enough time to look at the questions before they listen, then after the second listening, they have about one minute to respond to the questions in Finnish. The second passage is given below.

Test-takers hear:

> *a british woman has become the first female climber to conquer Mount Everest without oxygen or the help of others. Alison Hargreaves aged thirty-three reached the summit last Saturday. this is considered the most important climb by a woman. Ms Hargreaves is only the second climber in history, and the first woman, to reach the top of the twenty-nine thousand and twenty-eight foot mountain via the north ridge without artificial oxygen or someone to carry her gear. she spent more than a year preparing for the trip by training on Ben Nevis, where her husband, climber Jim Ballard, works part time. it was her second attempt on the summit. last year she was driven back by freezing winds when only one thousand five-hundred feet from the top.*

They hear the text again, and then read and respond to the following questions.

26. What was exceptional about Hargreaves' conquest of Mount Everest (mention two things)?

27. How long and with whose help had Hargreaves prepared for the attempt?

Generally, the tasks in Part 4 require summarising the whole of the test. Q26 and Q27 together really require reproducing most of the content. This requires a comprehensive understanding of the text on a linguistic level, but probably does not require making many pragmatic inferences or understanding inferred meanings.

Q27 is interesting in a number of respects. The speaker does not say anything about Hargreaves receiving help in her preparation. The only other person mentioned is her husband, and so the answer is obvious because there is no alternative. Logically, he may not have helped her at all, and may in fact have been opposed to her trip. Probably the test-developer was attempting to write an inference item, based on the assumption that her husband must have been helping. It would be interesting to see the item analysis for this item.

Summary

This test is clearly carefully planned and well made. The presentation does not have quite the same smooth professional feeling as the First Certificate, but these tests are produced at three levels for seven languages, and resources for each test will be less than those available for the First Certificate.

Examination of the items suggests that most of the tasks are engaging basic language skills: vocabulary, grammar and discourse knowledge. The tasks require processing reasonably fast, extensive texts, and understanding the basic information quite thoroughly. Certainly that applies to the Part 1 tasks; Part 2 tasks require finding explicitly stated information. I would assume that these tasks are much easier than the Part 1 tasks, and there might be a good case for putting Part 2 at the beginning of the test. Parts 3 and 4 require processing longer sections of text on a meaningful level.

From the perspective of the listening construct, there is little attempt to require pragmatic inferencing or sociolinguistic skills. The most obvious defect, however, is the absence of many oral features of spoken language: they do not require much processing of phonological modification, nor of hesitation phenomena, and there is no characteristically oral word choice, nor spoken expressions. The discourse structure also tends to be too coherent and polished.

However, we need to consider the situation in which such proficiency tests are made. Not only is there no clear target-language use situation, but there is no clear model of English to base the test on. Finnish English is not a widely accepted variety of English that could be used as a standard for the test, and many of the test-takers may not have had the opportunity to hear much real informal spoken English. In such foreign-language situations, it may be unfair to test realistic English. To some extent, the test-developers have to test the English that Finnish learners have been taught, and this test is to some extent an achievement test based on the English taught in the educational system. This is a fairly typical problem when making tests in a foreign-language environment.

The construct – basic vocabulary, grammar and discourse knowledge on language pronounced rather carefully by high-ability Finnish speakers of English – seems an appropriate one for such a test. The test assesses that construct well, with very little construct-irrelevant variance. Whether the construct could be expanded to include more oral features and more pragmatic inferencing items is something that would need to be decided in the light of the test purpose, and the testing context.

Certificate in Communicative Skills in English

The Certificate in Communicative Skills in English (CCSE) is published by UCLES, and provides a separate certificate in Reading, Writing, Listening and Speaking, at four levels. The test is based on the ideas of Morrow (1979) regarding communicative testing, reviewed in Chapter 3. There is a clear set of published descriptors for the four performance levels in each of the skills. The test reviewed here is the November 1998 test, at the most advanced level, which is approximately equivalent to the Council of Europe Common European Framework, Level C2.

Overall design

The listening test consists of seven parts, each one consisting of a longer text, or sometimes a group of similar texts, with a number of items attached. The overview is given opposite.

I will look at three parts: Part 1, Part 3 and Part 7.

Texts

The test publisher claims that only 'genuinely authentic material is used' (CCSE Handbook, 1995:69), and all the texts are original recordings made for a real-world purpose (although some of them may be re-recorded if the sound quality of the original is poor). This means that there is a predominance of broadcast material, although there

Task	Task type	No.	Task format
1	statement evaluation	8	test-takers listen to a text about a festival and then have to judge a number of written statements as correct, as incorrect, or as no relevant information given
2	multiple-choice questions	4	test-takers listen to a text of an actor speaking and then answer multiple-choice comprehension questions
3	true/false	6	test-takers listen to dialogue of an informal radio phone-in interview, and then answer true/false questions on the content
4	multiple matching	6	test-takers listen to a series of people expressing opinions on a windmill, then they read a series of statements and match the statements to the speakers
5	true/false	7	test-takers listen to an account of a holiday in England, and answer true/false questions on the content
6	multiple-choice statement completion	4	test-takers listen to a woman reading from her autobiography and then answer multiple-choice questions on the content
7	short-answer comprehension questions	3	test-takers listen to a radio programme, and write answers to short-answer questions

are some telephone messages and other pre-recorded materials. There are interactive texts as well as monologues.

The texts are clearly genuine. They are fast, realistic spoken texts, with the phonological modification typical of these texts. Some of them are relatively informal and unprepared, and thus have plenty of genuine oral features, while others are more planned. Some texts are played only once and others are played twice. The decision about whether to play the text once or twice seems to be based on the perceived difficulty of the task, rather than on any theoretical notion of what is appropriate.

Tasks

There are 38 items, of which 35 are selected responses with only two or three options, and three are constructed responses. Each item is dependent on understanding quite a lot of material, so they do provide a lot of information. However, this is a small number of items for a high-stakes, stand-alone test, especially one that allows as much guessing as this does. I would like to see far more items. The good thing is that although most of the items require selected responses, a number of different formats are used, which should reduce the method effect associated with any one item format.

In all cases test-takers see the tasks before listening. In some cases a rationale is provided for the activity. For example, in Part 1, the test-taker is told to listen to the information about the festival because it has been changed. This does add a little realism to the activity. However, although these are genuine texts, the test tasks bear little resemblance to the real-world use of these texts. Most of the texts are broadcast material intended for pleasure listening or general interest, not providing specific information. Although the texts are genuine, their use is not authentic at all.

Part 1

Test-takers listen to a pre-recorded telephone message with information about a festival, and then have to judge a number of written statements as correct, incorrect, or no relevant information given. All eight items are examined.

Test-takers look at the following grid:

	Correct information	Incorrect information	No relevant information
1　The festival runs from 20th May to 27th of May.			
2　It is open from 10am to midnight every day.			
3　It has never been held in Britain before.			

4	The unemployed get in free.			
5	People with Bristol Leisure card get a 50% discount.			
6	A meal is included in the ticket price.			
7	There are more than 700 ships at the festival.			
8	There is a disco every night.			

Test-takers then listen, and fill in the grid.

hello thanks for calling to hear about the international festival of the sea at Bristol harbour. it runs from Friday the twenty-fourth of May til Monday the twenty-seventh. and on each of those days it'll be open from ten in the morning to two A-M the next day. it's the first time a festival like this has ever been staged in Britain. it's a celebration of all things maritime. it's worth mentioning that if you live in the Bristol area and you've got a leisure card you'll got a whopping fifty percent off the ticket prices. once you've bought your festival ticket everything else is free. unless you want to buy something or have something to eat or drink at one of the many bars or cafes. anyway at the festival you'll find more than seven hundred vessels, classic traditional and modern. there are events all day and every day, some spontaneous and some set piece, events on the water, events in marquees on the dockside, and in visiting vessels. and every night there's a concert and a fantastic water pageant of sound and light.

The recorded message is fast and natural, and the ideas are strung together in realistic oral manner. The speaker is probably speaking from a semi-script – there are no false starts or corrections – but that is probably how such texts are constructed in the real world. The sound quality is rather poor, but in a manner that is authentic for telephone messages such as this. The message is played once, which is a little inauthentic in that a listener would normally have the option to listen to the message again. Six of the items require understanding clearly stated explicit information. Two items require the test-taker to realise that no relevant information was given. This device is quite often used by test-developers to increase the number of options on true/false items in order to reduce the effect of guessing – which is clearly desirable. Yet the task does seem unnatural. The other items require some necessary information to be identified and evaluated, but in the case of the *no relevant information* response, the test-taker is often left wondering whether the absence of information is due to their lack of understanding, or whether the information is actually absent. The eight items in this part require grammatical knowledge, including phonology and other oral features, perhaps some discourse knowledge, but they do not seem to require pragmatic or socio-linguistic knowledge.

Part 3

Test-takers listen to a dialogue of an informal radio phone-in inter-view, and then answer true/false questions on the content. Only the first part of the text and the first three questions are examined.

Test-takers look at the following, and respond by writing YES or NO.

1   He cooks more than once a week._____
2   He refuses to cook if there are guests._____
3   He is quite happy to make desserts._____

Then they listen to the interview, and answer the questions.

Interviewer:	*Hazel's in Kingston Park. good morning Hazel.*
Hazel:	*uh good morning.*
Interviewer:	*what's to do?*
Hazel:	*i've got a man that cooks so i just thought i would phone in and tell you.*
Interviewer:	*right now, does he do most of the cooking?*
Hazel:	*no.*
Interviewer:	*does he cook_ how often does he cook then?*
Hazel:	*oh at least a couple of times a week. and he ha_ and he'll cook as well when we have people round. he's got a couple of starters and a couple of puddings, and lots of main dishes and so we kind of split the meal if people come round and he does something and i do something.*
Interviewer:	*so it's_ but you still do the the bulk of the cooking in the house?*
Hazel:	*yeah, probably_ i mean he he would say its because i'm quicker and i've got more things that i can just knock up. but um i work funny hours so yaknow he will easily knock up two meals a week, which yaknow i think is great.*
Interviewer:	*so um do you think he's the rule or the exception??*
Hazel:	*um ah . . . well i've got quite a few friends who've got men that cook, who knock up the most amazing things. yaknow um, but i think he's the exception probably.*

The text is a very natural piece of spontaneous dialogue, although it was conducted on the radio. It is fast and informal, with characteristics of unplanned language. The choice of words and the discourse structure are quite typical of informal language use. The woman has a mild Scottish accent. Test-takers hear the text once. The questions all ask for clearly stated information, and do not require anything beyond a literal understanding of what was said.

Part 7

Test-takers listen to part of a radio programme, and write answers to open-ended comprehension questions. The whole task is described.

Test-takers read the following questions.

1 What is unusual about the prices in this place?
   _____
2 What do we learn about the woman who runs it?
   a _____
   b _____
3 What are her rules?
   a _____
   b _____

They then listen to the following interview, and answer the questions.

Interviewer:	*have you been here before then?*
Man:	*yeah, about thirty or forty times i should think*
Woman:	*even the tea's quite well priced. it gets cheaper as you go on, so presumably if you if you drink enough . . . hahaha*
Interviewer:	*what's this? it says first cup of tea thirty pence*
Woman:	*that's right. and then*
Interviewer:	*second cup twenty-five, third cup twenty. now what happens if you get onto your fourth cup?*
Woman:	*hahaha i don't know.*
Short Pause	
Interviewer:	*Mrs Godfrey you're the master mind behind the Dorchester Abbey tea rooms, how did it all begin?*
Mrs Godfrey:	*oh years ago, before the vicar before the vicar before last i asked_ actually i thought this room would be suitable for doing teas and i said when i retire from teaching can i run a tea shop and he said 'yes, start whenever you like' so i started twenty years ago.*

> Interviewer: *but it's very idiosyncratic here isn't it. i mean you keep your own tab, the tea gets cheaper the more cups you drink . . .*
> Mrs Godfrey: *yes, we have our rules*
> Interviewer: *you have your rules, what are the rules?*
> Mrs Godfrey: *well there's a warning on the on the wall there about not making the_ customers are exhorted not to waste butter or jam as it's apt to make the proprietress violent. you see that's the system here. and so we don't have any trouble with customers leaving butter on their plates. cos i get very fierce about that. i wont have anyone smoking in here. and basically yaknow, we are very pleased to see all these customers.*

Again this is a very authentic informal interview, and such texts can be heard regularly on British radio. There is typical phonological modification, and a number of informal oral characteristics, including some hesitations and false starts. There are even overlaps between the two speakers – when Mrs Godfrey says *'we have our rules'* she is actually speaking over something the interviewer is saying. This is a very natural piece of informal discourse. Again the tasks ask for clearly stated information, although it is necessary to locate it within the longer text. The test does not assess inferencing or understanding implied meanings.

Summary

In this chapter, I have frequently complained about tests using texts that lack genuine oral characteristics, but this test really does use genuine texts. The listener must deal with the characteristics of spoken language. Furthermore, in the two interviews, the test-taker has to deal with some of the characteristics of interactive discourse. This use of these genuine texts is probably the basis for the use of the word *communicative* in the test title, and claims for the construct validity are surely based on the authenticity of the texts.

However, it is interesting to consider whether they have situational authenticity. As a general proficiency test, there is no clear target-language use situation against which we could evaluate the situational authenticity of the texts. These texts do however represent only a narrow range of the text types normally encountered in general communicative situations, and this suggests that taken as a group the selection of texts does lack some degree of situational authenticity.

We can evaluate the interactional authenticity of the texts by comparing the competencies required by this test with those we believe are necessary for communicative competence. The test is assessing the ability to understand clearly stated information – grammatical knowledge and some discourse knowledge – plus most of what is unique to listening. This is an important construct, but it does fall short of typical descriptions of communicative competence. It lacks assessment of the ability to understand implied meanings, make inferences or understand sociolinguistic implications, and surely these are the characteristics that help define a communicative language test. Furthermore, the test is intended to target advanced second-language listeners, and this surely means that it needs to assess the more subtle aspects of comprehension – understanding implicit meanings and understanding 'between the lines'. Assessing only literally stated meanings does not seem sufficient for a test of this ability level.

In summary, I believe that this is a test of important language skills, but it falls short of being a test of communicative listening ability. In terms of the two-stage view of listening, it covers the first level very well, understanding literal linguistic information, but it does not cover the second level, the application of that to a wider communication situation.

Conclusion

In this chapter I have examined five different listening tests, and looked closely at how the items worked in order to consider what construct they were operationalising. I have then used these as a basis to illustrate some of the important issues in assessing listening.

The tests vary in how they assess listening. Both the lower-level test, the TOEIC, and the higher-level test, the CCSE, concentrated almost exclusively on understanding literal semantic meanings, although the TOEIC used short, scripted texts, with few discourse features, whereas the CCSE used longer, spontaneous texts, rich in discourse features. The three intermediate tests assess basic grammatical knowledge, but they also attempt to test discourse knowledge and pragmatic knowledge. None of the tests had much success testing sociolinguistic knowledge; probably because none of them was targeting a sufficiently clearly defined context of situation.

Four of the five tests had the same deficiency: namely, they failed to assess those aspects of language knowledge that are necessary for comprehension of texts with more oral features. I have already discussed why this happens: along with some possible solutions in Chapter 6. Although we may criticise test-developers for not concentrating more effort on comprehension of more oral texts, we should not underestimate the practical problems. Nevertheless, test-developers need to explore ways to address this important issue.

The CCSE avoids this problem by using genuine texts, such as announcements, recorded messages and radio broadcast material. This allows them to claim that their texts are authentic, but of course, listeners listen to a much wider variety of text types than these. Furthermore, many pre-recorded texts may be genuine, but still be carefully scripted or relatively formal. The need is not so much for genuine texts, but for informal, spontaneous texts. Ironically, it is the tests that make no pretence to be communicative, such as the TOEFL and the TOEIC, which use speech events from situations that are typically associated with more spontaneous speech. However, they use closely scripted, formal, written language, which results in texts that are poor examples of the genre.

Most listening-test developers choose between avoiding speech situations which require spontaneous, informal language, or including them, but with inauthentic scripted language. What test-developers should do is use spontaneous speech situations, but also ensure that they have the linguistic characteristics of unplanned, oral discourse. That would significantly improve the quality and utility of many listening tests.

CHAPTER NINE

....

Summary and future developments

In this final chapter, I shall summarise the main points I have made about the nature of listening, and the main ideas I have advocated for testing listening comprehension, and then I will discuss a number of issues I think should be addressed in order to make better assessments of listening.

An overview of listening comprehension

Before considering how to make listening tests, we need to understand the nature of the listening construct. Listening is a complex process in which the listener takes the incoming data, an acoustic signal, and interprets it based on a wide variety of linguistic and non-linguistic knowledge. The linguistic knowledge includes knowledge of phonology, lexis, syntax, semantics, discourse structure, pragmatics and sociolinguistics. The non-linguistic knowledge includes knowledge of the topic, the context and general knowledge about the world and how it works. Comprehension is an on-going process of constructing an interpretation of what the text is about, and then continually modifying that as new information becomes available.

Thus meaning is not something that is contained within a text, but it is actively constructed by the listener. The interpretation of the speaker's meaning is greatly influenced by the context in which the communication takes place. There are different types of context: co-text is the text that accompanies or precedes the text currently being listened to; the context of situation is the communicative situation in which the speech event is taking place; and the cognitive environment is everything that is in the listener's mind. Context is important because speakers often do not say exactly what they mean, but depend on the listener to use their knowledge of the context to make implications regarding the intended meaning. Much of the information communicated is never explicitly stated.

Listeners listen to spoken language, and there are a number of things to note about that. Firstly, the input is in the form of sound, and individual sounds are often very indistinct due to extensive phonological modification. Furthermore, stress and intonation often convey important information, especially by indicating the status of the information, or the speaker's attitude towards it. Secondly, listening takes place in real time, and once heard, a text is usually never repeated – after the speaker has finished, the listener does not have access to the text again. Thirdly, speech is linguistically different from writing: it is unplanned discourse, and has many distinctive oral features. It consists of short idea units, strung together in loose ways, with characteristic vocabulary and discourse structures. It usually contains hesitations, such as pauses, repetitions and corrections, and will often have errors of grammar and word choice.

Language is used for a variety of different functions; the two main ones are the interactional function, where the principal purpose is to maintain social relationships and the content is not very important, and the transactional function, where the principal purpose is to convey information. Most listening situations will consist of a mixture of the two.

Cognitive processing can operate in two basic modes: first, controlled processing, which is used when something is encountered for the first time, and which requires considerable cognitive processing capacity, and, second, automatic processing, which develops when a process has been repeated many times. Automatic processing is very fast and requires little cognitive processing capacity. Given the fast rate of most speech, successful listening processes should be entirely automatic; and all knowledge about the language should be usable automatically without any conscious thought. After the message has been processed, the language used to convey the message is usually forgotten quickly, and only a memory, or a mental representation, remains. These representations of meaning are stored in two main forms, either as propositions, which are rather like simple little facts, or as mental models, which are rather like analogue representations of the real world.

There is often no one simple interpretation of a particular text. Listeners have purposes for listening, and will attempt to arrive at an interpretation that is meaningful for their particular purpose. Furthermore, background knowledge varies from one listener to another, and so listeners may arrive at different interpretations of the same text, and these different interpretations may each be reasonable for the individual listener. This means that there is no correct interpretation for many texts, but rather just a number of reasonable interpretations.

Constructing tests of listening comprehension

As a general strategy, I advise developing listening tests that concentrate on those characteristics that are unique to listening. General language comprehension, or basic grammatical knowledge, can often be tested much easier and cheaper with reading tests. Even when the purpose is to promote washback by encouraging the teaching of listening in the classroom, it still makes sense to concentrate on the characteristics unique to listening.

The first step in test construction is to define the construct on a conceptual level, and then to operationalise that in a series of test tasks. When operationalising the construct there are two dangers: not covering the whole of the construct – construct-underrepresentation – and including things that do not belong in the construct – construct-irrelevant variance. Because listening comprehension cannot be examined directly, it is always necessary to give the test-taker some task, and then make inferences about the listener's comprehension based on performance on that task. Skills besides listening will always be involved in task performance, and there is always a possibility of construct-irrelevant variance affecting listening test scores.

In language testing, there are two main ways to define the construct on a conceptual level: we can define it either in terms of the underlying competencies, or in terms of tasks. The advantage of defining the construct in terms of competencies is that the construct definition is not tied to one particular language-use situation, so test results should better generalise across all language-use situations.

Although many of the meanings communicated by speech are not directly stated, on a practical level it is very difficult to test implied meanings or context-dependent interpretations, largely because inter-pretations can reasonably vary. Many test-developers may not have the skills or resources to develop tests of such complex and subtle constructs. In Chapter 4, I suggested a compromise which I called a default listening construct. This is the ability:

- to process extended samples of realistic, spoken language, automatically and in real time, and
- to understand all the linguistic information that is unequivocally included in the text, and
- to make whatever inferences are unambiguously implicated by the content of the passage.

This construct goes beyond basic linguistic competence, but avoids those aspects of language use that are difficult to assess. It includes: grammatical knowledge, discourse knowledge and quite a lot of pragmatic knowledge, and covers almost everything that is unique about listening comprehension. It is a competence-based construct.

When we come to operationalise a construct defined in terms of competencies, we need to determine which particular competencies are required for each task, in order to ensure that all the required competencies are adequately covered. This is not easy to do. An alternative approach is to define the construct in terms of target-language use tasks, and then replicate these tasks in the test. This helps to ensure that important competencies are automatically included in the test. This procedure is particularly useful when the target-language use situation is clearly defined – in testing for specific purposes, for example.

The theoretical rationale underlying this approach is the notion of authenticity, which is a powerful force for ensuring construct validity. Authenticity is of two types: situational authenticity and interactional authenticity. I have argued that although situational authenticity is useful, what is most important in testing language processing is that the knowledge and cognitive processes critical in the target-language use situation are those required to perform well in the testing situation. In other words, I believe interactional authenticity is what gets to the core of construct validity.

However, in many cases, there is no clearly defined target-language use situation, and even if there is, it is not always clear what the most important tasks are. There is also the need to show generalisability:

how can we show that performance on one task in one situation will generalise to performance on another task in another situation? By looking at the extent to which they share the same underlying competencies, perhaps?

This suggests a comprise between the two approaches. We can define the construct in terms of both competencies and tasks, perhaps using a two-dimensional matrix. Thus we can get the best of both approaches. For example, if we wish to improve on the default listening construct we would determine which were the most likely tasks in the target-language use situation, and then attempt to build our test items around those, replicating them as closely as possible. If there is no clear target-language use situation, such as in a general proficiency test, we could identify the most common communicative tasks, and use those to assess the most important competencies.

There are a large number of different tasks that can be used to test listening, and those were discussed in detail in Chapters 3 and 5. All tasks must have certain characteristics. Firstly, they must be passage dependent, in that it must be impossible to do the task without understanding the text. Secondly, they must provide unequivocal evidence of comprehension. This means that they must provide evidence that the test-taker has processed the language on a semantic level. In practical terms, this usually requires that the response be in a different form to that in which test-takers received the information.

The point was made earlier that inevitably all listening tasks will require construct-irrelevant skills, but the test-developer should try to ensure that these do not lead to construct-irrelevant variance in the test scores. However, that is not always possible, so it is important to choose tasks that require non-listening skills that are appropriate for that testing situation. Then, if the test-method effect does influence listening scores, the effect will not be so harmful. It is also important to remember that task processing can be very unpredictable. It is always advisable to pre-test all test items on a sample of test-takers similar to the target test-takers, and then analyse the results with standard item analysis procedures. Usually many tasks will need to be revised.

The most important characteristic of tasks is that they have interactional authenticity – that is they need to assess the knowledge, skills and abilities required by the construct definition, or assess the knowledge, skills and abilities critical to performance in the target-language use situation to which test performance is intended to generalise.

In Chapter 6, I discussed texts, and stressed that two things are particularly important. Firstly, the sound must be of sufficient quality that all test-takers can hear clearly and comfortably. Secondly, texts must have characteristics suitable for the construct definition: if you need to assess automatic processing, you need fast texts; if you want to assess phonological modification then you need texts with suitably modified pronunciation; and if you want to assess discourse, then you need longer texts. The particular text characteristics will obviously vary from one situation to another, but at the very least texts must use realistic spoken language. If the strategy is to focus on what is unique to listening, then it becomes even more important to use texts with a range of realistic oral features. An examination of published listening tests in Chapter 8 suggests that this is one area in which many tests are deficient.

Although most of the discussion has been about individual items, tests should be viewed as a whole. All the tasks taken together should operationalise the whole of the construct, in a balanced and comprehensive manner. And if they are to do that well, they must have certain measurement properties: they should be reliable and have construct validity. Ideally they should also have a positive impact, by avoiding bias, and providing a desirable washback effect.

Future developments in assessing listening

During the course of this book I have repeatedly stressed that, despite the complexities, it is possible to make good tests of listening. In this last section I wish to point out the issues that I think need to be addressed in order to move forward and make even better listening tests.

Providing suitable texts

In my view, the most pressing practical issue in the assessment of listening comprehension is the problem of providing texts that have the characteristics of real-world, spoken texts. Creating texts which have those oral characteristics is not easy, and most listening tests suffer from construct-underrepresentation in this regard.

The underlying cause of this is that most test-developers begin with a task they wish to construct, and then search for a suitable text after the task has been designed. This usually means creating or modifying texts to ensure that they have the right language or the right content for the task. It tends to result in scripted tasks which lack many of the characteristics of spoken language. In Chapter 6, I suggested that a better way is to start by collecting texts, good texts that have the right oral features, and then design the tasks around these. Of course not all texts are suitable for making test-tasks, but photographers expect to take a lot of pictures to get a few good ones, and perhaps listening-test developers need to record a lot of texts in order to get a few good ones.

Providing realistic texts for lower-ability listeners is a particular challenge. Most lower-ability listeners do not have the linguistic skills to process realistic texts, and in Chapter 6 I discussed ways of creating easier texts with realistic oral features, and also ways of using digital editing techniques to slow texts down while preserving the oral characteristics of interest. As test-developers, we need to explore ways of providing easier texts which still have the features of spontaneous oral language.

Visuals

In many communicative situations, the verbal information is also accompanied by visual information. This is an important variable in language comprehension. Not only does it serve to supplement the linguistic information, but it also helps define the context in which the spoken message will be interpreted. The common practice of playing a disembodied recording from an audio-player does not create a very realistic listening situation.

Recently, technologies have become available which allow the provision of visual information along with the audio. Videotape is now very common, and many test-developers will have access to video-cameras and video-players. Digital video is also possible, although the file sizes are huge. Still pictures are another possibility. Multi-media tests are appearing, and the spread of the Internet is serving to speed that trend. However, we do not know how video-texts affect listening comprehension, nor whether tests with video-texts are in any significant way different from audio-texts.

The point I made in Chapter 6 is worth repeating, namely that when testing language ability, the emphasis needs to be on processing linguistic information, not visual information. Furthermore, it seems sensible to bear in mind that adding visual information is probably only worthwhile if it provides us with better assessments of the listening construct. In some cases the visual information may serve to increase the cognitive load of the test-taker, and that may interfere with the testing process.

Research is clearly necessary. There are three main conditions that need to be explored: testing listening with no visual support, with still pictures or with full-motion video. The most important questions are whether visual support makes a difference to comprehension, and whether any differences are construct-relevant. We can approach these issues by evaluating the authenticity and interactiveness of video-based assessments. We also need to examine what happens when the visual information conflicts with the verbal information.

Collaborative listening

Most of our listening takes place in interactive situations with live speakers, and in these situations there are three main listener roles: the addressee, who is the person the speaker is addressing, participants who are not being directly addressed, and non-participants who are simply overhearers. Addressees have responsibilities. They must work together with the speaker and actively collaborate to construct the discourse: they monitor their comprehension, determine whether it is adequate, articulate any problems, work with the speaker to negotiate the meaning, and then indicate to the speaker when it is time to move on (Schober and Clark, 1989). This requires a set of important skills.

Non-addressed participants may aid the addressee in fulfilling these responsibilities. They can usually ask for clarification or repetitions as necessary, and will often collaborate to construct the discourse – or at least they will usually have the right to do so. In many cases they will become addressees themselves as the interaction continues, and listener and speaker roles change. The overhearer is in a very different position: they do not have the right, and often not even the opportunity, to enter the conversation. This means they cannot ask for clarification, nor modify the interaction to facilitate their comprehension. Thus, constructing a reasonable interpretation is much more difficult for the overhearer.

Many current listening tests put the listener in the role of over-hearer, and we need to know more about what effect this has on their level of comprehension. We need research to identify which are the most important interactive listening skills, and then we need to learn how to develop tests that assess these. Currently such skills are usually assessed as part of interactive speaking tests, but in most speaking tests the emphasis is on spoken production. It would obviously be sensible to find out more about listener roles in current oral interviews, and look at whether these can be modified to become better assessments of listening. Another area of exploration might be group interviews: we need to explore ways these can be adapted to assess collaborative listening skills.

Computer-based testing

Computer-based testing is developing rapidly (Dunkel, 1991b, 1996), and even large-scale listening tests, such as the TOEFL, are already delivered by computer. This is a significant advance in testing technology. However, the cost of developing these assessments is many times that of traditional paper-and-pencil versions, and there need to be significant advantages to make that worthwhile. The main advantages of computer-based test delivery are shorter testing times, instant score reporting, continual availability and distributed delivery over a network or over the Internet. In some situations these will be worth the extra cost. However, the product of assessment is information, in this case information about the test-takers' ability on the listening construct. If computer-based tests merely provide an alternative means of collecting the same information as paper-and-pencil tests, they may not be worth the additional cost.

The challenge for the future is to develop computer-based tests which provide better assessments of the constructs of interest, and particularly whether they can be used to test constructs closer to those engaged by real-world listening tasks. This probably means the integration of visual information, or creating realistic simulations of the listening situation – perhaps through virtual reality. It may even be possible to replicate interactive listening, and assess collaborative listening skills. The important issue is the extent to which we can use the power of the computer to test a richer and more realistic listening construct.

A theoretical basis for designing assessments of listening comprehension

The process of test construction requires first defining the listening construct, and then finding ways of operationalising that. At the present time, test-developers have to re-think this process for themselves every time they make a new listening test. It would be more convenient to have an established theoretical basis for constructing listening tests.

In Chapter 4, I attempted to address this. Firstly, I took the Bachman and Palmer (1996) model of language ability, which is the latest in a series of attempts to define communicative competence, and adapted that to describe listening comprehension. Secondly, I took that model and showed how it could be incorporated into a two-way matrix design to define a listening construct in terms of both underlying competence and performance tasks.

This is a start, but it does not yet provide an adequate theoretical basis for describing listening competence, nor for test design: there is no empirical validation for the description of listening ability, nor is there clear evidence for the utility of the matrix approach to test design. However, it is through such efforts that we can work towards developing theoretical models of listening and listening-test construction. We need an active process of generating ideas, and of evaluating those from both a theoretical and practical perspective.

Diagnosis of sub-skills

The other long-term goal is the need for diagnosis. Currently most tests provide a single score: this is sometimes a raw score of the number of items correct, and sometimes a score or band level on a pre-existing scale. The score represents the test-taker's level of attainment on the underlying construct, but it is usually very difficult to interpret scores in terms of meaningful levels of ability on the construct. Listening is a complex, multi-dimensional activity, and performance on listening test tasks requires a complex combination of knowledge, processing skills and strategies. We need tests to provide us with more interpretable information about the listener's ability.

Testers have traditionally been interested in sub-skills, and I described a number of taxonomies in Chapter 2. This is one way the issue of diagnosis can be approached. The first task would be to understand these sub-skills of listening much better. Then we need to be able to look at performance on a series of complex tasks and somehow tease out the effects of each particular sub-skill, and determine the test-taker's status on each. There are a number of promising techniques that might be able to do that, including statistical pattern recognition, regression techniques and neural nets. Hopefully, these will eventually help provide us with more meaningful test scores.

However, in Chapter 2, I raised the possibility that sub-skills may not actually exist, but may just be useful ways of describing what we do when we comprehend language. Such a question has considerable implications for describing the listening construct, as well as for diagnosing listening ability. Clearly more research is needed to explore ways of describing listening ability in meaningful ways that could be used as the basis for diagnostic assessments.

Conclusion

Testing listening is complex and challenging, but with care and effort it can be done, not only by professionals in large testing organisations, but also by teachers, or test-developers with limited resources. The important thing is to define a suitable construct, one that meets our needs and which can be operationalised with the resources available. Although compromises will need to be made, our current state of knowledge is sufficient to do a good job in most cases. Furthermore, many tests could be easily improved based on the knowledge and techniques available at the moment – especially in regard to phonology and those aspects of listening that make it unique. As our knowledge expands, there is every reason to believe that we will be able to make steady improvements in how we assess listening comprehension.

Bibliography

Abercrombie, D. (1967). *Elements of general phonetics*. Edinburgh: Edinburgh University Press.

Aitchison, J. (1994). Understanding words. In G. Brown, K. Malmkjaer, A. Pollitt, and J. Williams (eds.). *Language and understanding*. Oxford: Oxford University Press.

Aitken, K. G. (1978). Measuring listening comprehension. *English as a second language. TEAL Occasional Papers*, Vol 2. Vancouver: British Colombia Association of Teachers of English as an Additional Language. ERIC Document No. ED 155 945.

Alderson, C. A. (1981a) Reaction to the Morrow paper (3). In J. C. Alderson and A. Hughes (eds.), *Issues in Language Testing*. ELT *Documents, 111*, pp. 55–65. London: The British Council.

Alderson, J. C. (1981b). Report of the discussion on communicative language testing. In J. C. Alderson and A. Hughes (eds.), *Issues in Language Testing. ELT Documents, 111*, pp. 55–65. London: The British Council.

Alderson, J. C. (2000). *Assessing reading*. Cambridge: Cambridge University Press.

Alderson, J. C., Clapham, C. M., and Wall, D. (1995). *Language test construction and evaluation*. Cambridge: Cambridge University Press.

Alderson, J. C., and Wall, D. (1993). Does washback exist? *Applied Linguistics, 14*, 115–29.

Alderson, J. C., Wall, D., and Clapham, C. (1987). *An evaluation of the National Certificate of English, Sri Lanka, 1986. Volume 2.*

American Educational Research Association. (2000). *Standards for Educational and Psychological Testing 1999.*

Anderson, A., and Lynch, T. (1988). *Listening*. Oxford: Oxford University Press.

Anderson, A., Garrod, S. C., and Sanford, A. J. (1983). The accessibility of pronominal antecedents as a function of episode shifts in narrative text. *Quarterly Journal of Experimental Psychology, 35A*, 427–440.

Anderson, J. R. (1976). *Language, memory, and thought.* Hillsdale, NJ: Lawrence Erlbaum Associates.

Anderson, R. C. (1972). How to construct achievement tests to assess comprehension. *Review of Educational Research, 42*(2), 145–170.

Anderson-Hsieh, J., and Koehler, K. (1988). The effects of foreign accent and speaking rate on native speaker comprehension. *Language Learning, 38*, 561–613.

Antes, T. A. (1996). Kinesics: The value of gesture in language and in the language classroom. *Foreign Language Annals, 29*, 439–448.

Arbogast, B., Bicknell, J., Duke, T., Locke, M. and Shearin, R. (2000). *TOEIC Official Test Preparation Guide.* Princeton, NJ: Educational Testing Service.

Asher, J. J. (1969). The total physical response approach to second language learning. *The Modern Language Journal, 53*, 3–17.

Austin, J. L. (1962). *How to do things with words.* Oxford: Clarendon Press.

Bachman, L. F. (1990). *Fundamental considerations in language testing.* Oxford: Oxford University Press.

Bachman, L. F. (1991). What does language testing have to offer? *TESOL Quarterly, 25*(4), 671–704.

Bachman, L. F., and Palmer, A. (1996). *Language testing in practice.* Oxford: Oxford University Press.

Bae, J., and Bachman, L. F. (1998). A latent variable approach to listening and reading: Testing factorial invariance across two groups of children in the Korean/English two-way immersion program. *Language Testing, 15*(3).

Berne, J. E. (1995). How does varying pre-listening activities affect second language listening comprehension? *Hispania, 78*, 316–329.

Blau, E. (1990). The effect of syntax, speed and pauses on listening comprehension. *TESOL Quarterly, 24*, 746–53.

Blau, E. (1991) More on comprehensible input: The effect of pauses and hesitation markers on listening comprehension, ERIC DOC NO. ED340 234.

Bloom, B. S. (1956). *Taxonomy of educational objectives. Handbook 1: cognitive domain.* New York: Longman.

Bond, Z. S., and Garnes, S. (1980). Misperceptions of Fluent Speech. In R.A. Cole (ed.), *Perception and production of fluent speech.* Hillsdale, NJ: Lawrence Erlbaum Associates, pp. 115–32.

Bostrom, R. N. (1997). The testing of mother tongue listening skills. In C. M. Clapham and D. Corson (eds.), *Language testing and assessment: Encyclopedia of language and education, Vol. 7.* Dordrecht: Kluwer.

Boyle, J., and Suen, D. L. K. (1994). Communicative considerations in a large-scale listening test. In J. Boyle and P. Falvey (eds.), *English Language Testing in Hong Kong*, Hong Kong: The Chinese University Press.

Bransford, J. D., and Johnson, M. K. (1972). Contextual prerequisites for understanding: some investigations of comprehension and recall. *Journal of Verbal Learning and Verbal Behavior, 11*, 717–726.

Bransford, J. D., and Johnson, M. K. (1973). Considerations of some problems of comprehension. In W. G. Chase (ed.), *Visual information processing*. New York: Academic Press.

Bremer, K., Roberts, C., Vasseur, M., Simonot, M., and Broeder, P. (1996). *Achieving understanding: Discourse in international encounters*. London: Longman.

Brindley, G. (1998). Assessing Listening Abilities. *Annual Review of Applied Linguistics, 18*, 171–91.

Brown, G. (1990). *Listening to spoken English*. (2nd ed.). Longman: London.

Brown, G. (1995a). *Speakers, listeners and communication*. Cambridge: Cambridge University Press.

Brown, G. (1995b). Dimensions of difficulty in listening comprehension. In D. J. Mendelsohn and J. Rubin (eds.), *A guide for the teaching of second language listening*. San Diego: Dominie Press.

Brown, G., and Yule, G. (1983). *Teaching the spoken language*. Cambridge: Cambridge University Press.

Buck, G. (1988). Testing listening comprehension in Japanese university entrance examinations. *JALT Journal, 10*(1),15–42.

Buck, G. (1990). The testing of second language listening comprehension. Unpublished PhD thesis, Lancaster University.

Buck, G. (1991). The testing of listening comprehension: an introspective study. *Language Testing, 8*(1), 67–91.

Buck, G. (1992a). Listening comprehension: construct validity and trait characteristics. *Language Learning, 42*(3), 313–357.

Buck, G. (1992b). Translation as a language testing procedure: does it work? *Language Testing, 9*(2), 123–148.

Buck, G. (1994). The appropriacy of psychometric measurement models for testing second language listening comprehension, *Language Testing, 11*(2), 145–170.

Buck, G. (1997) The testing of listening in a second language. In C. M. Clapham and D. Corson (eds.), *Language testing and assessment. Encyclopedia of language and education, Vol. 7*. Dordrecht: Kluwer.

Buck, G., and Tatsuoka, K. (1998). Application of the rule–space procedure to language testing: Examining attributes of a free response listening test. *Language Testing, 15*(2), 119–157.

Buck, G., Tatsuoka, K., Kostin, I., and Phelps, M. (1997). The sub-skills of listening: Rule-space analysis of a multiple-choice test of second language listening comprehension. In A. Huhta, V. Kohonen, L. Kurki-Suonio and S. Luoma (eds.), *Current developments and alternatives in language assessment*. Tampere: University of Jyväskylä.

Burger, S., and Doherty, J. (1992). Testing receptive skills within a comprehension-based approach. In R. J. Courchene, J. I. Gidden, J. St. John and C. Therien (eds.). *Comprehension-based second language teaching*, pp. 299–318. Ottowa: University of Ottowa Press.

Burgoon, J. (1994). Nonverbal signals. In M. Knapp and G. Miller (eds.), *Handbook of Interpersonal Communication*, pp. 344–393. London: Routledge.

Campbell, D. T., and Fiske, D. W. (1959). Convergent and discriminant validation by the multitrait-multimethod matrix. *Psychological Bulletin, 56*, 81–105.

Canale, M. (1983). Some dimensions of language proficiency. In J. W. Oller Jr., (ed.), *Issues in language testing research*. Rowley, Mass.: Newbury House.

Canale, M., and Swain, M. (1980). Theoretical bases of communicative approaches to second language teaching and testing. *Applied Linguistics, 1*(1),1–47.

Carroll, B. J. (1980). *Testing communicative performance: an interim study*. Oxford: Pergamon Press Ltd.

Carroll, J. B. (1972). Defining language comprehension. In R. O. Freedle and J. B. Carroll (eds.), *Language comprehension and the acquisition of knowledge*. New York: John Wiley and Sons.

Carter, R., and McCarthy, M. (1997). *Exploring spoken language*. Cambridge: Cambridge University Press.

Carver, R. (1973). Effect of increasing the rate of speech presentation upon comprehension. *Journal of Educational Psychology, 65*, 118–126.

Cervantes, R., and Gainer, G. (1992). The effects of syntactic simplification and repetition on listening comprehension. *TESOL Quarterly, 26*, 345–74.

Chafe, W. L. (1985). Linguistic differences produced by differences between speaking and writing. In D. R. Olsen, N. Torrance and A. Hilyard (eds.), *Literacy, language and learning: the nature and consequences of reading and writing*. Cambridge: Cambridge University Press.

Chapelle, C. A. (1998). Construct definition and validity inquiry in SLA research. In L. F. Bachman and A. D. Cohen (eds.), *Interfaces between second language acquisition and language testing research*. Cambridge: Cambridge University Press.

Chaudron, C., and Richards, J. C. (1986). The effect of discourse markers on the comprehension of lectures. *Applied Linguistics, 7*(2), 113–127.

Chiang, C. S., and Dunkel, P. (1992). The effect of speech modification, prior knowledge, and listening proficiency on EFL lecture learning. *TESOL Quarterly, 26*(2), 345–374.

Chomsky, N. (1965). *Aspects of the theory of syntax*. Cambridge, MA: MIT Press.

Clark, H. H., and Clark, E. V. (1977). *Psychology and language: An introduction to psycholinguistics*. New York: Harcourt Brace Jovanovich.

Clark, H. H., and Haviland, S. E. (1974). Psychological processes as linguistic explanation. In D. Cohen (ed.), *Explaining linguistic phenomena*. Washington, D.C.: Hemisphere Publishing.

Cohen, A. (1975). Measuring intelligibility in foreign language leaning. In A. J. van Essen and J. P. Menting (eds.), *The context of foreign language learning*. Assen.

Cohen, A. (1977). Redundancy as a tool in measuring listening comprehension. In R. Dirven (ed.), *Hörverständnis im Fremdsprachenunterricht. Listening comprehension in foreign language teaching*. Kronberg/Ts.: Scriptor.

Cohen, A. D. (1994). *Assessing language ability in the classroom*. (2nd ed.). Boston, MA: Heinle and Heinle.

Cole, R. A., and Jakimik, J. (1980). A model of speech perception. In R. A. Cole (ed.), *Perception and production of fluent speech*. Hillsdale, NJ: Lawrence Erlbaum Associates.

Connor, U., and Read, C. (1978). Passage dependency in ESL reading comprehension tests. *Language Learning, 28*(1), 149–157.

Cooper, W. E. (1976). Syntactic control of timing in speech production: A study of complement clauses. *Journal of Phonetics, 4*, 151–157.

Cruttenden, A. (1997). *Intonation*. (3rd ed.). Cambridge: Cambridge University Press.

Crystal, D. (1995). *The Cambridge encyclopedia of the English language*. Cambridge: Cambridge University Press.

Dirven, R., and Oakeshott-Taylor, J. (1984). Listening comprehension (Part I). *Language Teaching, 17*, 326–342.

Douglas, D. (2000). *Assessing languages for specific purposes*. Cambridge: Cambridge University Press.

Dunkel, P. (1988). The content of L1 and L2 students' lecture notes and its relation to test performance. *TESOL Quarterly, 22*(2), 259–281.

Dunkel, P. (1991a). Listening in the native and second/foreign language: towards an integration of research and practice. *TESOL Quarterly, 26*(3).

Dunkel, P. (1991b). Computerized testing of non-participatory L2 listening comprehension proficiency: An ESL prototype development effort. *Modern Language Journal, 75*(1), 64–73.

Dunkel, P. (1996) Checking the utility and appropriacy of the content and measurement models used to develop L2 listening comprehension CATS: Implications for further development of comprehensive CATs. In M. Chalhoub-Deville (ed.), *Issues in computer adaptive testing of second language reading proficiency conference seminar papers*. University of Minnesota, Bloomington, MN.

Dunkel, P. and Davis, J. N. (1994). The effects of rhetorical signally cues on recall. In J. Flowerdew (ed.), *Academic listening: research perspectives*. Cambridge: Cambridge University Press.

Dunkel, P., Henning, G., and Chaudron, C. (1993). The assessment of an L2 listening comprehension construct: tentative model for test specification and development. *The Modern Language Journal, 77*(2), 180–191.

Eisenstein, M., and Berkowitz, D. (1981). The effect of phonological variation on adult learner comprehension. *Studies in Second Language Acquisition, 4*, 75–80.

Ellis, R. C. (2001). Memory for language. In P. Robinson (ed.), *Cognition and second language instruction*. Cambridge: Cambridge University Press.

Emery, P. G. (1980). Evaluating spoken English: a new approach to the testing of listening comprehension. *English Language Teaching Journal, 34*(2), 96–98.

Faerch, C., and Kasper, G. (1986). The role of comprehension in second language learning. *Applied Linguistics 7*, 257–274.

Fairclough, N. (1989). *Language and power*. London: Longman.

Feyten, C. (1991). The power of listening ability: an overlooked dimension in language acquisition. *The Modern Language Journal 75* (ii), 173–180.

Fishman, M. (1980). We all make the same mistakes: a comparative study of native and nonnative errors in taking dictation. In J. W. Oller, Jr. and K. Perkins (eds.), *Research in Language Testing*, pp. 187–194. Rowley, Mass.: Newbury House Publishers, Inc.

Flowerdew, J. (ed.). (1994). *Academic listening: research perspectives*. Cambridge: Cambridge University Press.

Foulke, E. (1968). Listening comprehension as a function of word rate. *The Journal of Communication, 18*, 198–206.

Foulke, E., and Sticht, T. G. (1969). Review of the research on the intelligibility and comprehension of accelerated speech. *Psychological Bulletin, 72*(1), 50–62.

Freedle, R., and Kostin, I. (1994). Can multiple-choice reading tests be construct valid? *Psychological Science*, 5, 107–110.

Freedle, R., and Kostin, I. (1996). *The prediction of TOEFL listening comprehension item difficulty for minitalk passages: implications for construct validity*. Princeton, NJ: ETS Research Report RR 96–29.

Freedle, R., and Kostin, I. (1999). Does text matter in a multiple-choice test of comprehension? The case for the construct validity of TOEFL's minitalks. *Language Testing, 16*(1), 2–32.

Friedman, H. L., and R. L. Johnson. 1971. Some actual and potential uses of rate controlled speech in second language learning. In P. Pimsleur and T. Quinn (eds.), *The psychology of second language learning*. Cambridge: Cambridge University Press.

Garnham, A. (1985). *Psycholinguistics: central topics*. London: Methuen.

Garro, L., and Parker, F. (1982). Some suprasegmental characteristics of relative clauses in English. *Journal of Phonetics, 10*, 149–161.

Gary, J., and Gary, N. (1981). Caution: talking may be dangerous to your linguistic health. The case for a much greater emphasis on listening comprehension in foreign language instruction. *IRAL, 19*(1), 1–14.

Gimson, A. C. (1980). *An introduction to the pronunciation of English.* 3rd edition. Edward Arnold.

Gradman, H. L., and Spolsky, B. (1975). Reduced redundancy testing: a progress report. In R. L. Jones and B. Spolsky (eds.), *Testing language proficiency.* Arlington, VA: Center for Applied Linguistics.

Graesser, A. C., Millis, K. K., and Zwaan, R. A. (1997). Discourse Comprehension. *Annual Review of Psychology 48*, 163–89.

Grice, H. P. (1975). Logic and conversation. In P. Cole and J. Morgan (eds.), *Syntax and semantics: Vol.3, Speech acts.* New York: Academic Press.

Griffiths, R. (1992). Speech rate and listening comprehension: Further evidence of the relationship. *TESOL Quarterly, 26*, 385–91.

Grosjean, F. (1980). Spoken word recognition and the gating paradigm. *Perception and Psychophysics, 28*(4), 267–283.

Gruber, P. (1997). Video media in listening assessment. *System 25*(3), 335–345.

Hale, G. A., and Courtney, R. (1994). The effects of note-taking on listening comprehension in the Test of English as a Foreign Language. *Language Testing, 11*(1), 29–48.

Halliday, M. A. K., and R. Hasan. (1976). *Cohesion in English.* New York: Longman.

Hanson, C., and Jensen, C. (1994). Evaluating lecture comprehension. In J. Flowerdew (ed.), *Academic listening: research perspectives.* Cambridge: Cambridge University Press.

Hatch, E. (1983). *Psycholinguistics: a second language perspective.* Rowley, MA: Newbury House.

Haviland, S. E., and Clark, H. H. (1974). What's new? Acquiring new information as a process in comprehension. *Journal of Verbal Learning and Verbal Behavior, 13*, 512–521.

Heaton, J. B. (1990). *Writing English language tests* (2nd ed.). Longman: London.

Hendrickx, J. 1977. Developing listening comprehension materials and tests. In R. Dirven (ed.), *Hörverständnis im Fremdsprachenunterricht. Listening comprehension in foreign language teaching,* Kronberg/Ts.: Scriptor.

Henning, G., Gary, N., and Gary, J. (1983). Listening recall: a listening comprehension test for low proficiency learners. *System, 11*, 287–293.

Henricksen, L. (1984). Sandhi variation: a filter of input for learners of ESL. *Language Learning, 34* (103–126).

Hildyard, A., and Olson, D. R. (1978). Memory and inference in the comprehension of oral and written discourse. *Discourse Processes, 1*, 91–107.

Hron, A. J., Kurbjuhn, I., Mandl, H., Schnotz, W. L. (1985). Structural inferences in reading and listening. In G. Rickheit and H. Strohner (eds.), *Inferences in Text Processing,* pp. 221–245. Amsterdam: North-Holland.

Hughes, A. (1989). *Testing for language teachers*. Cambridge: Cambridge University Press.

Hunnicutt, S. (1985). Intelligibility versus redundancy – conditions of dependency. *Language and Speech, 28,* 47–56.

Hymes, D. H. (1972). On communicative competence. In J. B. Pride and J. Holmes (eds.), *Sociolinguistics*. Harmondsworth: Penguin.

James, C. (1986). Listening and learning: protocols and processes. In B. Snyder (ed.), *Second language acquisition:, preparing for tomorrow*, pp. 38–48. Lincoln Wood, IL: National Textbook Company.

Jensen, C., and Hanson C. (1995). The effect of prior knowledge on EAP listening performance. *Language Testing, 12*(1), 99–119.

Johnson, M. K., Bransford, J. D., and Solomon, S. (1973). Memory for tacit implications of sentences. *Journal of Educational Psychology, 98,* 203–205.

Johnson R. L., and Friedman, H. L. (1971). Some temporal factors in the listening behaviour of second language students. In P. Pimsleur and T. Quinn (eds.), *The psychology of second language learning*. Cambridge: Cambridge University Press.

Johnson-Laird, P. N. (1983). *Mental models*. Cambridge: Cambridge University Press.

Johnson-Laird, P. N. (1985). Mental Models. In A. M. Aitkenhead and J. M. Slack (eds.), *Issues in cognitive modeling*. London: Lawrence Erlbaum Associates.

Just, M. A., and Carpenter, P. A. (1992). A capacity theory of comprehension: Individual differences in working memory. *Psychological Review,* 99, 122–149.

Kaga, M. (1991). Dictation as a measure of Japanese proficiency. *Language Testing, 8*(2), 112–124.

Kellerman, S. (1990). Lip service: The contribution of the visual modality to speech perception and its relevance to the teaching and testing of foreign language listening comprehension. *Applied Linguistics, 11,* 272–280.

Kellerman, S. (1992). 'I see what you mean': The role of kinesic behavior in listening and implications for foreign and second language learning. *Applied Linguistics, 13,* 239–258.

Kennedy, G. D. (1978). *The testing of listening comprehension*. RELC Monograph Series. Singapore: Singapore University Press.

Kintsch, W., and Yarbrough, J. C. (1982). Role of rhetorical structures in text comprehension. *Journal of Educational Psychology, 74*(6), 828–834.

Krashen, S. D. (1982). *Principles and practice in second language acquisition*. Oxford: Pergamon Press.

Krashen, S. D., and Terrel, T. (1983). *The natural approach: language acquisition in the classroom*. San Francisco: Pergamon.

Lado, R. (1961). *Language testing: the construction and use of foreign language tests*. London: Longman.

Leech, G. (1983). *Principles of pragmatics*. London: Longman.

Lewkowicz, J. A. (1991). Testing listening comprehension: a new approach? *Hong Kong Papers in Linguistics and Language Teaching 14*, 25–31.

Liebermann, P. (1963). Some effects of grammatical and semantic context on the production and perception of speech. *Language and Speech, 6*, 172–187.

Long, D. (1989). Second language listening comprehension: a schema-theoretic perspective. *Modern Language Journal, 73*, 32–40.

Long, R. L. (1990). What you don't know can't help you. *Studies in Second Language Acquisition, 12*, 65–80.

Lynch, B., and Davidson, F. (1994). Criterion-referenced language test development: linking curricula, teachers and tests. *TESOL Quarterly 28*, 727–744.

Lynch, T. (1998). Theoretical perspective on listening. *Annual Review of Applied Linguistics, 18*, 3–19.

McCarthy, M. (1998). *Spoken language and applied linguistics*. Cambridge: Cambridge University Press.

McNamara, T. F. (1996). *Measuring second language performance*. London: Longman.

Messick, S. (1989). Validity. In R. L. Linn (ed.), *Educational measurement* (3rd ed., pp. 13–103). New York: American Council on Education/ Macmillan.

Messick, S. (1994). The interplay of evidence and consequences in the validation of performance assessment. *Educational Researcher, 23*(2), 13–23.

Messick, S. (1996). Validity and washback in language testing. *Language Testing, 13*(3), 241–256.

Meyer, B. J., and Freedle, R. O. (1984). Effects of discourse type on recall. *American Educational Research Journal, 21*(1), 121–143.

Miller, G. A. (1956). The magical number seven plus or minus two: some limitations on our capacity for processing information. *Psychological Review, 63*(2), 81–97.

Morrow, K. (1979). Communicative language testing: Revolution or evolution?. In C. J. Brumfit and K. Johnson (eds.), *The communicative approach to language teaching*, pp. 143–57. Oxford: Oxford University Press.

Munby, J. (1978). *Communicative syllabus design*. Cambridge: Cambridge University Press.

Nagle, S. J., and Sanders, S. L. (1986). Comprehension theory and second language pedagogy. *TESOL Quarterly, 20*(1), 9–26.

National Board of Education. (1995). The framework of the Finnish national foreign language certificate. Helsinki: National Board of Education.

Nissan, S., DeVincenzi, F., and Tang, L. (1996). An analysis of factors affecting the difficulty of dialogue items in TOEFL listening comprehension. [TOEFL Research Report 51]. Princeton, NJ: Educational Testing Service.

Oakeshott-Taylor, Angela. (1977). Dictation as a test of listening comprehension. In *Hörverständnis im Fremdsprachenunterricht. Listening comprehension in foreign language teaching*, Rene Dirven (ed.). Kronberg/Ts.: Scriptor.

Oakeshott-Taylor, John. (1977). Information redundancy, and listening comprehension. In R. Dirven (ed.), *Hörverständnis im Fremdsprachenunterricht. Listening comprehension in foreign language teaching.* Kronberg/Ts.: Scriptor.

Ochs, E. (1979). Planned and unplanned discourse. In T. Givon (ed.), *Syntax and semantics, Vol. 12, Discourse and syntax.* New York: Academic Press.

Oller, J. W., Jr. (1971). Dictation as a device for testing foreign language proficiency. *English Language Teaching, 25*(3), 254–259.

Oller, J, W., Jr. (1979). *Language tests at school.* London: Longman.

Olsen, L. A., and Huckin, T. N. (1990). Point-driven understanding in engineering lecture comprehension. *English for Specific Purposes, 9,* 33–47.

Pearson, D., and Johnson, E. (1978). *Teaching Reading Comprehension.* New York: Holt, Rinehart and Winston.

Pickett, J. M., and Pollack, I. (1963). Intelligibility of excerpts from fluent speech: effects of rate of utterance and duration of excerpt. *Language and Speech, 6,* 151–164.

Pollack, I., and Pickett, J. M. (1963). The intelligibility of excerpts from conversation. *Language and Speech, 6,* 165–167.

Popham, W. J. (1989). *Modern education measurement* (2nd ed.). Englewood Cliffs, NJ: Prentice-Hall.

Postovsky, V. A. (1974). Effects of delay in oral practice at the beginning of second language learning. *Modern Language Learning, 58,* 229–239.

Powers, D., and Rock, D. (1999). Effects of coaching on SAT I: Reasoning test scores. *Journal of Educational Measurement, 36,* 93–118.

Preston, Ralph C. (1964). Ability of students to identify correct responses before reading. *The Journal of Educational Research, 58*(4),181–183.

Progosh, D. (1996). Using video for listening assessment: opinions of test-takers. *TESL Canada Journal 14*(1), 34–44.

Purpura, J. (1997). An analysis of the relationship between test takers cognitive and metacognitive strategy use and second language test performance. *Language Learning, 47*(2), 289–325.

Purpura, J. (1999). *Learner strategy use and performance on language tests: A SEM approach.* Cambridge: Cambridge University Press.

Richards, Jack C. (1983). Listening comprehension: approach, design, procedure. *TESOL Quarterly, 17*(2), 219–240.

Rivers, W. M. (1966). Listening comprehension. *Modern Language Journal, 50*(4), 196–202.

Roach, P. (2001). *English phonetics and phonology,* (3rd ed.). Cambridge: Cambridge University Press.

Rost, M. (1990). *Listening in language learning.* London: Longman.

Rost, M. (1994). On-line summaries as representations of lecture understanding. In J. Flowerdew (ed.), *Academic listening: research perspectives.* Cambridge: Cambridge University Press.

Rubin, J. (1995). The contribution of video to the development of competence in listening. In D. J. Mendelsohn and J. Rubin, *A guide for the teaching of second language listening*. San Diego: Dominie Press.

Rumelhart, D. E. (1980). Schemata: the building blocks of cognition. In J. R. J. Spiro, B. C. Bruce and W. F. Brewer (eds.), *Theoretical issues in reading comprehension*. Hillsdale, New Jersey: Lawrence Erlbaum Associates.

Rumelhart, D. E., and Ortony, A. (1977). The representation of knowledge in memory. In R. C. Anderson, R. J. Spiro and W. E. Montague (eds.), *Schooling and the acquisition of knowledge*. Hillsdale, NeJ: Lawrence Erlbaum Associates.

Sachs, J. S. (1967). Recognition memory for syntactic and semantic aspects of connected discourse. *Perception and Psychophysics*, 2:437–442.

Sanford, A. J., and Garrod, S. C. (1981). *Understanding written language: explorations in comprehension beyond the sentence*. Chichester: Wiley.

Schank, R. C., and Abelson, R. P. (1977). Scripts, plans, and knowledge. In P. N. Johnson-Laird and P. C. Wason (eds.), *Thinking: readings in cognitive science*. Cambridge: Cambridge University Press.

Schmidt-Rinehart, B. C. (1994). The effects of topic familiarity on second language listening comprehension. *The Modern Language Journal, 78* (ii), 179–189.

Schneider, W., and Shiffrin, R. M. (1977). Controlled and automatic information processing: I. Detection, search and identification. *Psychological Review, 84*, 1–55.

Schober, M. F., and Clark, H. H. (1989). Understanding by addressees and overhearers. *Cognitive Psychology, 21*, 211–232.

Scott, M. L., Stansfield, C. W., and Kenyon, D. (1996). Examining validity in a performance test: The listening summary translation exam (LSTE) – Spanish version. *Language Testing, 13*(1), 83–109.

Searle, J. R. (1969). *Speech acts*. Cambridge: Cambridge University Press.

Searle, J. R. (1975). Indirect speech acts. In P. Cole and J. L. Morgan (eds.), *Syntax and semantics, Vol. 3: Speech acts*. New York: Academic Press.

Sherman, J. (1997). The effect of question preview in listening comprehension tests. *Language Testing, 14*(2), 185–213.

Shiffrin, R. M., and Schneider, W. (1977). Controlled and automatic processing: II. Perceptual learning, automatic attending, and a general theory. *Psychological Review, 84*, 127–190.

Shohamy, E., and Inbar, O. (1991). Validation of listening comprehension tests: the effect of text and question types, *Language Testing, 8*(1), 23–40.

Sperber, D., and Wilson, D. (1986). *Relevance*. Oxford: Blackwell.

Spilich, G., Vesonder, G., Chiesi, H., and Voss, J. (1979). Text-processing of domain-related information for individuals with high and low domain knowledge. *Journal of Verbal Learning and Verbal Behavior, 18*, 275–290.

Stanley, J. A. (1978). Teaching listening comprehension: an interim report on a project to use uncontrolled language data as a source material for training foreign students in listening comprehension. *TESOL Quarterly, 12*(3), 285–295.

Sticht, T. (1971) *Learning by listening in relation to aptitude, reading, and rate-controlled speech: additional studies.* Human Resources Research Organisation. Technical Report NO. 71–5.

Tannen, D. (1982). The oral/literate continuum of discourse. In D. Tannen (ed.), *Spoken and written language: exploring orality and literacy.* Norwood, NJ: Ablex Publishing Co.

Tannen, D. (1985). Relative focus and involvement in oral and written discourse. In D. R. Olsen, N. Torrance and A. Hilyard (eds.), *Literacy, language and learning: the nature and consequences of reading and writing.* Cambridge: Cambridge University Press.

Tauroza, S., and Allison, D. (1990). Speech rates in British English. *Applied Linguistics, 11*, 90–105.

Tauroza, S., and Allison, D. (1994). Expectation-driven understanding in information systems lecture comprehension. In J. Flowerdew (ed.), *Academic listening: research perspectives.* Cambridge: Cambridge University Press.

Taylor, I., and Taylor, M. M. (1990). *Psycholinguistics: learning and using language.* Englewood Cliffs, NJ: Prentice Hall.

Templeton, H. (1977). A new technique for measuring listening comprehension. *ELT Journal, 31*(4), 292–299.

Thompson, I. (1995) Assessment of Second/Foreign Language Listening Comprehension. In D. J. Mendelsohn and J. Rubin (eds.), *A guide for the teaching of second language listening.* San Diego, CA: Dominie Press.

Tyler, L. K., and Marslen-Wilson, W. D. (1982). Speech comprehension process. In J. Mehler, E. Walker and M. Garrett (eds.), *Perspectives on cognitive representations.* Hillsdale, NJ: Lawrence Erlbaum Associates.

University Entrance Test in English for Speakers of Other Languages (UETESOL): Syllabus for 1995. (1995). Manchester, England: Northern Examinations and Assessment Board.

University of Cambridge Local Examinations Syndicate. (1995). Certificate of Communicative Skills in English Handbook. Cambridge: UCLES.

University of Cambridge Local Examinations Syndicate. (1997). First Certificate Handbook. Cambridge: UCLES.

University of Cambridge Local Examinations Syndicate. (1998). Business English Certificates Handbook. Cambridge: UCLES.

Valette, R. M. (1967). *Modern language testing.* New York: Harcourt Brace Jovanovich.

Valette, R. M. (1977). *Modern language testing.* (2nd ed.). New York: Harcourt Brace Jovanovich.

Van Dijk, T., A., and Kintsch, W. (1983). *Strategies of discourse comprehension.* London: Academic Press.

Van Lier, Leo. (1995). *Introducing language awareness.* Harmondsworth, Middlesex: Penguin.

Voss, B. (1979). Hesitation phenomena as sources of perceptual errors for non-native speakers. *Language and Speech, 22,* 129–144.

Voss, B. (1984). *Slips of the ear: investigation into the speech perception behavior of German speakers of English.* Tübingen: Narr.

Wall, D. (1997). Impact and Washback in Language Testing. In C. M. Clapham and D. Corson (eds.), *Language testing and assessment. Encyclopedia of language and education, Vol. 7.* Dordrecht: Kluwer.

Weir, C. (1990). *Communicative language testing.* New York: Prentice Hall.

Weir, C. (1993). *Understanding and developing language tests.* New York: Prentice Hall.

Wendell, W. W., and A. C. Bickley. (1967). Sources of information for responses to reading test items. *Proceedings, 75th Annual Convention, APA,* 293–294.

Widdowson, H. (1978). *Teaching language as communication.* Oxford: Oxford University Press.

Winitz, H. (1981). A reconsideration of comprehension and production in language training. In H. Winitz (ed.), *The comprehension approach to foreign language instruction.* Rowley, MA.: Newbury House.

Wu, Y. (1998). What do tests of listening comprehension test? – A retrospection study of EFL test-takers performing a multiple-choice task. *Language Testing, 15*(1), 21–44.

Index